ALGORITHMS

AUTHORS

Dr. Piyoosh P
Assistant Professor,
Department of Computer Science and Engineering, College of Engineering Trivandrum (CET), Trivandrum, Kerala (India).

Dr. Arnab Sarkar
Associate Professor,
Advanced Technology Development Centre (ATDC),
IIT Kharagpur, West Bengal (India).

REVIEWER

Dr. Pratistha Mathur
Professor,
Department of Information Technology,
School of Information Technology,
Manipal University Jaipur, Rajasthan (India)

KHANNA BOOK PUBLISHING CO. (P) Ltd.
4C/4344, Ansari Road, Darya Ganj,
New Delhi, India

All India Council for Technical Education
Nelson Mandela Marg, Vasant Kunj,
New Delhi, India

Dear Readers,

To prevent the piracy, this book is secured with HIGH SECURITY HOLOGRAM on the front title cover. In case you don't find the hologram on the front cover title, please write us to at contact@khannabooks.com or whatsapp us at +91-99109 09320 and avail special gift voucher for yourself.

Specimen of Hologram on front Cover title:

Moreover, there is a SPECIAL DISCOUNT COUPON for you with EVERY HOLOGRAM.

How to avail this SPECIAL DISCOUNT:

Step 1: Scratch the hologram

Step 2: Under the scratch area, your "coupon code" is available

Step 3: Logon to www.khannabooks.com

Step 4: Use your "coupon code" in the shopping cart and get your copy at a special discount

Step 5: Enjoy your reading!

ISBN: 978-93-55384-54-6
Book Code: DIP448EN

Algorithms

by Piyoosh P & Arnab Sarkar

First Edition: 2025

Originally Published by:
All India Council for Technical Education, Ministry of Education, GOI

Exclusively Published & Distributed by:
Khanna Book Publishing Co. (P) Ltd.
4C/4344, Ansari Road, Daryaganj,
New Delhi (INDIA)

Visit us at: **www.khannabooks.com**
Write us at: **contact@khannabooks.com**

To view complete list of books, Please scan the QR Code:

KPH

Printed in Bharat.

प्रो. टी. जी. सीताराम
अध्यक्ष
Prof. T. G. Sitharam
Chairman

सत्यमेव जयते

आज़ादी का अमृत महोत्सव

अखिल भारतीय तकनीकी शिक्षा परिषद्
(भारत सरकार का एक सांविधिक निकाय)
(शिक्षा मंत्रालय, भारत सरकार)
नेल्सन मंडेला मार्ग, वसंत कुंज, नई दिल्ली–110070
दूरभाष : 011–26131498
ई–मेल : chairman@aicte-india.org

ALL INDIA COUNCIL FOR TECHNICAL EDUCATION
(A STATUTORY BODY OF THE GOVT. OF INDIA)
(Ministry of Education, Govt. of India)
Nelson Mandela Marg, Vasant Kunj, New Delhi-110070
Phone : 011-26131498
E-mail : chairman@aicte-india.org

FOREWORD

Engineers are the backbone of any modern society. They are the ones responsible for the marvels as well as the improved quality of life across the world. Engineers have driven humanity towards greater heights in a more evolved and unprecedented manner.

The All India Council for Technical Education (AICTE), have spared no efforts towards the strengthening of the technical education in the country. AICTE is always committed towards promoting quality Technical Education to make India a modern developed nation emphasizing on the overall welfare of mankind.

An array of initiatives has been taken by AICTE in last decade which have been accelerated now by the National Education Policy (NEP) 2020. The implementation of NEP under the visionary leadership of Hon'ble Prime Minister of India envisages the provision for education in regional languages to all, thereby ensuring that every graduate becomes competent enough and is in a position to contribute towards the national growth and development through innovation & entrepreneurship.

One of the spheres where AICTE had been relentlessly working since past couple of years is providing high quality original technical contents at Under Graduate & Diploma level prepared and translated by eminent educators in various Indian languages to its aspirants. For students pursuing 2nd year of their Engineering education, AICTE has identified 87 books, which shall be translated into 12 Indian languages - Hindi, Tamil, Gujarati, Odia, Bengali, Kannada, Urdu, Punjabi, Telugu, Marathi, Assamese & Malayalam. In addition to the English medium, books in different Indian Languages are going to support the students to understand the concepts in their respective mother tongue.

On behalf of AICTE, I express sincere gratitude to all distinguished authors, reviewers and translators from the renowned institutions of high repute for their admirable contribution in a record span of time.

AICTE is confident that these outcomes based original contents shall help aspirants to master the subject with comprehension and greater ease.

T.G. Sitharam

(Prof. T. G. Sitharam)

ACKNOWLEDGEMENT

The authors are grateful to the authorities of AICTE, particularly Prof. T. G. Sitharam, Chairman; Dr. Abhay Jere, Vice-Chairman; Prof. Rajive Kumar, Member-Secretary, Dr. Ramesh Unnikrishnan, Advisor-II and Dr. Sunil Luthra, Director, Training and Learning Bureau for their planning to publish the books on Algorithms. We sincerely acknowledge the valuable contributions of the reviewer of the book Dr. Pratistha Mathur, Professor, Department of Information Technology, School of Information Technology, Manipal University Jaipur for making it students' friendly and giving a better shape in an artistic manner.

We are very grateful to Dr. Rajesh Devaraj, Senior System Software Engineer, Nvidia Graphics, Bangalore, for his immense help in designing the problems, finding solutions to them, and generating examples. We are thankful to the efforts from postgraduate students at College of Engineering Trivandrum, Rohith L R, Aishwarya Suresh Mohod and Vishnupriya M V. The book could be possible only with their support in drafting and drawing of sketches.

This book is an outcome of various suggestions of AICTE members, experts and authors who shared their opinion and thought to further develop the engineering education in our country. Acknowledgements are due to the contributors and different workers in this field whose published books, review articles, papers, photographs, footnotes, references and other valuable information enriched us at the time of writing the book.

Dr. Piyoosh P

Dr. Arnab Sarkar

PREFACE

The book is expected to be the first course on this subject and is generally meant for students who already have some introductory knowledge of programming. The book shall cover the basic foundations of designing correct and efficient sequential algorithms through a process of mathematical analysis and logical design steps. Such algorithms can then be translated into software programs for deployment in practice. In this first course, analysis involves understanding of an algorithm's complexity through asymptotic analysis of its time requirement under worst-case scenarios, through step counting and the substitution method.

We have organized the book into five units. The first unit deals with fundamentals and is oriented to help students get a primary idea on the concept of an algorithm and the importance of designing correct and efficient algorithms. Through a series of small examples, students can understand how to properly define a problem, measure its inherent complexity and explore different ways of developing an algorithmic solution to the problem. The unit explains the concept of data structures as systematic methods for organizing and accessing data associated with an algorithm. In the second unit, we discuss sorting techniques. In Computer Science, a systematic study of sorting problems is an essential step in learning the art of designing efficient algorithms. Also, sorting often helps reduce the complexity of other problems. We describe techniques for searching elements in a given data structure, along with mechanisms for insertion and deletion, as part of the third unit. The fourth unit is dedicated to the discussion on graphs, a data structure for modeling relationships between objects. We present different types of graphs, various operations associated with them, along with algorithms for important problems involving graphs. We discuss strings in the last unit of this book. Strings are commonly considered as a data type in many programming languages. We discuss the Trie data structure, a unique tree-based data structure designed specifically for storing and searching strings. The unit also discusses regular expressions and data compression techniques with strings.

We wish that the material in this book will enable novice student enter into the wonderful world of algorithms and efficient programming.

Dr. Piyoosh P

Dr. Arnab Sarkar

OUTCOME BASED EDUCATION

For the implementation of an outcome based education the first requirement is to develop an outcome based curriculum and incorporate an outcome based assessment in the education system. By going through outcome based assessments, evaluators will be able to evaluate whether the students have achieved the outlined standard, specific and measurable outcomes. With the proper incorporation of outcome based education there will be a definite commitment to achieve a minimum standard for all learners without giving up at any level. At the end of the programme running with the aid of outcome based education, a student will be able to arrive at the following outcomes:

Programme Outcomes (POs) are statements that describe what students are expected to know and be able to do upon graduating from the program. These relate to the skills, knowledge, analytical ability, attitude and behaviour that students acquire through the program. The POs essentially indicate what the students can do from subject-wise knowledge acquired by them during the program. As such, POs define the professional profile of an engineering diploma graduate.

National Board of Accreditation (NBA) has defined the following seven POs for an Engineering diploma graduate:

PO-1. Basic and Discipline specific knowledge: Apply knowledge of basic mathematics, science and engineering fundamentals and engineering specialization to solve the engineering problems.

PO-2. Problem analysis: Identify and analyses well-defined engineering problems using codified standard methods.

PO-3. Design/development of solutions: Design solutions for well-defined technical problems and assist with the design of systems components or processes to meet specified needs.

PO-4. Engineering Tools, Experimentation and Testing: Apply modern engineering tools and appropriate technique to conduct standard tests and measurements.

PO-5. Engineering practices for society, sustainability and environment: Apply appropriate technology in context of society, sustainability, environment and ethical practices.

PO-6. Project Management: Use engineering management principles individually, as a team member or a leader to manage projects and effectively communicate about well-defined engineering activities.

PO-7. Life-long learning: Ability to analyse individual needs and engage in updating in the context of technological changes.

COURSE OUTCOMES

By the end of the course the students are expected to learn:

CO-1: The backgrounds related to the fundamentals of programming models as well as important data structures that are necessary towards the understanding of algorithms discussed in the course.

CO-2: The foundations for designing correct and efficient sequential algorithms through a process of mathematical analysis and logical design steps.

CO-3: Important algorithmic strategies for sorting, searching, graphs, strings, etc.

CO-4: Mechanisms for analyzing the efficiency of an algorithm by obtaining a measure of its complexity through asymptotic analysis of the time required for execution under worst-case scenarios.

CO-5: How to translate designed algorithms into software programs that can be deployed in practice.

Mapping of Course Outcomes with Programme Outcomes to be done according to the matrix given below:

Course Outcomes	EXPECTED MAPPING WITH PROGRAMME OUTCOMES (1- Weak Correlation; 2- Medium correlation; 3- Strong Correlation)						
	PO-1	PO-2	PO-3	PO-4	PO-5	PO-6	PO-7
CO-1	3	3	3	2	1	2	3
CO-2	3	3	3	2	1	2	3
CO-3	3	3	3	2	1	2	3
CO-4	3	3	3	2	1	2	3
CO-5	3	3	3	3	1	2	3

GUIDELINES FOR TEACHERS

To implement Outcome Based Education (OBE) knowledge level and skill set of the students should be enhanced. Teachers should take a major responsibility for the proper implementation of OBE. Some of the responsibilities (not limited to) for the teachers in OBE system may be as follows:

- Within reasonable constraint, they should manoeuvre time to the best advantage of all students.
- They should assess the students only upon certain defined criterion without considering any other potential ineligibility to discriminate them.
- They should try to grow the learning abilities of the students to a certain level before they leave the institute.
- They should try to ensure that all the students are equipped with the quality knowledge as well as competence after they finish their education.
- They should always encourage the students to develop their ultimate performance capabilities.
- They should facilitate and encourage group work and team work to consolidate newer approach.
- They should follow Blooms taxonomy in every part of the assessment.

Bloom's Taxonomy

Level	Teacher should Check	Student should be able to	Possible Mode of Assessment
Creating	Students ability to create	Design or Create	Mini project
Evaluating	Students ability to Justify	Argue or Defend	Assignment
Analysing	Students ability to distinguish	Differentiate or Distinguish	Project/Lab Methodology
Applying	Students ability to use information	Operate or Demonstrate	Technical Presentation/ Demonstration
Understanding	Students ability to explain the ideas	Explain or Classify	Presentation/Seminar
Remembering	Students ability to recall (or remember)	Define or Recall	Quiz

GUIDELINES FOR STUDENTS

Students should take equal responsibility for implementing the OBE. Some of the responsibilities (not limited to) for the students in OBE system are as follows:

- Students should be well aware of each UO before the start of a unit in each and every course.
- Students should be well aware of each CO before the start of the course.
- Students should be well aware of each PO before the start of the programme.
- Students should think critically and reasonably with proper reflection and action.
- Learning of the students should be connected and integrated with practical and real life consequences.
- Students should be well aware of their competency at every level of OBE.

ABBREVIATIONS AND SYMBOLS

List of Abbreviations

General Terms			
Abbreviations	**Full form**	**Abbreviations**	**Full form**
CO	Course Outcome	PO	Programme Outcome
UO	Unit Outcome	Hz	Hertz
LHS	Left Hand Side	RHS	Right Hand Side
LIFO	Last-In-First-Out	FILO	First-In-Last-Out
FIFO	First-In-First-Out	LILO	Last-In-Last-Out
BST	Binary Search Tree	AVL	Adelson-Velsky and Landis
BF	Balance Factor	DAG	Directed Acyclic Graph
BFS	Breadth-First Search	DFS	Depth-First Search
FFA	Ford-Fulkerson Algorithm	PNG	Portable Network Graphics
LZW	Lempel-Ziv-Welch	MPEG	Moving Picture Experts Group
JPEG	Joint Photographic Experts Group	MP3	MPEG Audio Layer 3

List of Symbols

Symbols	Description	Symbols	Description
//	To add comments inside algorithms	$\cup$	Union operation between two sets or multisets
$\cap$	Intersection operation between two sets or multisets	-	Difference operation between two sets or multisets
O	Big-Oh notation	Ω	Omega notation
Θ	Theta notation	O(1)	Constant time
$O(log\ n)$	Logarithmic time	$O(n)$	Linear time
$O(n\ log\ n)$	Linear logarithmic time	$O(n^k)$	Polynomial time
$O(2^n)$	Exponential time	$h(k)$	Hash value of key k
G	Graph	V	Set of vertices or nodes
E	Set of edges	$C(S)$	Compressed version of bitstream S
$c(u,v)$	Capacity of an edge (u,v)	$f(u,v)$	Flow value corresponding to an edge (u,v)

LIST OF FIGURES

CONTENTS

1 Fundamentals

UNIT SPECIFICS

Through this unit we have discussed the following aspects:

- Concept of algorithms and considerations related to their efficient design
- The data and program model in terms of which algorithms are designed
- Storing and operating on data in an organized fashion through data structures
- Important data structures - sets, multisets, stacks and queues
- Complexity and its usefulness in determining an algorithm's efficiency
- for measuring time complexity

RATIONALE

This fundamental unit on algorithms helps students to get a primary idea on the concept of an algorithm and the importance of designing correct and efficient algorithms. Through a series of small examples, students can understand how to properly define a problem, measure its inherent complexity and explore different ways of developing an algorithmic solution to the problem. The unit explains the concept of data structures as systematic methods for organizing and accessing data associated with an algorithm. It discusses in detail four important data structures namely, sets, multisets, stacks and queues. Finally, the concept of algorithmic complexity has been introduced with a focus on time complexity. It discusses how the measure of complexity can be used to compare the efficiencies of different algorithms for a given problem.

PRE-REQUISITES

Rudimentary knowledge of computer programming

UNIT OUTCOMES

List of outcomes of this unit is as follows:

U1-O1: Define an algorithm

U1-O2: Describe the computation model needed for designing an algorithm

U1-O3: Explain the concepts of data structures and data abstraction

U1-O4: Realize the role of complexity associated with an algorithmic solution

U1-O5: Apply techniques for measuring time complexity order ('big-Oh')

Unit-1 Outcome	EXPECTED MAPPING WITH COURSE OUTCOMES (1 - Weak Correlation; 2 - Medium Correlation; 3 - Strong Correlation)				
	CO-1	CO-2	CO-3	CO-4	CO-5
U1-O1	3	3	1	3	1
U1-O2	3	3	1	3	1
U1-O3	3	3	1	3	1
U1-O4	3	3	1	3	1
U1-O5	3	3	1	3	1

1.1 INTRODUCTION

In very general terms, a structured mechanism for solving a problem is an *algorithm*. When we are talking about writing a computer program to solve a problem, a more precise definition of *algorithm* would be: *a sequence of instructions which processes data fed at its input and delivers some outputs within a finite number of steps.*

In this book, we will try to gain an understanding or insight on the following major aspects related to algorithm design and analysis:

- How can efficient algorithms be designed for various types of problems?
- How can we measure the efficiency of an algorithm?
- Given an algorithm for a problem, how can its efficiency be compared with other algorithms for the same problem?

1.2 COMPUTATION MODEL

Algorithms process data presented at its input in order to produce appropriate output(s) and may be considered to be a generalization of computer programs. Hence, we firstly need to develop a computation model (or program model) so that algorithms can be designed in terms of that model. This computation model has two principal components: a model for storing and representing data (*Data Model*) and a model sketching the structured mechanisms for processing data so that a desired function can be effectively described (*Program Model*).

1.2.1 Basic Data Model

The basic data holding element in a computer is termed as a *variable*. Let us consider the mathematical equation: '$x + y = 2$'. In this equation, x and y are the names of two variables that hold some values or data. These variables can hold only one value at a given time, and their values can be changed. The variables x and y in the above equation can hold any value, like real numbers (0.25, 0.5, etc.) or integer numbers (-2, 0, 1, 2, etc.). To solve the equation, these variables need to be related to the kind of value (say, only integer numbers) that they can take. *Data type* is the term used in computer science to store a specific type of value for a variable. Examples of data types are char, string, int, float, etc. Data type determines the type and size of data associated with variables. For example, in many computers, the *char* data type takes 1 byte of memory and stores character data, the *int* data type takes 2 bytes of memory and stores integer data etc.

Arrays or Indexed Variables: In general, variables are frequently used in algorithms to store data. Variables can be of different types but capable of holding only one value at a given time. For example, a variable may hold an integer, real number, or character value. Arrays may be considered an extended version of variables. Specifically, an array is a collection of variables of the same type. For example, let us consider an integer variable "Num" and it can hold only one integer value at a given time. If we want to store multiple integer values (say, 10 values) as part of "Num", we can declare it as an array variable like "Num[1, 2, …, 10]". This declaration implies that "Num" can hold 10 different values: Num[1], Num[2], …, Num[10]. We can manipulate the values stored in arrays using the index of each entry in it. Here, we use the index starting from 1. Example: "Num[5] = 10".

1.2.2 Program Model

As mentioned above, an algorithm is composed of a finite sequence of instructions. Each such instruction must be clear and unambiguous. We should also be able to perform each instruction with a finite effort and within bounded time. An example of an instruction would be: "a = b + c"; the instruction has a clear meaning: *the values in variables 'b' and 'c' are added and the result is stored/loaded in variable 'a'*. It is also possible to perform this instruction with finite computing and storage resources within bounded time. Instructions within an algorithm can indicate the repetition of one or more instructions. However, in spite of such repetition, an algorithm must terminate after executing a finite number of instructions.

In this book, we will present algorithms using a pseudo-language. This language has been developed by using C-like instructions (C programming language constructs) and combining them with informal English statements. A detailed overview of this pseudo-language is discussed below.

Procedure: Algorithmic descriptions of all functions are encapsulated within a procedural block (equivalent to functions in C). The template of such a procedure is presented below:

```
Procedure procedure_name (argument_1, argument_2, …)
    Input argument_1, argument_2, …
     Statement_Num_1
     Statement_Num_2
    …
     Statement_Num_N
        Return Value
End Procedure
```

The procedural block starts with the keyword "**Procedure**" and ends with the keyword "**End Procedure**". Each procedure is identified using a unique name and it is mentioned immediately after the keyword "**Procedure**". In general, the purpose of the procedure is to process an input and produce an output. The input arguments to the procedure are listed within brackets, after the name of the procedure. In the first line of the procedure, we explicitly call-out the input arguments using the keyword "**Input**". In some cases, there will be no input to the procedure. In such cases, empty brackets will be present and input arguments will not be listed using the "**Input**" keyword.

Inside a procedure block, there are a set of statements describing an algorithm and these statements are executed in a sequential order from the first statement to the last one. These statements can be of different types, namely: (i) initialization statements, (ii) print statements, (iii) assignment statements, (iv) conditional statements, (v) iterative statements. The output of the procedure needs to be returned to its caller. For this purpose, the "**Return**" keyword is used before the actual return value. In some cases, the procedure may not have any specific value to return; rather, it may simply print an output. In such a scenario, this "**Return**" keyword will not be used.

Initialization Statements: Statements of this type are used to declare variables to be used in an algorithm. A declared variable may also be initialized to a certain value, if needed. Consider as an example, the statement: "Initialize sum = 0". This statement declares the variable "sum" and initializes it to the value "0".

Print Statements: The print statement is used to output the values of a sequence of one or more variables on screen. It can also be used to print a string represented as a sequence of characters within double-quotes. Let us consider three variables a, b and c, having values 5, "Ram is a" and 10.2, respectively. Then the print statement: "print a b "good boy" c" will produce the following output on screen: "5 Ram is a good boy 10.2".

Assignment Statements: These are of the form: "LHS = Expression". Here, LHS (Left Hand Side) is a placeholder (variable) and RHS (Right Hand Side) is a unary/binary/n-ary expression consisting of arithmetic/logical operations. An example would be, "A = (B + C) - (B && C)".

Conditional Statements: These statements are used to capture conditions which may evaluate to either "True" or "False". The format of a simple conditional statement is as follows:

```
If condition
     Statement_Num_1
     Statement_Num_2
     ...
     Statement_Num_N
End If
```

Here, *condition* denotes a logical expression of the form "var1 cond_op var2", where 'var1' and 'var2' are variables, and 'cond_op' is a conditional operator which can be either: '==' (equality test), or '>' (greater than), or '!=' (not equal), or '<' (less than), or '<=' (less than or equal to), or '>=' (greater than or equal to).

If the condition evaluates to 'True', then the statements placed between "**If**" and "**End If**" keywords are executed; otherwise, not. To support multiple condition checks along with a distinct set of actions, we have the following construct: "**If**", "**Else If**", and "**Else**".

```
If condition_1
     Statement_1_cond_1
     Statement_2_cond_1
     ...
     Statement_N_cond_1
Else If condition_2
     ...
Else If condition_n
     Statement_1_cond_n
     Statement_2_cond_n
     ...
     Statement_N_cond_n
Else
```

```
        Statement_Num_1
        Statement_Num_2
        ...
        Statement_Num_N
End If
```

Iterative Statements: In order to support repetitive execution of a block of statements under a particular condition, iterative statements are used. One such construct is "**Repeat until**" whose syntax is given below:

```
Repeat until condition
        Statement_Num_1
        Statement_Num_2
        ...
        Statement_Num_N
End Repeat
```

As long as the condition is evaluated to 'True', the statements placed between the keywords "**Repeat until**" and "**End Repeat**" are executed. Similarly, we have the "**For each**" construct to iterate over each element of a 'list', from its first to the last element.

```
For each element in a list
        Statement_Num_1
        Statement_Num_2
        ...
        Statement_Num_N
End For
```

Comment Statements: An algorithm written by one person may be difficult for another person to read and understand. In order to make the steps of an algorithm more lucid, liberal use of comment statements is often recommended. In this book, we use the notation "//" to add comments inside algorithms. If a statement starts with "//", then that statement should be interpreted as a comment.

We will now take a few very simple examples to show how algorithms may be presented using the program model discussed above.

Example-1: Write a procedure to print the list of first 100 odd numbers (starting from 1).

Solution Approach: To print the first 100 odd numbers (beginning from 1), there is a need to use a variable which will take values from 1 to 200. If the value present in that variable is not divisible by 2, then that value is an odd number. So, the value in that variable can be printed as an output. This process needs to be repeated from 1 to 200, to find the first 100 odd numbers. Such a procedure is presented in *print_odd_numbers*.

```
Procedure print_odd_numbers()
        Initialize count = 1
        Repeat until count <= 200
                If ((count % 2) != 0)
                        Print count
                End If
                Increment count by 1
```

```
L8:         End Repeat
L9:     End Procedure
```

Explanation: The procedure *print_odd_numbers()* starts with the keyword "Procedure" (Line no. 1) and it ends with the keyword "End Procedure" (Line no. 9). Inside this procedure, a new variable named "count" is initialized to 1 (Line no. 2). To find whether the value present in "count" is an odd number, modulo division operation is used (Line no. 4). That is, (count % 2) returns the remainder, when count is divided by 2. If the remainder is not equal to 0, then it implies that the value in count is an odd number. Such a conditional check is performed using the "If" statement (Line no. 4) and it ends with the "End If" keyword (Line no. 6). Then, the value in the "count" variable is printed (Line no. 5). Since this operation needs to be repeated until the "count" value reaches 200, a "Repeat until" loop is introduced (Line no. 3) and it ends with the keyword "End Repeat" (Line no. 8). Within this "Repeat until" block, the value of "count" gets incremented by 1 (Line no. 7). The "Repeat until" block gets executed as long as "count" value is less than or equal to 200 (Line no. 3).

Example-2: Write a procedure to print the largest number among three distinct numbers.

Solution Approach: Let us assume that we need to write a procedure that takes as input three distinct numbers, say, No_A, No_B, and No_C, and produces the largest among them as an output. To find the maximum number among these three numbers, there is a need to compare each number against the other numbers. If No_A is the maximum, then it must be greater than No_B and No_C. In a similar manner, No_B can be compared against No_A and No_C, to check whether No_B is the largest number. If both No_A and No_B are not the largest number, then No_C ultimately becomes the largest number. This has been captured in the procedure *find_max_among_three_numbers().*

```
Procedure find_max_among_three_numbers(No_A,No_B,No_C)
        Input No_A, No_B, No_C
        If ((No_A > No_B) && (No_A > No_C))
            Print "No_A is largest"
        Else If ((No_B > No_A) && (No_B > No_C))
            Print "No_B is largest"
        Else
            Print "No_C is largest"
        End If
End Procedure
```

Example-3: Write a procedure to print the largest number in a given input array.

Solution Approach: Let us consider an input array (say, random_numbers) with K numbers in it. To find the largest number among K numbers in random_numbers, initialize the first element in the array as the largest element (say, P). Compare P against its next element. If the next element is bigger than P, then store the next element in P. Otherwise, move to the next element and perform comparison. This process will be repeated until all elements in the input array are traversed. Finally, P will contain the largest element in random_numbers. This has been captured in the procedure *find_largest_number()*.

```
Procedure find_largest_number
                              (random_numbers[1, 2, …, K])
        Input random_numbers[1, 2, …, K]
        // Let P be the largest element
        Initialize P = random_numbers[1]
```

```
        For each element R in random_numbers[1, 2, …, K]
            If (R > P)
                update P = R
            End If
        End For
        Print P
End Procedure
```

Example-4: An array *A*[1, 2, …, N] contains N distinct numbers. Write a procedure to search for a given number Num_X, in *A*. If it is present, print its location in *A*.

Solution Approach: To find whether the given number Num_X is present in A, compare Num_X against each element in A. To print the corresponding location in which Num_X is present, use an index variable (initialized to 1) while traversing through the array. If Num_X is found, then the index of the variable containing Num_X is the required location in A. The procedure *find_a_number()* depicts the steps related to the above discussed solution.

```
Procedure find_a_number(A[1, 2, …, N],Num_X)
        Input A[1, 2, …, N], Num_X
        Repeat until index <= N
            If (Num_X == A[index])
                Print Num_X is present at location
                                                  index in A
                Return
            End If
            Increment index by 1
        End Repeat
        Print Num_X is not present in A
End Procedure
```

1.3 DATA STRUCTURE AND DATA ABSTRACTION

We now focus towards the notions of 'data structures' and 'data abstraction'. As discussed earlier, *data types* determine the type of data that a variable can store, as well as size of the memory location necessary to store one data element of such type. In many programming languages, data types are classified into two types: *basic* and *composite* data types. Commonly used basic data types are int, char, float etc. Many programming languages allow users to define composite data types, which are obtained as a user-defined collection of basic and/or composite data types. In this book, we use the keyword '**struct**' to define composite data types. For example, a composite data type named 'xyz' which is obtained as a combination of three variables having data types char, int and float respectively, can be defined as:

```
struct xyz {
        char var1;
        int var2;
        float var3;
};
```

A variable, say 'var4', of type 'xyz', can be declared as, 'xyz var4'. Content of the variable 'var1' of 'abc' can be accessed using the '.' (dot) operator: 'abc.var1'. It may be observed that composite data types ('struct') provide a mechanism for storing data associated with a procedure in a well-structured fashion. This brings us to the notion of a data structure.

Definition: *Data structure* is the organized representation of a collection of related data elements, as well as representation of a set of operations (or functions/procedures) that can be applied to these data elements. It provides a specific format for storing, accessing, retrieving, and organising data within an algorithmic procedure.

Data structures are known to be the backbone of computer algorithms as they help the programmer to efficiently handle data and thus enhance the performance of the developed procedure. Commonly used data structures include arrays, stacks, queues, sets, trees, graphs etc. For example, a stack data structure uses Last-In-First-Out (LIFO) order to arrange data within it. To achieve this ordering, the stack defines two main operations (or procedures) — PUSH() and POP(). The PUSH() operation inserts an element onto the stack, while POP() deletes an element from the stack. As an algorithm designer, we simply use these operations or procedures to manage data within a stack, and we need not look into the detailed implementation of these operations when manipulating data associated with a stack. This brings us to the concept of *data abstraction.*

Definition: *Data abstraction* is the process of providing only essential details of a procedure and hiding its background implementation from the end user.

In the previous section, we saw that the procedure block is an effective mechanism for encapsulating and localizing a sequence of statements representing a distinct part of an algorithm which deals with a specific aspect of its overall behaviour. Let us now look at procedures from the perspective of data abstraction. Procedures can be viewed as a generalization of the notion of an operator. As operators transform operands applied to them and produce a result, procedures process data fed at its input and deliver one or more outputs. Thus, procedures can be considered a mechanism which allows a designer to build user-defined operators. However, similar to basic operators, how the data at the input of a procedure is manipulated to produce the result remains hidden inside the procedure and is not visible from outside. This therefore, may be considered as a form of data abstraction.

1.4 SETS AND MULTISETS

Sets and multisets are two important data structures often used in computer algorithms. *Set* is a collection of unique elements. On the other hand, a *Multiset* can contain multiple instances of the same element. That is, duplicates are not permitted in a Set, however, they are permitted in a Multiset. For example, [1, 2, 3, 1, 2] is a Multiset, but it is not a Set. This is because the elements 1 and 2 are repeated twice.

On Sets, algebraic operations like union, intersection and difference are supported. Let us discuss these standard operations using a few examples.

Union (U): A U B contains unique elements from sets A and B.

[1, 2] U [3, 4] = [1, 2, 3, 4]

[1, 2] U [1, 2] = [1, 2]

Intersection (∩): A ∩ B contains elements that are common in both the sets A and B.

[1, 2] ∩ [3, 4] = [ ] (empty set)

[1, 2] ∩ [1, 2] = [1, 2]

Difference (-): A - B contains all elements in A that are not present in B.

[1, 2] - [3, 4] = [1, 2]

[1, 2] - [1, 2] = [ ] (empty set)

Similar to Sets, the above discussed operations are supported in Multisets as well. We now discuss these operations with respect to Multisets.

Union (U): A U B contains common elements from multisets A and B. In case of repeated elements, the number of occurrences/instances of an element in (A U B) is equal to the maximum of the number of occurrences/instances of that element in A and B.

[1, 2, 2, 2, 3] U [1, 1, 2, 4] = [1, 1, 2, 2, 2, 3, 4]

Intersection (∩): A ∩ B contains common elements from multisets A and B. In case of repeated elements, the number of occurrences/instances of an element in (A ∩ B) is equal to the minimum of the number of instances of that element in A and B.

[1, 2, 2, 2, 3] ∩ [1, 1, 2, 2, 4] = [1, 2, 2]

Difference (-): A - B contains all elements in A that are not part of B. In case of repeated elements, the number of instances of an element in (A - B) is equal to the difference of number of instances of that element in A and B. If the difference is 0 or negative, then that number will not be part of the resulting set.

[1, 2, 2, 2, 3] - [1, 1, 2, 4] = [2, 2, 3]

In programming languages like C++, Java and Python, both set and multiset are valid data structures. Typically, the following APIs (Application Program Interface) are allowed on multisets:

- Multiset() : Create an empty multiset
- add (item) : add an item
- isEmpty() : Is the multiset empty?
- size() : number of items in the multiset

For example, we can create a new multiset named A using the procedure Multiset(). After creation, A = [] is an empty set. To insert an element/item (say, 5), we use A.add(5). Now, A = [5]. To check the number of items in A, we use A.size(). This will return 1. Typically, remove(item) operation is not supported, to allow the possibility of collecting items and iterating through all of them. However, we can still implement remove(item) API to remove an item from Multiset. To remove the item 5 from Multiset A, we can use A.remove(5). Subsequently, A becomes an empty set. To confirm this, A.isEmpty() can be used. Further, the operations such as union, intersection and difference can also be implemented using APIs and employed to perform operations on Multisets.

1.5 STACKS AND QUEUES

Stack and queue are two simple yet powerful data structures used to store data in an ordered fashion. These two data structures differ on the mechanisms for arranging and accessing elements in them.. In this section, we first start with stack and its basic operations.

1.5.1 Stack

Before going to the details of stack, we first discuss a real world scenario where the concept of stack is applicable. Consider a scenario in which plates are organised in a kitchen plate rack stand. Whenever we clean a plate, it is placed on the top of the rack, above the previously cleaned plate. Here, the plates are placed on the rack as they are cleaned, and a newly cleaned plate is always kept at the top of the rack. When we require a plate, we first take the plate that is placed at the top of the rack. The last plate that is cleaned and placed at the top of the rack is the first one to be used. This ordered way of arranging items or data is known as Last-In-First-Out (LIFO) or First-In-Last-Out (FILO) policy.

Definition: A simple data structure that follows LIFO or FILO order to store information is known as 'Stack'. In a stack, the position at which the data is inserted or deleted is termed the 'TOP' of the stack.

The stack defines two types of operations. Insertion of an element at the TOP of the stack is termed "PUSH," and deletion of an element from the TOP of the stack is called "POP." Generally, a simple array is used to implement stack. Fig. 1.1 depicts a stack and its PUSH and POP operations.

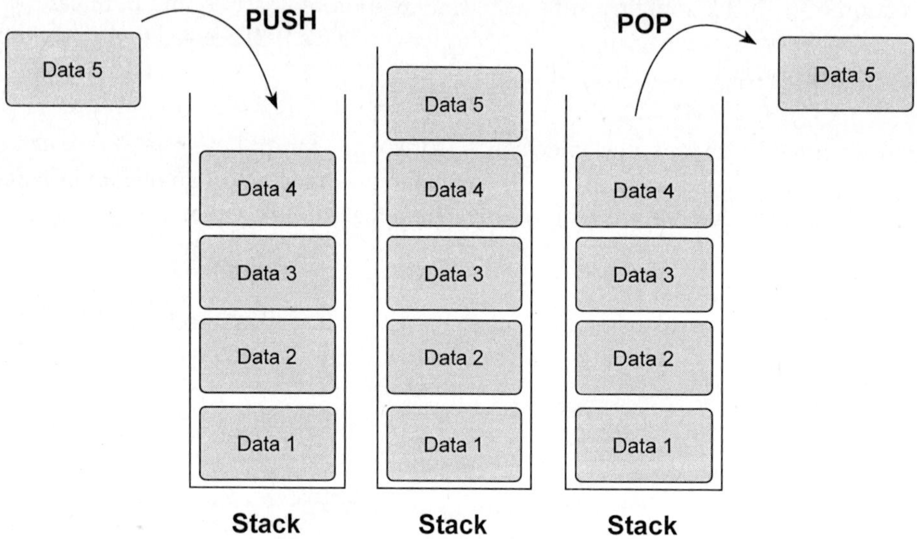

Fig. 1.1: Stack and its operations

The PUSH and POP operations of a stack are defined as follows.

```
Procedure PUSH(int ITEM)
        Input Stack_Array[1, 2, …, N], ITEM
        // Let TOP be the top of the stack
        If (TOP == N)
                Print Overflow
        Else
                Increment TOP by 1
                Stack_Array[TOP] = ITEM
        End If
End Procedure
```

```
Procedure POP()
        Input Stack_Array[1, 2, …, N]
        // Let TOP be the top of the stack
        If (TOP != 0)
```

```
                    Decrement TOP by 1
            Else
                    Print Underflow
            End If
    End Procedure
```

Let us consider a stack (say, Stack_Array) that supports a maximum of N elements within it. The variable TOP keeps track of the top element of the stack. Initially, the value of TOP is set to be 0. If a new element (say, ITEM) is inserted onto the Stack_Array, the value of TOP is incremented by 1, and the ITEM is stored in the Stack_Array[TOP]. This insertion operation may continue till the value of TOP becomes N. If the value of TOP is N, no further insertion is possible onto the stack, resulting in an 'Overflow' situation. The deletion of an element from a stack is possible only if the value of TOP is not 0. In this case, an element is deleted from the stack by decrementing the value of TOP by 1. If the value of TOP is 0, no further deletion is possible from the stack, resulting in an 'Underflow' situation.

Example-5: Consider a stack of size 4. Initially, the value of TOP is set to 0. When we perform the first push operation to insert the data '100' onto the stack, the value of top is incremented to 1. Now, we perform three more PUSH operations to insert data '200', '300', and '400' respectively onto the stack. Each such PUSH operation increments the value of TOP by 1, and finally the value of TOP becomes 4 which is equal to the maximum size of the stack. No further PUSH operation is possible when the stack is full. Fig. 1.2 depicts these PUSH operations.

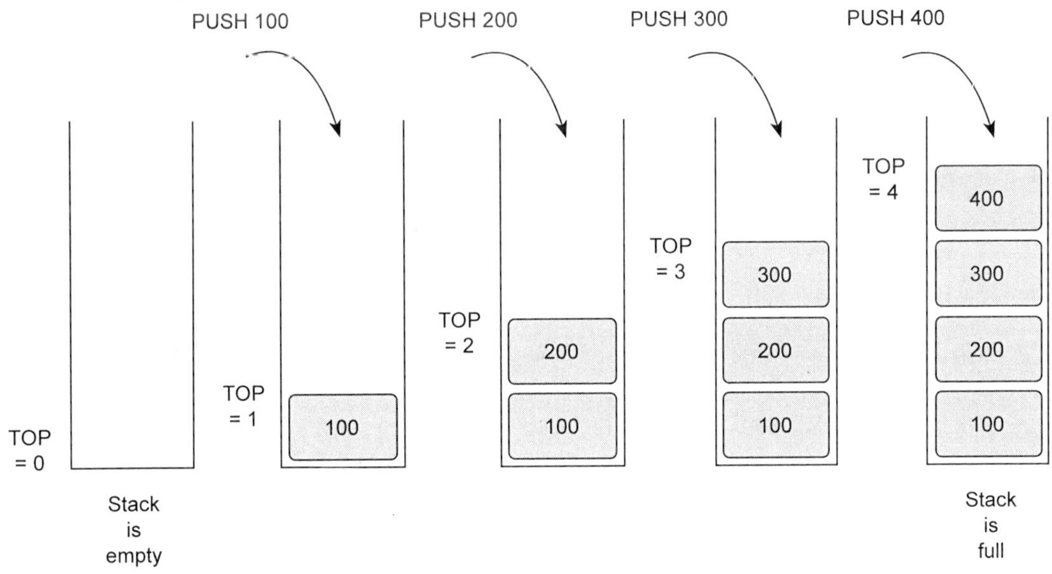

Fig. 1.2: PUSH operations

Now, we perform a set of POP operations to delete the stack elements. The first POP operation deletes the top element of the stack by decrementing the value of TOP by 1. That is, the top element 400 is deleted from the stack by decrementing the value of TOP to 3. In a similar way, if we perform three consecutive POP operations, the elements 300, 200, and 100 repectively are deleted from the stack by decrementing TOP by 1 on each such operation. Now, the stack is empty (the value of TOP is 0) and no further POP operation is possible on the stack. Fig. 1.3 shows these POP operations.

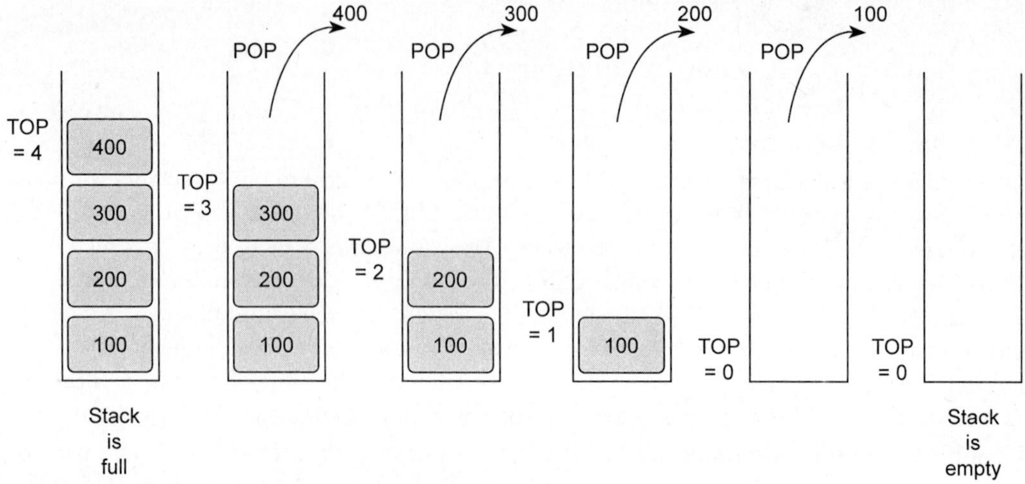

Fig. 1.3: POP operations

Applications of stack:

- Recursion
- Parentheses Checking
- String Reversal
- Backtracking
- Expression Conversion
- Syntax Parsing
- Undo/Redo
- Forward and backward features in web browsers
- Depth First Search Algorithm
- Memory Management

1.5.2 Queue

Similar to stack, *queue* is also a simple data structure used to store data in an ordered manner. However, the way of arranging and accessing data in a queue is opposite to that of a stack. Before going to the details of queue, we first discuss a real world scenario where the concept of queue is applicable.

Consider a line at a movie ticket counter. When you enter the line, you are at the end of it. The person at the front of the line is the first one to be served and depart the line. You will be served only when all the people in front of you are served and depart. Here, the first person who enters the line for a movie ticket is the first one to be served and exit the line. This ordered way of arranging data is known as the First-In-First-Out (FIFO) or Last-In-Last-Out (LILO) policy.

Definition: A simple data structure that follows FIFO or LILO order to store information is known as a "queue". In a queue, insertions are done at one end, termed "REAR", and deletions are done at the other end, termed "FRONT."

Similar to stack, queue also defines two types of operations. The insertion of an element into the queue is termed as ENQUEUE and the deletion of an element from the queue is called DEQUEUE.

Generally, a simple array is used to implement the queue. Fig. 1.4 depicts a queue and its ENQUEUE and DEQUEUE operations.

Fig. 1.4: Queue and its basic operations

The ENQUEUE and DEQUEUE operations of a queue are defined as follows.

```
Procedure ENQUEUE(int ITEM)
        Input Queue_Array[1, 2, …, N], ITEM
        // Let REAR and FRONT be the rear and front
                                    positions of a queue
        If (REAR == N)
               Print Overflow
        Else If (FRONT == REAR == 0)
               FRONT = REAR = 1
               Queue_Array[REAR] = ITEM
        Else
               Increment REAR by 1
               Queue_Array[REAR] = ITEM
        End If
End Procedure
```

```
Procedure DEQUEUE()
        Input Queue_Array[1, 2, …, N]
        // Let REAR and FRONT be the rear and front
                                       positions of a queue
        If (FRONT == REAR == 0)
               Print Underflow
        Else If (FRONT == REAR)
               FRONT = REAR = 0
        Else
               Increment FRONT by 1
        End If
End Procedure
```

Let us consider a queue (say, Queue_Array) that supports a maximum of N elements within it. The variables REAR and FRONT denote the rear and front positions of a queue, respectively. Initially, the queue is empty and the values of both FRONT and REAR are set to 0. When the first element (say, ITEM) is added into the queue, both FRONT and REAR become 1, and the ITEM is stored in the

Queue_Array[REAR]. On each new element insertion, the value of REAR is incremented by 1, and that element is stored in the Queue_Array[REAR]. This insertion operation may continue till the value of REAR becomes N. If the value of REAR is N, no further insertion is possible into the queue resulting in an "Overflow" situation. An element is deleted from a queue through its FRONT position. The value of FRONT is incremented by 1 on each deletion operation. If the values of FRONT and REAR are 0, the queue is said to be empty and no further deletion is possible from the queue. The deletion of an element from an empty queue results in an 'Underflow' situation.

Example-6: Consider a queue of size 4, and is denoted as Queue[1,2,3,4]. Initially, the queue is empty and the values of both FRONT and REAR are set to 0. When the first data '100' is added into Queue, both FRONT and REAR become 1, and 100 is stored at Queue[1]. When a new data '200' is added into Queue, the value of REAR is incremented to 2, and 200 is stored at Queue[2]. Now, we perform two more ENQUEUE operations to add data '300' and '400' into Queue, and are stored at positions Queue[3] and Queue[4], respectively. Each such ENQUEUE operation increments the value of REAR by 1, and finally the value of REAR becomes 4 which is equal to the maximum size of the queue. No further ENQUEUE operation is possible since the queue is already full. Fig. 1.5 depicts these ENQUEUE operations.

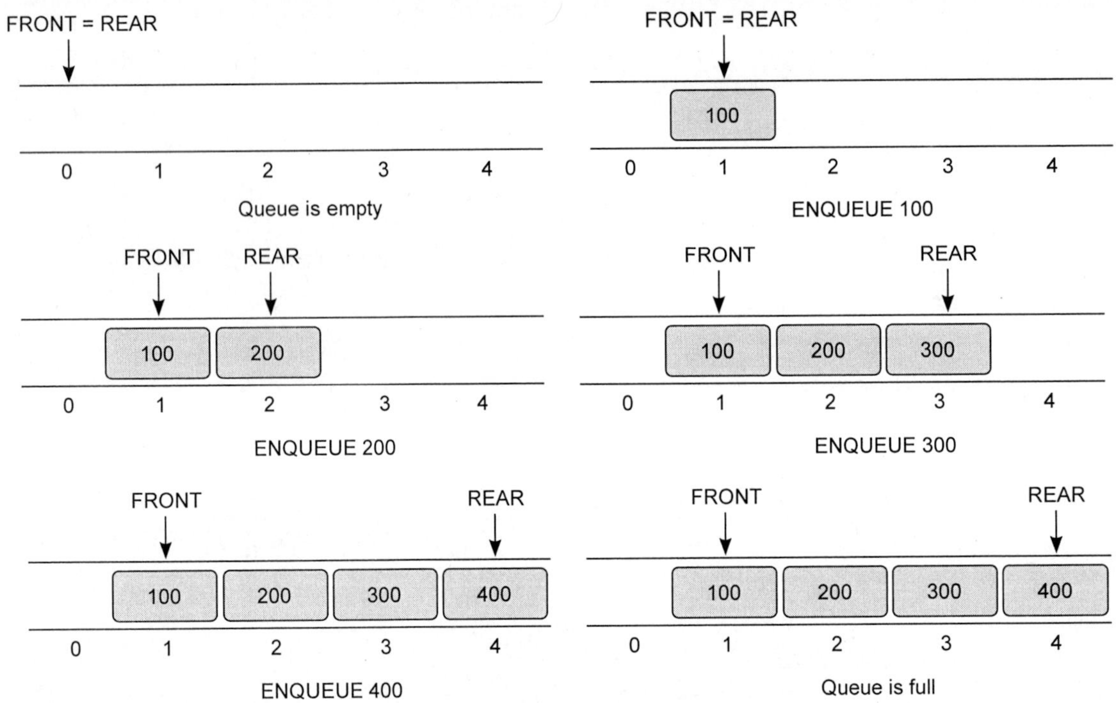

Fig. 1.5: Enqueue operations

Now, we perform a set of DEQUEUE operations to delete the queue elements. The DEQUEUE operation is performed at the FRONT position of Queue. Currently, the values of FRONT and REAR are 1 and 4, respectively. The first DEQUEUE operation deletes the data stored at Queue[1] by incrementing the value of FRONT to 2. In a similar way, if we perform three consecutive DEQUEUE operations, the data '200', '300', and '400' repectively, are deleted from the queue by incrementing FRONT by 1 on each such operation. When we delete the last data 400 from Queue[4], the values of FRONT and REAR become the same, that is, 4, and are then reset to 0. When the values of FRONT and REAR are 0, the queue is said to be empty and no further DEQUEUE operation is possible from the queue. Fig. 1.6 shows these DEQUEUE operations.

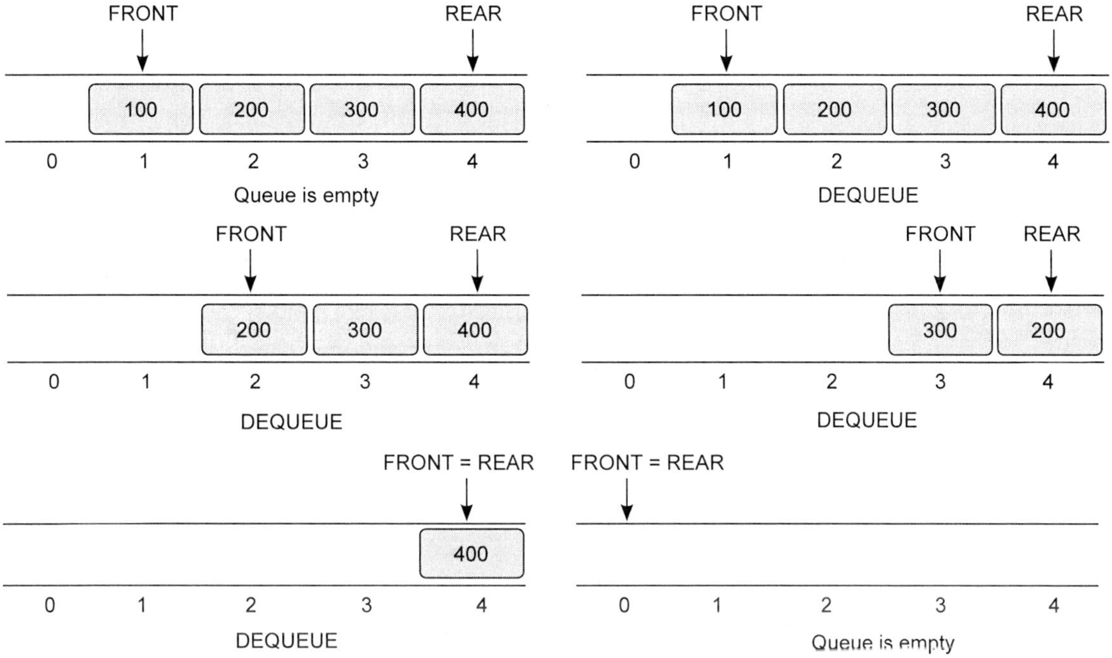

Fig. 1.6: Dequeue operations

Applications of queue:

- Call center phone systems use queues to hold people calling them in order.
- Handling of interrupts in real-time systems.
- Waiting lists for a single shared resource like CPU, Disk, Printer.
- Song list in a media player.

1.6 ASYMPTOTIC COMPLEXITY AND WORST-CASE ANALYSIS

Given a problem statement, we can design an algorithm to solve it and then, implement this algorithm in any programming language of our choice. As part of this process, we try to find answers to the following questions:

1. Does the designed algorithm satisfy all conditions provided in the problem statement?
2. Are the algorithm steps documented correctly?
3. Does the implemented program/procedure execute and produce correct results for all possible input combinations mentioned in the problem statement?

The above questions are really important in the design of an algorithm. After designing the algorithm, there is a need to evaluate its performance. The performance evaluation of an algorithm is a process of identifying the amount of resources (such as time and space) needed to get the final results. So, the efficiency (or complexity) of an algorithm is described in terms of space and time complexity.

Space complexity: The amount of memory required to complete the execution of an algorithm.

Time complexity: The amount of time taken to complete the execution of an algorithm.

In most cases, running time is more important than the memory requirement of an algorithm. Hence in this section, we will focus on the time complexity analysis of an algorithm. One of the naive approaches to find the running time is to execute it on a computing machine/CPU with specific input data and measure the amount of time taken for its execution. However, this approach will work correctly for that specific input and the employed CPU only. Hence, measurement of the exact running time of an algorithm for a specific input on a given CPU is not very useful. Instead of computing exact running time, we use asymptotic analysis to measure the order of growth in running time of an algorithm, with respect to growth in the size of the input.

To illustrate asymptotic analysis, let us consider the following example.

Example-7: Compute the sum of the first n natural numbers: 1 + 2 + 3 + … + n.

Solution Approaches: There can be multiple ways to solve this problem. Let us discuss two possible ways. Approach-1: Iteratively add each number starting from 1 to n. Approach-2: Use the formula (n * (n + 1)) / 2 to find the answer directly. Now, we represent both these approaches using the following procedures:

```
L1:   Procedure sum_of_N_numbers_approach_1(n)
L2:       Input n
L3:       Initialize variables: sum to 0, count to 1
L4:       Repeat until count <= n
L5:           sum = sum + count
L6:           Increment count by 1
L7:       End Repeat
L8:       Print sum
L9:   End Procedure
```

```
L1:   Procedure sum_of_N_numbers_approach_2(n)
L2:       Input n
L3:       Initialize variable sum to 0
L4:       sum = (n * (n + 1)) / 2
L5:       Print sum
L6:   End Procedure
```

Comparison between Approaches 1 and 2:

In *sum_of_N_numbers_approach_2()*, a formula has been used to directly compute the final answer. Here, irrespective of the value of n, the statements within the entire procedure get executed only once. So, the number of statements/steps executed remains constant for Approach-2. On the other hand, the number of steps executed by the procedure *sum_of_N_numbers_approach_1()* depends on the input value n, since the repeat loop (in Line no. 4) will be executed n times. Thus, the number of steps executed is linearly dependent on n for Approach-1. From this comparison, we can conclude that the running time of Approach-1 is higher than Approach-2.

The above approach of analyzing the number of steps involved in the computation of final result forms the basis for asymptotic analysis of an algorithm. Based on the possibility of the number of steps that will be executed for a specific input instance of an algorithm, the running time can be categorized as follows:

- **Worst-case running time**

  This is the scenario in which the algorithm takes the highest amount of time for its execution. So, this provides an upper bound on the execution time of the algorithm over all possible input combinations.

- **Best-case running time**

  This represents the lower bound on the execution time of an algorithm over all possible combinations of inputs that it can take.

- **Average-case running time**

  This captures the average amount of time taken for the execution of an algorithm.

To illustrate the above discussed concept on the worst-case, average-case, and best-case running times, let us consider the following algorithm/procedure *sequential_search()*. This procedure takes a list containing a set of items and an item to be searched (search_item). It searches for search_item in the list by starting from the first item. If search_item is found, it prints the location of search_item in the list. Otherwise, it prints NOT_FOUND.

```
Procedure sequential_search (list[1, 2, …,n],
                                            search_item)
        Input list[1, 2, …, n], search_item
        Initialize count = 0
        For each item in the list
                Increment count by 1
                If item matches with the search_item
                        Print "item's location"
                End If
    End For
    Print "NOT_FOUND"
End Procedure
```

For the above procedure/algorithm, let us consider the following list as an input: [1, 2, 3, 4, 5, 6, 8, 9, 10].

- The worst-case running time for this algorithm occurs when search_item is 10. Specifically, sequential_search takes 10 and starts comparison with 1. Since 10 does not match with 1, 10 will be compared with the next item (i.e., 2). This process will be repeated until 10 is found and this leads to the comparison of all items in the list. A similar situation occurs when *search_item* is not present in the list.
- We know that the search always starts from the first item in the list. So, the best-case running time occurs when search_item is 1.
- Average-case running time occurs when search_item lies almost in the middle of the input list. In this scenario, average-case occurs when search_item is 5.

As part of asymptotic analysis, the following notations are used as short forms to describe running-times:

- Big-Oh notation (O)

- It measures the worst-case running time of an algorithm

- Big-Omega notation (Ω)
  - It measures the best-case running time of an algorithm
- Big-Theta notation (Θ)
  - It measures the average-case running time of an algorithm

In this book, we will discuss Big-Oh notation since computing the worst-case running time of an algorithm is an important aspect of algorithm analysis.

Big-Oh notation (O)

Let T(n) be the running time (growth rate) of an algorithm. According to Big-Oh notation, T(n) is the order of function 'p' of 'n'. That is,

T(n) = O(p(n))

This means that T(n) is less than a constant multiple of p(n) for n >= n_0. For a given constant c, the above expression of T(n) can be re-written as follows:

T(n) <= c * p(n),   where c > 0

So, as the value of n is increased beyond no, the function p(n) provides an upper bound (c * p(n)) on the growth rate of T(n). This has been pictorially depicted in the figure below.

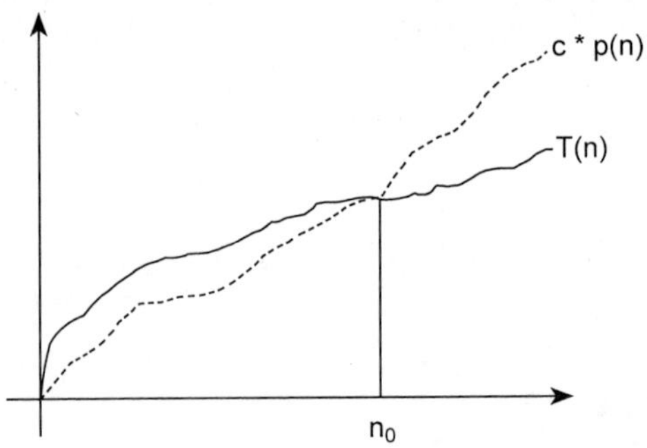

For example, let us consider (k1 * n) and (k2 * log n) with k1 < k2. When n starts growing from 0 to infinity, the values returned by (k1 * n) may be greater than (k2 * log n) since k1 < k2. However, after reaching a certain value of n (say, n_0), the values returned by (k1 * n) will always be greater than (k2 * log n). With respect to the figure shown above, we can relate T(n) to (k2 * log n) and p(n) to (k1 * n). Here, (k1 * n) overtakes (k2 * log n), when n reaches n_0.

Now, let us apply the concept of Big-Oh to constructs that are described in our programming model.

- **Simple statement**

  Let us consider the following procedure:

```
Procedure ex_simple_stmt(No_A, No_B, No_C)
        Input No_A, No_B, No_C
        No_A = No_B + No_C
End Procedure
```

  This is an example of a simple statement (No_A = No_B + No_C) which performs simple addition. Theoretically, the execution of this operation takes one unit of time on a computing machine. Then, T(n) = 1. With respect to Big-oh notation, we can express this relation as follows:

$T(n) <= 1 * 1$ where $c = 1$ and $n_0 = 0$

Comparing the above equation with the general equation of Big-Oh, we can find that p(n) = 1. Hence, the above relation can be re-written as follows: T(n) = O(1).

- **Sequence of statements**

  Let us consider the following procedure:

```
Procedure ex_sequence_stmt(No_A, No_B, No_C)
        Input No_A, No_B, No_C
        No_C = No_A
        No_A = No_B
        No_B = No_C
Print No_A, No_B, No_C
End Procedure
```

  The execution time of a sequence of statements is the sum of execution time of individual statements (excluding the input). In the above procedure, there are four statements and thus, T(n) = 4. With respect to Big-oh notation, we can express this relation as follows:

  $T(n) <= 4 * 1$ where $c = 4$ and $n_0 = 0$

  With respect to the general equation of Big-Oh, we get p(n) = 1. Therefore, T(n) = O(1).

- **Looping statement**

  Let us consider the procedure *sum_of_N_numbers_approach_1()* that we have discussed. In this procedure,

  No. of simple statements = 3 (Line nos. 3, 8)

  No. of Loops = 1 (Line nos. 4 to 7)

  No. of statements within loop = 3 (1 comparison, 2 additions)

  Here, the loop will execute for n times.

  Thus, $T(n) = 3 + (n * 3) = 3n + 3$

  If $n >=4$, then $3n + 3 <= 4n$. We can say

  $T(n) <= 4n$ where $c = 4$, $n_0 = 0$

  $T(n) = O(n)$

- **Nested Looping statement**

  Let us consider the following procedure that contains nested "for each" loops in it:

```
Procedure sample_nested_loop(list1[1, 2, …, n],
                                 list2[1, 2, …, n])
        Input list1[1, 2, …, n], list2[1, 2, …, n]
        For each item in the list1
                For each item in the list2
                        Print list1[item]
                        Print list2[item]
                End For
        End For
End Procedure
```

In the above procedure, the inner "for each" loop (Line nos. 4 to 7) is executed for n times for a single execution of the outer "for each" loop (Line nos. 3 to 8). So, the statements in Line nos. 5 and 6 will be executed for n * n times. Thus, $T(n) = n^2$.

To satisfy Big-Oh notation, it can be written as,

$T(n) = 1 * n^2$ where $c = 1$ and $n_0 = 0$

In the above equation, we can see that $p(n) = n^2$. Thus, $T(n) = O(n^2)$.

- **Conditional statement**

  To discuss this, let us consider the following procedure:

```
L1:  Procedure sample_cond_loop(Num_X, list1[1, 2, …, n],
                                       list2[1, 2, …, n])
L2:       Input Num_X, list1[1, 2, …, n], list2[1, 2, …, n]
L3:       If (Num_X == 1)
L4:            Num_X = Num_X + 1
L5:       Else
L6:            For each item in the list1
L7:                 For each item in the list2
L8:                      Print list1[item]
L9:                      Print list2[item]
L10:                End For
L11:           End For
L12:      End If
L13: End Procedure
```

In the above procedure, we know that either Line no. 4 or Line nos. 6 to 11 will be executed, depending on the value of Num_X. The time complexity of "If" and "Else" parts are $O(1)$ and $O(n^2)$, respectively. The maximum of these two is $O(n^2)$. Hence, the time complexity of this entire procedure is $O(n^2)$.

Example-8: Compute the time complexity of the following equations:

1. $T(n) = 2022$

   $T(n) <= 2022 * 1$, where $c = 2022$, $n_0 = 0$.

   Hence, $T(n) = O(1)$
2. $T(n) = 5 * n + 12$

   $T(n) <= 5 * n + 12 <= 6 * n$, where $c = 6$, $n_0 = 12$.

   Hence, $T(n) = O(n)$
3. $T(n) = 20 * n^2 + 2$

   $T(n) <= 20 * n^2 + 2 <= 21 * n^2$, where $c = 21$, $n_0 = 2$.

   Hence, $T(n) = O(n^2)$
4. $T(n) = 20 * n^3 + 2 * n + 5$

   $T(n) <= 20 * n^3 + 2 * n + 5 <= 21 * n^3$, where $c = 21$, $n_0 = 5$.

   Hence, $T(n) = O(n^3)$

Based on Big-Oh notation, we have the following categories of time complexities:

- O(1) Constant time
- O(log n) Logarithmic time
- O(n) Linear time
- O(n log n) Linear Logarithmic time
- $O(n^k)$ Polynomial time (where, k > 1)
- $O(2^n)$ Exponential time

Further Insights

At the start of this section, we discussed two algorithms/approaches to compute the sum of n natural numbers. If we apply the concept of Big-Oh notation for these algorithms, then

T(n) = O(n) for *sum_of_N_numbers_approach_1()*

T(n) = O(1) for *sum_of_N_numbers_approach_2()*

From the above running times, we can see that approach-2 is more efficient than approach-1.

Growth rate of algorithms

For different types of algorithms, the growth rate for different values of input size n have been presented in the following table:

n	log n	n log n	n^2
1	0	0	1
2	1	2	4
16	4	64	256
256	8	2048	65536
1024	10	10240	1048576

The pictorial representation of the growth rate for different values of input size ***n*** is also presented below:

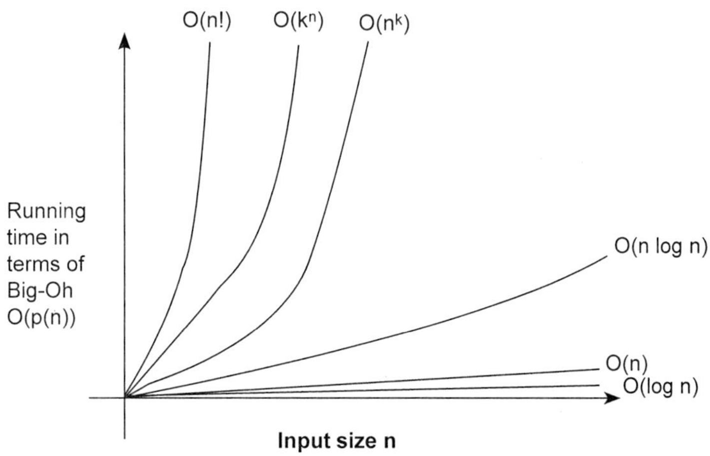

UNIT SUMMARY

A sound grasp of algorithms is necessary for any computer engineer. This introductory unit first introduces the concept of algorithms as a well-defined finite sequence of steps for solving a problem. It discusses the computation model in terms of which algorithms have been written in this book. It explains the notions of data structures and data abstraction as mechanisms for organizing data and associated operations in an algorithm. The unit then goes on to discuss in detail a few important data structures along with illustrative examples. Finally, the concepts of asymptotic complexity and worst-case analysis of an algorithm's efficiency has been dealt with. Mechanisms for measuring an algorithm's time complexity and using this measure for comparing the efficiencies of different alternative strategies for solving a given problem, have also been discussed.

EXERCISES

Multiple Choice Questions

1. What is the value stored in the variables No_A and No_B after the execution of the following sequence of assignment statements: No_A = 10, No_B = 20, No_C = 2, No_A = No_B % No_C, No_B = No_B / No_C.
   (a) 10, 20 (b) 2, 0
   (c) 1, 10 (d) 0, 10
2. What is the value stored in the variables No_A and No_B after the execution of the following sequence of assignment statements: No_A = 10, No_B = 20, No_C = 0, No_C = No_A, No_A = No_B, No_B = No_C.
   (a) 10, 20 (b) 20, 10
   (c) 10, 10 (d) 20, 20
3. Which one of the following conditions can be used to check whether the given number (say, Num_X) is an odd number?
   (a) (Num_X == 2) (b) (Num_X %2 != 0)
   (c) (Num_X / 2 == 0) (d) None of the above
4. Let us consider the following [1, 2, 3, 4]. This can be called as ______.
   (a) Set (b) Multiset
   (c) Both (a) and (b) (d) None of the above
5. Let us consider the following [1, 2, 3, 3, 4]. This can be called as ______
   (a) Set (b) Multiset
   (c) Both (a) and (b) (d) None of the above
6. Find A U B, if set A = [1, 3, 5] and set B = [2, 4]
   (a) [1, 5, 3] (b) [4, 2]
   (c) [1, 5, 2, 4, 3] (d) [2, 1, 3]
7. Find A - B, if A = [1, 3, 5] and B = [2, 4]
   (a) [1, 3, 5] (b) [2, 4]

(c) [1, 2, 3, 4, 5] (d) [1, 2, 3]

8. Find A - B, if A = [1, 3, 5] and B = [1, 2, 4]
   (a) [1, 3, 5] (b) [2, 4]
   (c) [1, 2, 3, 4, 5] (d) [3, 5]
9. Balanced parentheses problem is solved using ___ data structure?
   (a) Queue (b) Set
   (c) Array (d) Stack
10. Recursion is implemented using ____ data structure?
   (a) Multiset (b) Queue
   (c) Stack (d) Set
11. Which of the following is not an application of stack.
   (a) Resources like CPU, DISK scheduling (b) Recursion
   (c) String Reversal (d) Parentheses Checking
12. A data structure in which insertion is performed on one side and deletion is performed only on the other side is known as ____.
   (a) Stack (b) Set
   (c) Queue (d) Tree
13. The order followed by a queue is ____.
   (a) Last-In-First-Out (LIFO) (b) First-In-First-Out (FIFO)
   (c) First-In-Last-Out (FILO) (d) None of the above
14. Consider a queue which is implemented using an array of size n. The queue is said to be *full* if
   (a) FRONT == REAR + 1 (b) FRONT == (REAR + 1) mod n
   (c) REAR == FRONT (d) REAR == n
15. Let us consider the following procedure *sample_iterator_1()*:

```
Procedure sample_iterator_1(list[1, 2, …, n])
        Input list[1, 2, …, n]
        For each item in the list
                Print list[item]
        End For
End Procedure
```

   What is the total running time of the *sample_iterator_1()* procedure?
   (a) 1 (b) 100
   (c) n (d) n/2
16. Let us consider the following procedure *sample_iterator_2()*:

```
Procedure sample_iterator_2(list1[1, 2, …, N1],list2
                                        [1, 2, …, N2])
        Input list1[1, 2, …, N1],list2 [1, 2, …, N2]
        For each item in the list1
                Print list1[item]
```

```
        End For
    End Procedure
```

What is the total running time of the *sample_iterator_2()* procedure?

(a) N (b) N1

(c) N1 + N2 (d) N2

17. Let us consider the following procedure *sample_iterator_3()*:

```
Procedure sample_iterator_3(list1[1, 2,…, N1],list2[1,
                                                2, …, N2])
    Input list1[1, 2, …, N1], list2[1, 2, …, N2]
    For each item in the list1
        For each item in the list2
            Print list1[item]
        Print list2[item]
        End For
    End For
End Procedure
```

What is the total running time of the *sample_iterator_3()* procedure?

(a) N (b) N1 / N2

(c) N1 + N2 (d) N1 * N2

18. Let us consider the following procedure *sample_iterator_4()*:

```
Procedure sample_iterator_4(list1[1, 2,…, N1],list2[1,
                                                2, …, N2])
    Input list1[1, 2, …, N1], list2[1, 2, …, N2]
    For each item in the list1
            Print list1[item]
    End For
    For each item in the list2
            Print list2[item]
    End For
End Procedure
```

What is the total running time of the *sample_iterator_4()* procedure?

(a) N (b) N1 / N2

(c) N1 + N2 (d) N1 * N2

19. Let us consider the following procedure *sample_iterator_5()*:

```
Procedure sample_iterator_5(list1[1, 2,…, N1],list2[1,
                                                2, …, N2])
    Input list1[1, 2, …, N1], list2[1, 2, …, N2]
    For each item in the list1
            Print list1[item]
    End For
```

```
        For each item in the list1
            For each item in the list2
                Print list1[item]
                Print list2[item]
            End For
        End For
        For each item in the list2
                Print list2[item]
        End For
    End Procedure
```

What is the total running time of the *sample_iterator_5()* procedure?

(a) N1 / N2 (b) N1 + N2 + (N1 * N2)
(c) N1 + N2 (d) N1 * N2

20. What is the time-complexity for $T(n) = 20 * n^2 + 1000 * n + 100000$, in Big- Oh notation?

(a) O(100000) (b) $O(n^2)$
(c) O(n) (d) O(1)

21. What is the time-complexity for $T(n) = n^{100} + 100^{100} * n^{10}$, in Big-Oh notation?

(a) O(100) (b) $O(n^{10})$
(c) $O(n^{100})$ (d) O(1)

22. Which one of the following statements is true?

(a) $O(1) < O(n) < O(\log n) < O(n^2)$ (b) $O(1) < O(\log n) < O(n) < O(n^2)$
(c) $O(n) < O(\log n) < O(1) < O(n^3)$ (d) $O(n) < O(1) < O(n^2) < O(\log n)$

23. Let us consider two algorithms namely, Algo_1 and Algo_2, which are used to solve the same problem. The time-complexity of Algo_1 and Algo_2 are O(n) and O(log n), respectively. Which one of the following statements is true?

(a) Algo_1 is efficient than Algo_2 (b) Algo_2 is efficient than Algo_1
(c) Both Algo_1 and Algo_2 are efficient (d) None of them are efficient

Answers for Multiple Choice Questions

1. (d), 2. (b), 3. (b), 4. (c), 5. (b), 6. (c), 7. (a), 8. (d), 9. (d), 10. (c), 11. (a), 12. (c), 13. (b), 14. (d), 15. (c), 16. (b), 17. (d), 18. (c), 19. (b), 20. (b), 21. (c), 22. (b), 23. (b)

Short and Long Answer Type Questions

1. Write a procedure to print the first 100 numbers (starting from 1) using the "Repeat until" statement.
2. Write a procedure to print all the elements in a given input array.
3. Write a procedure to print the largest number among two numbers.
4. Write a procedure to check whether the given integer number (say, Num_X) is an odd number.
5. Write a procedure to print the list of first 100 even numbers (starting from 1).

6. Write a procedure to print the smallest number in a given input array.
7. Let us consider the array *Random_Num*[1, 2, …, n] with n integer numbers. Write a procedure to compute and print the average of all n numbers in *Random_Num*.

Hint: Solution approach is given below.

```
Procedure compute_avg_of_numbers(Random_Num[1,2,…,n])
        Input Random_Num[1,2,…,n]
        Initialize variables Sum = 0, Avg = 0
        For each element R in Random_Num[1, 2, …, n]
            Sum = Sum + R
        End For
        Compute Avg = Sum / n;
        Print Avg
End Procedure
```

8. Let us consider the array *Random_Num*[1, 2, …, n] with n integer numbers. Write a procedure to find the number of occurrences of the given number Num_X in *Random_Num*.

Hint: Solution approach is given below.

```
Procedure find_frequency(Random_Num[1,2,…,n], Num_X)
    Input Random_Num[1,2,…, n], Num_X
        Initialize count = 0
        Repeat until index <= n
            If (Num_X == Random_Num[index])
                Increment count by 1
            End If
            Increment index by 1
        End Repeat
        Print Num_X is present in Random_Num for count
                                                    times
End Procedure
```

9. Consider the following multisets: A = [1, 2, 3, 4], B = [1, 5, 4], C = [1, 2, 3]. Find (A - B) U C.
10. Consider the following sets: A = [1, 2, 3, 4], B = [1, 5, 4], C = [1, 2, 3]. Find (A - B) U C.
11. Consider the following sets: A = [1, 2, 3, 4], B = [1, 5, 4], C = [1, 2, 3]. Find (A U B) $\cap$ C.
12. Let us consider the following procedure *multiset_manipulation_1()*:

```
Procedure multiset_manipulation_1()
    A = Multiset()
    A.add(1)
    A.add(1)
    B = Multiset()
    B.add(2)
    A = A union B
    For each item R in Multiset A
```

```
            If R != 1
                  Print item R
            End If
      End For
End Procedure
```

What is the output of the above procedure?

13. Let us consider the following procedure *Multiset_manipulation_2():*

```
Procedure Multiset_manipulation_2()
      A = Multiset()
      A.add(1)
      A.add(2)
      B = Multiset()
      B.add(2)
      B.add(3)
      C = Multiset()
      C = A intersection B
      B = A union B
      For each item R in C intersection B
            If R == 1
                  R = R - 1
                  Print itcm R
            Else
                  R = R + 1
                  Print item R
            End If
      End For
End Procedure
```

What is the output of the above procedure?

14. What is a stack? Discuss different stack operations with an example.
15. List out various applications of stack.
16. Consider a stack in which the following operations are performed sequentially. PUSH(10), PUSH(20), PUSH(20), POP, PUSH(10), POP, POP, PUSH(20), POP, POP. Write the correct order of popped out values.

Hint: Answer – 20, 10, 20, 20, 10

17. Consider a stack that can be used to solve the following problem of parentheses balancing (( ) (( )) (( ))). By analysing this problem, find out the maximum number of parentheses that can be added into the stack at any point in time.

Hint: Answer – 3

18. What is a Queue? What are the different operations that can be performed over Queue?
19. List out various applications of queue.

20. Consider five people named A, B, C, D and E standing in a queue. A is just standing behind B and B is the second one in the queue. C is standing between A and E. Identify the positions of people in the queue. Who is the second last person in the queue?

Hint: Answer – Queue is D B A C E. The second last person is C.

21. Let us consider the following procedure *sample_iterator_6()*:

```
Procedure sample_iterator_6(value)
        Input value
        If value is 1
                Return 1
        End If
        Return value * sample_iterator_6(value - 1)
End Procedure
```

What is the total running time of the *sample_iterator_6()* procedure?

22. Let us consider the following procedure *sequential_search()* with the input *list*: [10, 5, 3, 4, 15, 6, 28, 9, 1]

```
Procedure sequential_search()
        Input list, search_item
        Initialize count = 0
        For each item in the list
                Increment count by 1
                If item matches with the search_item
                        Print "item's location"
                End If
        End For
        Print "NOT_FOUND"
End Procedure
```

(a) The best-case running time occurs when search_item is _____.

(b) The worst-case running time occurs when search_item is _____.

23. Let us consider the following procedure *sequential_search()*. This procedure takes a list containing a set of items and an item to be searched (search_item). It searches for search_item in the list by starting from the first item. If search_item is found, it will print the location of search_item in the list. Otherwise, it prints NOT_FOUND.

```
Procedure sequential_search()
        Input list, search_item
        Initialize count = 0
        For each item in the list
                Increment count by 1
                If item matches with the search_item
                        Print "item's location"
```

```
            End If
        End For
        Print "NOT_FOUND"
    End Procedure
```

(a) For the *sequential_search()* procedure, let us consider **list** = {1, 2, 5, 4, 5, 6, 7}, **search_item** = 5. For this input, what is the **count** value?

(b) For the *sequential_search()* procedure, Let us consider **list** = {1, 2, 5, 4, 5, 6, 7}, **search_item** = 8. For this input, what is the **count** value?

(c) What are the lowest and highest possible values for **count** in the *sequential_search()* procedure, for the input list containing **n** (where, n > 1) elements in it?

(d) For the *sequential_search()* procedure, best case and worst case input combination occurs when **search_item** is the _____ and _____ element in the input **list**, respectively. Assume that the search_item is present in the input **list**.

Hint: Answers – a) 3, b) 7, c) 1, n, d) first, last

24. Let us consider the following procedure: binary_search(). This procedure takes a list containing a set of items which are already sorted in non-decreasing order and an item be searched (search_item). It searches search_item in the list. If found, it will return the location of search_item in the list. Otherwise, it returns NOT_FOUND. (Note: floor(x) refers to the largest integer not greater than x).

```
Procedure binary_search(list[1, 2, …, n], search_item)
      Input list[1, 2, …, n], search_item
            Initialize low = 1, high = n, count = 0
      Repeat until low <= high
Update count by 1
Calculate middle = floor ((low + high) / 2);
If an element at the middle position in list
matches with search_item
                  Return middle
End If
If an element at the middle position in list is greater
                                         than search_item
                  Update high = middle - 1
End If
If an element at the middle position in list is lesser
                                        than search_item
                  Update low = middle + 1
End If
            End Repeat
            Return NOT_FOUND
End Procedure
```

(a) For the *binary_search()* procedure, let us consider **list** = {1, 2, 3, 4, 5, 6, 7}, **search_item** = 5. For this input, what is the **count** value?

(b) For the *binary_search()* procedure, Let us consider **list** = {1, 2, 3, 4, 5, 6, 7}, **search_item** = 8. For this input, what is the **count** value?

(c) What are the lowest and highest possible values for **count** in the *binary_search()* procedure, for the input list containing **n** (where, n > 1) elements in it?

(d) For the *binary_search()* procedure, if the input list is not sorted, then its running time becomes ______.

Hint: Answers – a) 3, b) 3, c)1, log n, d) O(n log n)

KNOW MORE

This section talks about a set of additional information that helps the reader to improve the knowledge on the topics discussed in Unit-1.

Characteristics of an Algorithm:

An algorithm must have the following characteristics:

1. **Input:** The information that may be passed on to the algorithm externally for computation is known as input. An algorithm must receive zero or more well-defined inputs for its proper computation.
2. **Output:** The result that is generated as part of the computation is known as the output. An algorithm must generate one or more outputs that correspond to the expected result(s).
3. **Finiteness:** An algorithm must stop or terminate after a finite number of steps.
4. **Definiteness:** All the statements or steps in an algorithm must be clear and unambiguous.
5. **Effectiveness:** An algorithm must be efficient in terms of both time and memory. It should be free from any redundant or unnecessary statements or steps that make it ineffective.

Iterative Vs. Recursive Procedures

Algorithms can be classified into two broad categories – iterative and recursive. Iteration and recursion are essentially two different ways of repeatedly executing a set of instructions. Iterative algorithms use loops and conditional statements for such repetitive instruction execution. For example, given the problem of printing the largest number in a given input array, the solution presented in 'Example-3' above is an instance of an iterative algorithm.

In comparison, a recursive algorithm expresses repetition by using a procedure which calls itself on smaller sub-problems. This strategy allows a large problem to be broken down into smaller pieces and to obtain the solution to a large complex problem in terms of (often) more easily derivable solutions to smaller sub-problems. As an illustration, let us see how a simple recursive solution can be obtained for the problem in Example-3.

Example: Write a recursive procedure for printing the largest number in a given input array.

Solution Approach: A generic recursive solution approach would be as follows. As before, let us consider an input array (say, random_numbers) with ***n*** numbers in it. Now, split the array into two smaller sub-arrays, say, random_numbers [1...p] and random_numbers [p+1...n]. Recursively find the maximum elements in random_numbers [1...p] and random_numbers [p+1...n]. Let them be max1 and max2, respectively. The larger of max1 and max2 is returned as the maximum element of the original array random_numbers [1…n].

```
Procedure find_largest_number(random_numbers[1, 2, …, n])
        Input random_numbers[1, 2, …, n]
        // Let max be the largest element
        max = find_max(random_numbers[1, 2, …, n])
        Print max
End Procedure
Procedure find_max(random_numbers[1, 2, …, n])
        Input random_numbers[1, 2, …, n]
        If (n == 1)
                Return random_numbers[1]
        End If
        // Choose any integer p between 1 and n-1
        max1 = find_max(random_numbers[1, 2, …, p])
        max2 = find_max(random_numbers[p+1, …, n])
        If (max1 > max2)
                Return max1
        Else
                Return max2
        End If
End Procedure
```

It may be noted that in the above procedure, we have a choice on the value of 'p', and that all allowable values of 'p' give us the correct solution. This 'choice' allows us to explore multiple alternative ways of constructing a recursive solution from constituent sub-problems, and possibly determine the best alternative in terms of algorithmic efficiency.

Solution Analysis: The following recurrence relation can be derived from the solution procedure above:

$T(n) = O(1)$, if $n = 1$

$T(n) = T(p) + T(n-p) + O(1)$, if $n > 1$

It is easy to see that for this simple problem, $T(n) = O(n-1) = O(n)$, irrespective of our choice for the value of 'p'.

REFERENCES AND SUGGESTED READINGS

Syllabus Referred Textbooks:

1. Algorithms, 4th Edition. R. Sedgewick, and K. Wayne. Addison-Wesley, (2011)
2. Introduction to Algorithms, Fourth Edition, Thomas H. Cormen, Charles E. Leiserson, Ronald L. Rivest and Clifford Stein, The MIT Press, (2022)
3. Introduction to the Theory of Computation, Third Edition, M. Sipser. Course Technology, Boston, MA, (2013)

4. Design And Analysis Of Algorithms, Third Edition, Gajendra Sharma, Khanna Book Publishing Company (P) Limited, (2015)

Other Textbook References:

1. Data Structures and Algorithms Made Easy, Second Edition, Narasimha Karumanchi, CareerMonk Publications, (2011)
2. Data Structure Through C, Yashavant P. Kanetkar, BPB Publications, (2003)
3. Algorithms: Design and Analysis, Harsh Bhasin, Oxford University Press, (2015)

Dynamic QR Code for Further Reading

Scan Me

2 Sorting

UNIT SPECIFICS

Through this unit we have discussed the following aspects:

- Importance of the sorting problem in Computer Science
- Simple $O(n^2)$ sorting algorithms along with analysis on their efficiency
- Design and analysis of two more efficient strategies, Quicksort and Mergesort
- Choice of the right sorting strategy for a given problem at hand

RATIONALE

Sorting, or arranging items in an appropriate order, is a fundamental component towards solving many larger, more complicated problems. In Computer Science, a systematic study of sorting problems is an essential step in learning the art of designing efficient algorithms. Also, sorting often helps reduce the complexity of other problems.

This chapter focuses on the discussion of a few important sorting strategies through the textual description of these strategies, presentation of their pseudo-codes with running examples and also analyses of their algorithmic efficiencies.

PRE-REQUISITES

Rudimentary knowledge of computer programming

UNIT OUTCOMES

List of outcomes of this unit is as follows:

U2-O1: Describe basic importance of the sorting problem
U2-O2: Describe and distinguish between prominent sorting approaches
U2-O3: Explain the working of various sorting strategies through running examples
U2-O4: Realize the algorithmic efficiency of different sorting strategies
U2-O5: Apply an appropriate sorting strategy for a given problem at hand

Unit-2 Outcome	EXPECTED MAPPING WITH COURSE OUTCOMES (1 - Weak Correlation; 2 - Medium Correlation; 3 - Strong Correlation)				
	CO-1	CO-2	CO-3	CO-4	CO-5
U2-O1	3	3	2	2	1
U2-O2	3	3	2	2	1
U2-O3	3	3	3	3	1
U2-O4	3	3	3	3	1
U2-O5	3	3	3	3	1

2.1 THE SORTING PROBLEM

Since time immemorial, a lot of human endeavour and effort has gone into *sorting* or arranging a given set of items or elements in a particular order. This is because such an order often provides a more organized or structured view of the set of items and allows humans to derive further information about the items. In a majority of scenarios, the sorting order is usually monotonic, either *ascending* (more accurately *non-descending*, to take care of scenarios when the given set has multiple elements having the same value) or *descending* (*non-ascending*).

In Computer Science, the problem of sorting (along with searching) has traditionally attracted a lot of research, possibly because of the complexity involved in solving it, despite its relatively straight-forward problem definition. Given an unsorted sequence (represented as an array) of integer numbers, say A[75, 10, 7, 6, 20, 40, 50, 30, 99, 30], as input to a sorting algorithm, the sorted output in non-decreasing order becomes: A[6, 7, 10, 20, 30, 30, 40, 50, 75, 99]. We will study five important sorting algorithms in this chapter, namely Bubble sort, Selection sort, Insertion sort, Mergesort and Quicksort. We will analyze each of these algorithms, both in terms of their design complexity as well as algorithmic efficiency.

2.2 BUBBLE SORT

This was one of the first sorting techniques, which was initially described and investigated as a computer algorithm in 1956. An overview of the approach is as follows: At the beginning, for an n element array, the 1st one is compared with the 2nd and swapped if the 2nd element is found to be smaller. Then, the 2nd element is compared with the 3rd and possibly swapped, if the 3rd element is found to be smaller. In a similar fashion, all the elements (excluding the nth (last) element) are compared with their next elements and possibly exchanged, if required. This concludes the algorithm's first iteration. The largest element in the array is put in the final (nth) place after the first iteration. In the second iteration, pairwise comparisons between consecutive elements in the array are similarly conducted, starting from the 1st element up to the $(n\text{-}1)^{th}$ (last but one) element. When the second iteration completes, the second largest element gets placed in the last but one ($(n\text{-}1)^{th}$) position of the array. In this way, the entire array gets sorted after n-1 iterations.

2.2.1 Pseudocode

```
Procedure Bubble_Sort (IN_LST[1, 2, …, n])
        Input IN_LST[1, 2, …, n]
        For each i from 1 to n-1
                For each j from 1 to n-i
                        If IN_LST[j] > IN_LST[j+1]
                                bbl_val = IN_LST[j]
                                IN_LST[j] = IN_LST[j+1]
                                IN_LST[j+1] = bbl_val
                        End If
                End For
        End For
End Procedure
```

2.2.2 Example

Let us consider the input array, A[75, 10, 7, 6, 20, 40, 50, 30, 99, 30]

Iteration-1 (i = 1):

Iteration-1 (j = 1):

Swap A[1] = 75 with A[2] = 10

[10, 75, 7, 6, 20, 40, 50, 30, 99, 30]

Iteration-2 (j = 2):

Swap A[2] = 75 with A[3] = 7

[10, 7, 75, 6, 20, 40, 50, 30, 99, 30]

.

.

.

Iteration-n-i (j = 9):

Swap A[9] = 99 with A[10] = 30

[10, 7, 6, 20, 40, 50, 30, 75, 30, 99]

Iteration-2 (i = 2):

Iteration-1 (j = 1):

Swap A[1] = 10 with A[2] = 7

[7, 10, 6, 20, 40, 50, 30, 75, 30, 99]

Iteration-2 (j = 2):

Swap A[2] = 10 with A[3] = 6

[7, 6, 10, 20, 40, 50, 30, 75, 30, 99]

.

.

.

Iteration-n-i (j = 8):

Swap A[1] = 75 with A[2] = 30

[7, 6, 10, 20, 40, 30, 50, 30, 75, 99]

.

.

.

Iteration-n-1 (i = 9):

Iteration-n-i (j = 1):

[6, 7, 10, 20, 30, 30, 40, 50, 75, 99]

So, the final sorted output is: A [6, 7, 10, 20, 30, 30, 40, 50, 75, 99].

2.2.3 Complexity Analysis

Two "For" loops, one nested inside the other, are used in the procedure above. The outer iterative loop is repeated n-1 times. On the other hand, the inner iterative loop has been iterated n-i times for the ith iteration of the outer iterative loop. Each iteration of the inner iterative loop has a constant time overhead (O(1)). As a result, the algorithm's *worst-case overall time complexity* becomes:

$$T(n) = (n - 1 + n - 2 + \ldots + 1) \times O(1) = O(((n - 1) \times (n - 2)) / 2) = O(n^2)$$

Bubble sort only needs to carry out *O(n)* comparisons in the best scenario when the input array has already been sorted, making its complexity O(n).

2.3 SELECTION SORT

One of the simplest sorting methods is *selection sort.* It begins by identifying the least element in the input array. Then, the strategy swaps this least element with the first. The second-smallest element is then found and substituted for the first. This process is repeated until every element in the array is organised in a sorted manner.

2.3.1 Pseudocode

```
Procedure Selection_Sort(IN_ARY[1, 2, …, n])
        Input IN_ARY[1, 2, …, n]
        For each i from 1 to (n - 1)
                //Let IN_ARY[i] be the ith smallest element
                min_index = i
                For each j from i to n
                        If IN_ARY[j] < IN_ARY[min_index]
                                min_index = j
                        End If
                End For
                //Put ith smallest element in its final
                position
                swap (IN_ARY[i], IN_ARY[min_index])
```

```
L13:          End For
L14:    End Procedure
```

2.3.2 Example

Let us consider the input array, A [75, 10, 7, 6, 20, 40, 50, 30, 99, 30].

(**Note:** For readability purposes, we print the values of i and min_index at line no. 12 in the Selection_Sort() procedure presented above.)

Iteration-1 (i = 1):

1st smallest element: 6 (min_index = 4)
Swap A[1] = 75 with A[4] = 6
[6, 10, 7, 75, 20, 40, 50, 30, 99, 30]

Iteration-2 (i = 2):

2nd smallest element: 7 (min_index = 3)
Swap A[2] = 10 with A[3] = 7
[6, 7, 10, 75, 20, 40, 50, 30, 99, 30]

Iteration-3 (i = 3):

3rd smallest element: 10 (min_index = 3)
Swap A[3] = 10 with A[3] = 10
[6, 7, 10, 75, 20, 40, 50, 30, 99, 30]

Iteration-4 (i = 4):

4th smallest element: 20 (min_index = 5)
Swap A[4] = 75 with A[5] = 20
[6, 7, 10, 20, 75, 40, 50, 30, 99, 30]

Iteration-5 (i = 5):

5th smallest element: 30 (min_index = 10)
Swap A[5] = 75 with A[10] = 30
[6, 7, 10, 20, 30, 40, 50, 75, 99, 30]

Iteration-6 (i = 6):

6th smallest element: 30 (min_index = 10)
Swap A[6] = 40 with A[10] = 30
[6, 7, 10, 20, 30, 30, 50, 75, 99, 40]

Iteration-7 (i = 7):

7th smallest element: 40 (min_index = 10)
Swap A[7] = 50 with A[10] = 40
[6, 7, 10, 20, 30, 30, 40, 75, 99, 50]

Iteration-8 (i = 8):

8th smallest element: 50 (min_index = 10)

Swap A[8] = 75 with A[10] = 50
[6, 7, 10, 20, 30, 30, 40, 50, 99, 75]

Iteration-9 (i = 9):

9th smallest element: 75 (min_index = 10)
Swap A[9] = 99 with A[10] = 75
[6, 7, 10, 20, 30, 30, 40, 50, 75, 99]

The final sorted array is: **A [6, 7, 10, 20, 30, 30, 40, 50, 75, 99]**

2.3.3 Complexity Analysis

It can be seen that the procedure *Selection_Sort()*, contains two "For" loops. Specifically, the outer "For" loop (in Line no. 3) iterates from i = 1 to (n - 1). The inner "For" loop (in Line no. 6) iterates from j = i to n. Considering both the "For" loops together, there will be n iterations, when "i = 1". Similarly, when "i = 2", there will be (n - 1) iterations. Finally, when "i = (n - 1)", there will be only two iterations. More precisely, the sum of the number of steps is provided below:

$$n + (n - 1) + (n - 2) + (n - 3) + \ldots + 3 + 2 = n^2 - 1 = O(n^2)$$

It may be noted that selection sort's running time is unaffected by input. That is, it always requires n^2 iterations in all situations (best/average/worst), regardless of whether or not we have an already sorted input array.

2.4 INSERTION SORT

Consider a real-world scenario where we have a set of playing cards in our hands for a card game. The cards are selected one at a time and inserted into an appropriate position among a set of already sorted cards. The insertion sort algorithm works in a similar fashion.

The given input array (say, A[1, 2, 3, .., n]) is logically divided into two lists: one sorted and the other unsorted. Initially, we assume that the first entry (A[1]) of the array is in the sorted list, and all other elements (A[2, 3, .., n]) are part of the unsorted list. At the first iteration, the first entry (A[2]) in the unsorted list is selected and compared with the first one (A[1]) in the sorted list. If A[2] is less than A[1], we swap A[2] with A[1]. Otherwise, the element A[2] is inserted into the sorted list by adding it on the right side of A[1]. In the next iteration, we select the first element (A[3]) in the unsorted list and compare it with the elements of the sorted list (A[1] and A[2]). Then, we insert A[3] at its correct place in the sorted list. Repeat this procedure until the sorted list contains all of the unsorted list's components. Insertion sort is considered as an important basic sorting algorithm due to its effective but straightforward construction.

2.4.1 Pseudocode

```
Procedure Insertion_Sort(IN_ARY[1, 2, …, n])
        Input IN_ARY[1, 2, …, n]
        For each i from 1 to n-1
                Initialize j = i+1
                Repeat until j>1 and (IN_ARY[j]<IN_ARY[j-1])
                        swap(IN_ARY[j], IN_ARY[j-1])
```

```
L7:                     Decrement j by 1
L8:                 End Repeat
L9:         End For
L10:    End Procedure
```

2.4.2 Example

Let us consider the input array, A [75, 10, 7, 6, 20, 40, 50, 30, 99, 30]

Iteration-1 (i = 1):

a) j = 2, Swap A[2] = 10 with A[1] = 75, Decrement j by 1
b) j = 1, condition j > 1 in line no. 5 fails
[10, 75, 7, 6, 20, 40, 50, 30, 99, 30]

Iteration-2 (i = 2):

a) j = 3, Swap A[3] = 7 with A[2] = 75, Decrement j by 1
b) j = 2, Swap A[2] = 7 with A[1] = 10, Decrement j by 1
c) j = 1, condition j > 1 in line no. 5 fails
[7, 10, 75, 6, 20, 40, 50, 30, 99, 30]

Iteration-3 (i = 3):

a) j = 4, Swap A[4] = 6 with A[3] = 75, Decrement j by 1
b) j = 3, Swap A[3] = 6 with A[2] = 10, Decrement j by 1
c) j = 2, Swap A[2] = 6 with A[1] = 7, Decrement j by 1
d) j = 1, condition j > 1 in line no. 5 fails
[6, 7, 10, 75, 20, 40, 50, 30, 99, 30]

Iteration-4 (i = 4):

a) j = 5, Swap A[5] = 20 with A[4] = 75, Decrement j by 1
b) j = 4, condition A[j] < A[j-1] in line no. 5 fails
[6, 7, 10, 20, 75, 40, 50, 30, 99, 30]

Iteration-5 (i = 5):

a) j = 6, Swap A[6] = 40 with A[5] = 75, Decrement j by 1
b) j = 5, condition A[j] <A[j-1] in line no. 5 fails
[6, 7, 10, 20, 40, 75, 50, 30, 99, 30]

Iteration-6 (i = 6):

a) j = 7, Swap A[7] = 50 with A[6] = 75, Decrement j by 1
b) j = 6, condition A[j] <A[j-1] in line no. 5 fails
[6, 7, 10, 20, 40, 50, 75, 30, 99, 30]

Iteration-7 (i = 7):

a) j = 8, Swap A[8] = 30 with A[7] = 75, Decrement j by 1
b) j = 7, Swap A[7] = 30 with A[6] = 50, Decrement j by 1

c) j = 6, Swap A[6] = 30 with A[5] = 40, Decrement j by 1
d) j = 5, condition A[j] <A[j-1] in line no. 5 fails
[6, 7, 10, 20, 30, 40, 50, 75, 99, 30]

Iteration-8 (i = 8):

a) j = 9, condition A[j] <A[j-1] in line no. 5 fails
[6, 7, 10, 20, 30, 40, 50, 75, 99, 30]

Iteration-9 (i = 9):

a) j = 10, Swap A[10] = 30 with A[9] = 99, Decrement j by 1
b) j = 9, Swap A[9] = 30 with A[8] = 75, Decrement j by 1
c) j = 8, Swap A[8] = 30 with A[7] = 50, Decrement j by 1
d) j = 7, Swap A[7] = 30 with A[6] = 40, Decrement j by 1
e) j = 6, condition A[j] <A[j-1] in line no. 5 fails
[6, 7, 10, 20, 30, 30, 40, 50, 75, 99]

The final sorted array is: **A [6, 7, 10, 20, 30, 30, 40, 50, 75, 99]**

2.4.3 Complexity Analysis

The input determines how long insertion sort takes to complete. Whether or not the input array is already sorted affects how long it takes to run. The outer loop ("For" loop; line 3) runs for n-1 iterations if the input array has already been sorted, and the inner "Repeat untill" loop (line 5) does not run at all in the best-case situation. The best-case complexity is therefore O(n). The complexity increases, though, if the input array is reverse-sorted already. In this worst-case situation, the outer iterative loop runs (n-1) times. On the other hand, the inner iterative loop runs (n-2). Therefore, its overall *worst-case complexity* is given by:

$$T(n) = O(1) \times (1 + 2 + 3 + \ldots (n - 2) + (n - 1)) = O(n (n - 1) / 2) = O(n^2).$$

In case of an unsorted array, the average complexity case occurs and it is the same as the complexity for the worst-case (i.e., $O(n^2)$).

2.5 MERGESORT

One of the most well-liked and efficient sorting methods is mergesort, which is frequently selected in practical applications due to its efficient average and worst-case running times. It sorts the given unsorted array by dividing and conquering. The detailed steps are described below.

The procedure *Merge_Sort()* sorts the entire array A[1,.., n] by taking two variables, say, left and right, that point to the leftmost and rightmost indices of A, respectively, along with the given array A as inputs.

Divide: A[left,.., middle] and A[middle+1,.., right] are two half-sized sub-arrays that are created from the unsorted array by locating its middle index (middle = (left + right)/2).

Conquer: The sub-arrays A[left,.., middle] and A[middle+1,.., right] are sorted recursively using the procedures *Merge_Sort(A, left, middle)* and *Merge_Sort(A, middle+1, right)*, respectively. When a sub-array of size one is encountered, the recursive call will terminate.

Combine: The procedure *Merge(A, left, middle, right)* shown inside *Merge_Sort()* is used to combine the sub-arrays into the final sorted array.

2.5.1 Pseudocode

```
Procedure Merge_Sort(A[1, 2, …, n], left, right)
        Input A[1, 2, …, n], left, right
        If left > = right
                return
        End If
        middle = (left + right)/2
        Merge_Sort(A, left, middle)
        Merge_Sort(A, middle+1, right)
        Merge(A, left, middle, right)
End Procedure
```

```
Procedure Merge(A[1, 2, …, n], left, middle, right)
        Input A[1, 2, …, n], left, middle, right
        Initialize i = left, j = middle + 1
        For each k from left to right
                // Declare a temporary array B[1,2, …, n]
                 to hold the elements of A
                B[k] = A[k]
        End For
        For each k from left to right
                If (i > middle)
                  A[k] = B[j++]
            Else If (j > right)
                  A[k] = B[i++]
            Else If (B[j] < B[i])
                  A[k] = B[j++]
            Else
                  A[k] = B[i++]
            End If
     End For
End Procedure
```

2.5.2 Example

Let us consider the input array, A [75, 10, 7, 6, 20, 40, 50, 30, 99, 30]. Fig. 2.1 depicts the steps for sorting the given input array using the mergesort. Here, the number mentioned inside the "circle" denotes the order in which the steps are processed.

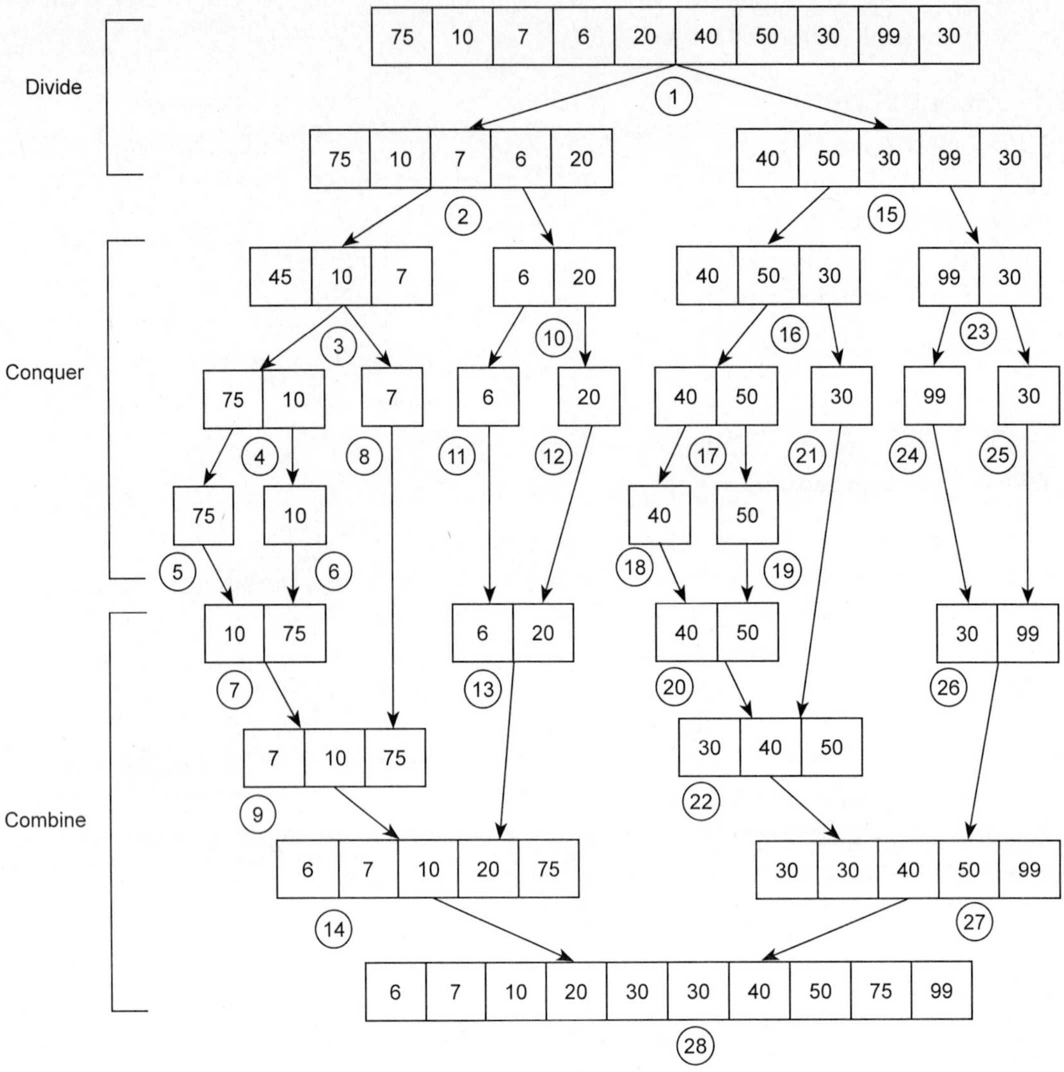

Fig. 2.1: Mergesort steps

Initially, we pass the array A along with left = 1, and right = 10 as inputs to the procedure *Merge_Sort()*. The input array A is then split into two equal-sized sub-arrays using the formula: middle = (1 + 10) / 2 = 5. The sub-arrays [75,.., 20] and [40,.., 30] are then passed onto the recursive procedural calls *Merge_Sort(A, 1, 5)* and *Merge_Sort(A, 6, 10)*, respectively, which again divides each of these arrays into smaller sub-arrays. The recursive function terminates when it encounters a sub-array of size 1 (base condition). That is, no further division is possible from that sub-array. For example, steps 5 and 6 indicate the generation of two sub-arrays of size 1, that is, [75] and [20]. The algorithm then combines these two sub-arrays and produces a sorted array [10, 75] using the procedure *Merge()*. We then backtrack and combine the sub-array [7] with this array [10, 75] to generate a new sorted array [7, 10, 75]. These processes of recursive calling and merging are repeated until we generate the final sorted array [6, 7, 10, 20, 30, 30, 40, 50, 75, 99].

2.5.3 Complexity Analysis

Recurrence relations are used to compute the running time of recursive algorithms. A recurrence relation is typically an equation that expresses the value of a function on smaller inputs. For example, let T(n) be the worst-case time complexity of the mergesort on an input array of size n. When n = 1, that is, the input array contains only one element, mergesort takes constant time. The complexity of mergesort is evaluated when n > 1 using the divide-and-conquer approach that was previously discussed. This can be shown by the recurrence relation below:

$$T(n) = O(1) \qquad \text{if } n = 1$$
$$T(n) = 2T(n/2) + O(n) \qquad \text{if } n > 1$$

Divide: This step requires constant time since this step just finds the middle of the sub-array.

Conquer: In the conquer stage, two sub-arrays of almost identical size n/2 are sorted recursively. Each such sub-array consumes T(n/2) time, leading to an overall time complexity of 2T(n/2).

Combine: The combine step uses the Merge() procedure that takes O(n) time.

When we add the time complexities of divide, conquer and merge parts, the time complexity of merge sort becomes:

$$\begin{aligned} T(n) &= O(1) + 2T(n/2) + O(n) \\ &= 2T(n/2) + O(n) \\ &= O(n \log n) \end{aligned}$$

It should be noted that input has no bearing on how long mergesort takes to complete. This means that in all scenarios (best/average/worst), regardless of whether the input array is already sorted, it always takes O(n log n) time. This is due to the fact that the mergesort always splits the input array into equal-sized halves and then combines them in O(n) time.

Solving Recurrences:

Typically, recurrence relations can be solved using methods like the substitution, recursion tree, and master methods. In this section, we will look at the substitution method. It consists of two steps: (i) Make an educated guess about the final solution; (ii) employ mathematical induction to prove that the solution actually works. This method can be used to compute lower and upper bounds on recurrences. Let us compute an upper bound on the recurrence corresponding to mergesort as an example.

$$T(n) = 2T(n/2) + O(n)$$

Since the input array is partitioned into two halves and O(n) computations are performed in each iteration, we can make a rough guess for T(n) as O(n log n). In the substitution method, we need to show that $T(n) \leq C\, n \log n$ for the constant $C > 0$. Let us first demonstrate that this bound holds good for all positive values of $M < n$. Specifically, we choose $M = n / 2$. Substituting this for the recurrence results in:

$$T(n/2) \leq C\, n/2 \log n/2$$

Applying the above in equation(1),

$$\begin{aligned} T(n) &\leq 2\,(C\, n/2 \log n/2) + n \\ T(n) &\leq C\, n \log n/2 + n \\ T(n) &= C\, n \log n - C\, n \log 2 + n \\ T(n) &= C\, n \log n - C\, n + n \\ T(n) &\leq C\, n \log n \end{aligned}$$

The above step holds as long as $C \geq 1$. We must now demonstrate that the above solution holds true for the boundary conditions using mathematical induction. To identify the boundary values, let us employ the asymptotic analysis, i.e., $T(n) \leq C\, n \log n$ for $n \geq n_0$, where n_0 is a constant. Setting n_0 to 1 leads to $T(1) \leq C\, 1 \log 1 = 0$, which contradicts the recurrence relation $T(1) = 1$ if $n = 1$. So, let $n_0 = 2$.

$$T(n) = 2T(n/2) + O(n)$$
$$T(2) = 2\,T(1) + 2 = 4.$$

So, we can set $n_0 = 2$ as the base case of inductive proof. To complete the proof, we need to choose C, which is large enough such that $T(2) \leq C\, 2 \log 2$. It can be seen that any choice of $C \geq 2$ satisfies the base case $n_0 = 2$ to hold (i.e., $4 \leq 2 * 2 \log 2$; $4 \leq 4$. Note: Here, the base for the logarithm is 2 since the mergesort splits the input problem into two halves). As a result, the mergesort algorithm's worst-case complexity is $T(n) = O(n \log n)$.

2.6 QUICKSORT

This is one of the popular sorting techniques and it is often preferred in real-world applications due to its efficient average-case running time. It uses a divide-and-conquer strategy to sort the input unsorted array A[p,..., r]:

Divide: The input A[p, …, r] is partitioned into sub-arrays A[p, …, q-1] and A[q+1, …, r] such that elements in, (i) A[p, …, q-1] are less than or equal to A[q], (ii) A[q+1, …, r] are greater than A[q]. This partitioning has been explained using the procedure *Partition()*.

Conquer: Recursively invoking the *Quick_Sort()* procedure will sort the sub-arrays A[p, ..., q-1] and A[q+1, ..., r].

Combine: The sub-arrays can be joined to create the final sorted array because they are already sorted.

2.6.1 Pseudocode

```
Procedure Quick_Sort(IN_LST[1, 2, …, n], p, r)
        Input IN_LST[1, 2, …, n], p, r
        If p < r
                q = Partition(IN_LST, p, r)
                Quick_Sort(IN_LST, p, q-1)
                Quick_Sort(IN_LST, q+1, r)
    End If
End Procedure
```

```
Procedure Partition(IN_LST[1, 2, …, n], p, r)
        Input IN_LST[1, 2, …, n], p , r
        Initialize pivot = IN_LST[r]
        Initialize i = p - 1
        For each j from p to r - 1
                If IN_LST[j] <= pivot
                        i = i + 1
                        swap (IN_LST[i], IN_LST[j])
            End If
    End For
```

```
        swap (IN_LST[i+1], IN_LST[r])
        Return i + 1
    End Procedure
```

2.6.2 Example

Let us consider the input array, A [75, 10, 7, 6, 20, 40, 50, 30, 99, 30].

Here, p = 1, r = 10. Then, Quick_Sort(A[75, 10, …, 30], 1, 10). Since 1 < 10, q = Partition(A, 1, 10), pivot = A[r] = 30, i = p - 1 = 0.

Iteration-1 (j = 1, i = 0):

A[1] = 75 is not less than the pivot 30.

[75, 10, 7, 6, 20, 40, 50, 30, 99, 30]

Iteration-2 (j = 2, i = 0):

A[2] = 10 <= 30.

i = i + 1 = 1. Swap A[1] with A[2].

[**10**, 75, 7, 6, 20, 40, 50, 30, 99, 30]

Iteration-3 (j = 3, i = 1):

A[3] = 7 <= 30.

i = i + 1 = 2. Swap A[2] with A[3].

[**10, 7**, 75, 6, 20, 40, 50, 30, 99, 30]

Iteration-4 (j = 4, i = 2):

A[4] = 6 <= 30.

i = i + 1 = 3. Swap A[3] with A[4].

[**10, 7, 6**, 75, 20, 40, 50, 30, 99, 30]

Iteration-5 (j = 5, i = 3):

A[5] = 20 <= 30.

i = i + 1 = 4. Swap A[4] with A[5].

[**10, 7, 6**, 20, 75, 40, 50, 30, 99, 30]

Iteration-6 (j = 6, i = 4):

A[6] = 40 is not less than 30.

[**10, 7, 6**, 20, 75, 40, 50, 30, 99, 30]

Iteration-7 (j = 7, i = 4):

A[7] = 50 is not less than 30.

[**10, 7, 6, 20**, 75, 40, 50, 30, 99, 30]

Iteration-8 (j = 8, i = 4):

A[8] = 30 <= 30.

i = i + 1 = 5. Swap A[5] with A[8].

[**10, 7, 6, 20, 30**, 40, 50, 75, 99, 30]

Iteration-9 (j = 9, i = 5):

A[9] = 99 is not less than 30.

[**10, 7, 6, 20, 30**, 40, 50, 75, 99, 30]

After Iteration-9 (i = 5):

i = i + 1 = 6. Swap A[6] with A[10].

[**10, 7, 6, 20, 30, 30**, 50, 75, 99, 40]. Return value = 6. Then, q = 6.

This will lead to the following splits:

Quick_Sort(A[10, 7, …, 40], 1, 5)

Quick_Sort(A[10, 7, …, 40], 7, 10)

Now, let us consider the first split Quick_Sort(A[10, 7, …, 40], 1, 5). Here, p = 1, r = 5, pivot = A[5] = 30. It may be noted that A[j] <= pivot, for all values of j (1 to 4), since this sub-array has already been in a sorted order. Hence, the return value i = 0 from Partition(A[10, 7, …, 40], 1, 5). Thus, there will be no more recursive calls from the first split.

Let us consider the second split Quick_Sort(A[10, 7, …, 40], 7, 10). Here, p = 7, r = 10, pivot = A[10] = 40. After the execution of Partition(A[10, 7, …, 40], 7, 10), the resulting array: [**10, 7, 6, 20, 30, 30, 40**, 75, 99, 50] with the return value 8. In the next invocation of Quick_Sort(A[10, 7, …, 50], 9, 10), the pivot 50 gets swapped with 75 and results in [**10, 7, 6, 20, 30, 30, 40, 50**, 99, 75]. It takes one more invocation of *Quick_Sort()* to get the final sorted array: [**6, 7, 10, 20, 30, 30, 40, 50, 75, 99**].

2.6.3 Complexity Analysis

Let us first examine the running time of the Partition() procedure, which is used internally by the Quick Sort() procedure. For the given array of size n, Partition() chooses a pivot element and compares it against all the remaining elements. Finally, the input array is partitioned into two parts: sub-array containing elements that are less than or equal to the pivot element and sub-array with the elements greater than the pivot. As a result, the running time of Partition() is O(n). Now, let us analyze the worst / best / average-case behaviors of Quick_Sort().

- Worst-case behavior

  This situation occurs when the Partition() procedure partitions the input array with size n into one sub-array of size (n-1) and another sub-array with 0 elements. Further, let us assume that such an imbalance partitioning occurs at every recursive call. Then,

  $$T(n) = T(n-1) + T(0) + O(n)$$
  $$T(n) = T(n-1) + O(n)$$

  Here, T(0) = 1 since there is no element to sort. If we solve the above recurrence relation using the substitution method, then it will result in $O(n^2)$. In particular, adding up the number of steps taken at each stage of the recursion yields an arithmetic series: (n + (n-1) + (n-2) + … + 1). So, $T(n) = O(n^2)$.

- Best-case behavior

  This scenario occurs when the Partition() procedure always splits the input array of size n into two sub-arrays of size (almost) equal to (n/2). Then,

  $$T(n) = 2T(n/2) + O(n) = O(n \log n).$$

- Average-case behavior
  This is similar to the best-case scenario. If the partition always produces two sub-arrays with a total number of elements greater than zero in each, then T(n) becomes O(n log n).

UNIT SUMMARY

For an input array of η elements, the table below summarises the best, average, and worst-case running times for the sorting algorithms covered in this chapter:

Sorting Approach	Best	Average	Worst
Bubble	$\Omega(\eta)$	$\Theta(\eta^2)$	$O(\eta^2)$
Selection	$\Omega(\eta^2)$	$\Theta(\eta^2)$	$O(\eta^2)$
Insertion	$\Omega(\eta)$	$\Theta(\eta^2)$	$O(\eta^2)$
Merge	$\Omega(\eta \log \eta)$	$\Theta(\eta \log \eta)$	$O(\eta \log \eta)$
Quick	$\Omega(\eta \log \eta)$	$\Theta(\eta \log \eta)$	$O(\eta^2)$

EXERCISES

Multiple Choice Questions

1. What are the best, average, worst-case complexities of bubble sort, for an input array with *k* elements?
   (a) k, k^2, k^2
   (b) k, k log k, k^2
   (c) k, k^2, k^3
   (d) k^2, k^2, k^3
2. In the following options, what is true about bubble sort?
   (a) $O(n^2)$ for a sorted input.
   (b) $O(n^2)$ for a reverse sorted input.
   (c) Always consumes $O(n^2)$ for sorting an input array.
   (d) Always consumes O(n log n) for sorting an input array.
3. What are the best, average, worst-case complexities of selection sort, for an input array with *k* elements?
   (a) k, k^2, k^3 (b) k, k, k
   (c) k^2, k^2, k^2 (d) k^2, k^2, k^3
4. Let us consider the input array [10, 10, 10, 10, 10]. How many iterations (including both inner and outer loops) will be taken by the selection sort algorithm to produce the final sorted output (in non-decreasing order)?
   (a) 10 (b) 12
   (c) 14 (d) 25

5. Let us consider the input array [50, 40, 30, 20, 10]. How many iterations (including both inner and outer loops) will be taken by the selection sort algorithm to produce the final sorted output (in non-decreasing order)?
   (a) 0 (b) 1
   (c) 25 (d) 15
6. Let us consider the input array [100, 120, 140, 160, 180]. How many iterations (including both inner and outer loops) will be taken by the selection sort algorithm to produce the final sorted output (in non-decreasing order)?
   (a) 0 (b) 1
   (c) 15 (d) 25
7. In the following options, what is true about the selection sort?
   (a) O(n) for a sorted input.
   (b) O(log n) for a reverse sorted input.
   (c) Always consumes $O(n^2)$ for sorting an input array.
   (d) Always consumes O(n log n) for sorting an input array.
8. Suppose the given input array is sorted or nearly sorted. ________ sort is the best algorithm to sort this given input.
   (a) Selection (b) Quick
   (c) Insertion (d) Merge
9. For insertion sort, the best, average, worst-case complexities are __, __, __, for an input array with *f* elements?
   (a) f log f, f^2, f^2 (b) f, f^2, f^2
   (c) f log f, f^2, f (d) f log f, f log f, f log f
10. What is true about insertion sort in the following options?
    (a) $O(n^2)$ for a sorted input.
    (b) $O(n^2)$ for a reverse sorted input.
    (c) Always consumes $O(n^2)$ for sorting an input array.
    (d) Always consumes O(n log n) for sorting an input array.
11. Let us consider the input array [100, 120, 140, 160, 180]. How many iterations (including both inner and outer loops) will be taken by insertion sort to produce final sorted output (in non-decreasing order)?
    (a) 5 (b) 4
    (c) 15 (d) 10
12. What are the best, average, worst-case complexities of mergesort, for an input array with ✗ elements?
    (a) ✗ log ✗, ✗2, ✗2 (b) ✗2, ✗2, ✗2
    (c) ✗ log ✗, ✗2, ✗ (d) ✗ log ✗, ✗ log ✗, ✗ log ✗
13. In the following options, what is true about the mergesort algorithm?
    (a) $O(n^2)$ for a sorted input.
    (b) $O(n^2)$ for a reverse sorted input.

(c) Always consumes $O(n^2)$ for sorting an input array.
(d) Always consumes O(n log n) for sorting an input array.

14. What are the best, average, worst-case running time complexities of quicksort, for an input array with Ɣ elements?

(a) Ɣ log Ɣ, Ɣ^2, Ɣ^2 (b) Ɣ^2, Ɣ^2, Ɣ^2
(c) Ɣ log Ɣ, Ɣ^2, Ɣ (d) Ɣ log Ɣ, Ɣ log Ɣ, Ɣ^2

15. Let us consider the input array [10, 10, 10, 10, 10]. Apply the Partition procedure (with p = 1, r = 5) in the quicksort algorithm to produce the two partitions of the input array. How many elements are there in the first and second partitions?

(a) 4, 0 (b) 2, 3
(c) 4, 2 (d) 0, 3

16. Let us consider the input array [50, 40, 30, 20, 10]. Apply the Partition procedure (with p = 1, r = 5) in the quicksort algorithm to produce the two partitions of the input array. How many elements are there in the first and second partitions?

(a) 4, 0 (b) 2, 3
(c) 4, 2 (d) 0, 4

17. Let us consider the input array [100, 120, 140, 160, 180]. Apply the Partition procedure (with p = 1, r = 5) in the quicksort algorithm to produce the two partitions of the input array. How many elements are there in the first and second partitions?

(a) 4, 0 (b) 2, 3
(c) 4, 2 (d) 0, 3

18. In the following options, what is true about the quicksort algorithm?

(a) If the input is sorted already, O(n) time to sort it.
(b) Always consumes $O(n^2)$ to sort the input array.
(c) Always consumes O(n log n) to sort the input array.
(d) Consumes O(n log n) in best / average scenario; On the other hand, $O(n^2)$ in worst-case.

Answers for Multiple Choice Questions

1. (a), 2. (b), 3. (c), 4. (c), 5. (d), 6. (c), 7. (c), 8. (c), 9. (b), 10. (b), 11. (b),
12. (d), 13. (d), 14. (d), 15. (a), 16. (d), 17. (a), 18. (d)

Short and Long Answer Type Questions

1. Explain the stepwise procedure of bubble sort algorithm. What are the merits and demerits of bubble sort.
2. Illustrate the steps of sorting the given input array [50, 40, 30, 20, 10] using bubble sort.
3. Consider the input array [21, 13, 11, 16, 3]. On this input, apply the selection sort algorithm and show the step by step execution (considering the outer loop of selection sort).

   Hint:

   Iteration-1: [3, 13, 11, 16, 21]
   Iteration-2: [3, 11, 13, 16, 21]

Iteration-3: [3, 11, 13, 16, 21]
Iteration-4: [3, 11, 13, 16, 21]

4. Write the selection sort procedure to sort a given array in descending order.
   Hint: Solution approach is given below.

```
Procedure Selection_Sort(γ[1, 2, …, x])
      Input γ[1, 2, …, x]
      For each z from 1 to (x - 1)
            //Let γ[z] be the zth largest element
            maximum_index = z
            For each j from z to x
                  If γ[j] > γ[maximum_index]
                              maximum_index = j
                  End If
            End For
            // Put the zth largest element in its final
            position
            swap (γ[z], γ[maximum_index])
      End For
End Procedure
```

5. Explain the stepwise procedure of insertion sort algorithm.
6. Consider the input array [50, 40, 30, 20, 10]. Illustrate the steps of sorting this array using insertion sort.
7. Explain the stepwise procedure of mergesort algorithm.
8. Consider the input array [40, 35, 30, 25, 20, 15, 10, 5]. Illustrate the steps of sorting this array using mergesort.
9. Consider the input array [21, 13, 11, 16, 3]. On this input, apply the Partition() procedure in the quicksort algorithm and show the step by step execution.
   Hint:
   Iteration-1: [21, 13, 11, 16, 3]
   Iteration-2: [21, 13, 11, 16, 3]
   Iteration-3: [21, 13, 11, 16, 3]
   Iteration-4: [21, 13, 11, 16, 3]
   Iteration-5: [3, 13, 11, 16, 21]
10. Write the quicksort procedure to sort the given array in descending order.
    Hint: In the Partition() procedure, replace "A[j] <= pivot" with "A[j] >= pivot."

KNOW MORE

This section talks about a set of additional information that helps the reader to improve the knowledge on the topics discussed in Unit-2.

IN-PLACE SORT

When a sorting algorithm uses only a constant amount of extra storage or variables to perform the sorting operation over the given input array, then it is termed as a "IN-PLACE SORT" algorithm. Selection sort, Bubble sort, Insertion sort, and quicksort are a few examples of "IN-PLACE SORT." On the other hand, mergesort requires additional space (O(log n)) to keep track of subarrays in its divide-and-conquer strategy.

STABLE SORT

When an algorithm for sorting maintains the same relative order between elements with equal values in the input array even after producing the sorted output, it is referred to as "STABLE SORT". For example, let us consider an input array [10, 10, 30, 20]. If a sorting algorithm does not change the order of equal elements (i.e., 10, 10) even after producing the sorted output, then it is called "stable sort". The examples of "STABLE SORT" are bubble sort, mergesort, and insertion sort. On the other hand, selection sort and quicksort are not stable.

QUICKSORT IMPROVEMENTS

Quicksort was proposed by C.A.R. Horae in 1960. Since its introduction, many researchers have proposed improvements to it. We can infer from Quicksort's running time study that pivot element choice is a key factor in deciding how well Quicksort works. The "*median-of-3 method*" is one of the most used methods.

The pivot is chosen at random as the median of a group of three elements from the subarray. This approach is expected to generate the balanced partitioning of subarrays.

REFERENCES AND SUGGESTED READINGS

Syllabus Referred Textbooks:

1. All textbooks prescribed in the syllabus.

Other Textbook References:

1. Data Structures and Algorithms Made Easy, Second Edition, Narasimha Karumanchi, CareerMonk Publications, (2011)
2. Data Structure Through C, Yashavant P. Kanetkar, BPB Publications, (2003)

Dynamic QR Code for Further Reading

Scan Me

3 Searching

UNIT SPECIFICS

Through this unit we have discussed the following aspects:

- Importance of the searching problem in Computer Science
- Concept of symbol tables
- Simple searching algorithms along with analysis on their efficiency
- Characteristics of a tree data structure
- Basic operations on binary and balanced search trees
- Design and analysis of hash based searching strategy
- Choice of the right searching strategy for a given problem at hand

RATIONALE

Searching is the operation of determining whether an element exists in a given data structure. Search strategies are evaluated based on how quickly they are able to find a solution. How appropriate a search algorithm is, also often depends on which data structure it is being applied on. Therefore, searching can many-a-times be made more efficient through the use of specially designed data structures such as sorted lists, search trees and hash tables.

Two other problems which are often studied along with searching are insertion and deletion strategies. Efficient techniques for insertion and deletion on a chosen data structure often help to make search more efficient.

PRE-REQUISITES

Rudimentary knowledge of computer programming and data structure

UNIT OUTCOMES

List of outcomes of this unit is as follows:

U3-O1: Describe basic importance of the searching problem

U3-O2: Describe and distinguish between sequential and interval searching strategies

U3-O3: Explain binary and balanced search trees through running examples

U3-O5: Realize the usage of hash tables in the searching problem

U3-O5: Apply an appropriate searching strategy for a given problem at hand

Unit-3 Outcome	EXPECTED MAPPING WITH COURSE OUTCOMES (1 - Weak Correlation; 2 - Medium Correlation; 3 - Strong Correlation)				
	CO-1	CO-2	CO-3	CO-4	CO-5
U3-O1	3	3	2	2	1
U3-O2	3	3	2	2	1
U3-O3	3	3	3	3	1
U3-O4	3	3	3	3	1
U3-O5	3	3	3	3	1

3.1 INTRODUCTION

Along with sorting, *searching* an item within a given list, is also an age-old associated problem which has been extensively studied in computer science. As an example of the searching problem, consider the following: Given a list of integer numbers, say A[75, 10, 7, 6, 20, 40, 50, 30, 99, 30], searching is the process of finding answers to queries such as, whether the element 20 exists in the list; the answer to this query will be returned as TRUE. A call to this search procedure would be of the form: *Search(A[], 20)*. On the other hand, the call: *Search(A[], 15)*, will return FALSE. Along with *search*, two other commonly associated operations are *deletion* of a looked-up element from a list and *addition* of a new element into a list.

All of us have faced the problem of manually searching an item/element of interest, say a song, an address, the name of a student etc., from a given large-sized list. Hence, efficient automated techniques for searching, adding or deleting elements within lists, are necessary. Along with this, design of effective list organization mechanisms for enhanced search efficiency, are also very important and hence, studied.

3.2 SYMBOL TABLES

Often, lists of elements are represented as *symbol tables* where the elements are a set of *<name, value> pairs,* along with possibly other *attributes* containing additional information about the elements. Operations on symbol tables include, querying whether a particular name already exists, as well as *adding* or *deleting* a name along with its associated value and other attributes. These *values,* also called *keys,* are often used to organize the elements of a symbol table in the form of well-defined data structures such as unsorted or sorted sequential lists, trees, binary search trees, balanced binary search trees etc. For example, a sorted sequential list representation of the symbol table, ST[<A,75>, <B,10>, <C,7>, <D,6>, <E,20>, <F,40>, <G,50>, <H,30>, <I,99>, <J,30>] would be say, Sorted-ST[<D,6>, <C,7>, <B,10>, <E,20>, <H,30>, <J,30>, <F,40>, <G,50>, <A,75>, <I,99>]. In the subsequent sections, we will not generally explicitly refer to symbol tables when dealing with particular search strategies, but only refer to them as lists of values (or *keys*) for convenience. However, such values may be implicitly assumed to have associated names and other attributes.

3.3 SEQUENTIAL AND INTERVAL SEARCH

Consider a scenario in which you are searching for a word in a dictionary. You can perform this search operation mainly in two ways. In the first method, you can start the search from the beginning page and keep flipping the pages until you encounter the page where the word lies. On the other hand, you can perform the search by first locating the dictionary's middle pages. Then you can decide to look for the word on the right or left-side pages of the middle. The process of finding the middle and searching for the word on the right or left-side pages of the middle is repeated until you encounter the page where the word lies. The second approach (known as *interval* or *binary search*) is a fast and efficient technique as compared to the first method (known as *sequential* or *linear search*). In the next sections, we will discuss these searching techniques in detail.

3.4 SEQUENTIAL SEARCH

It is the simplest searching algorithm and is also known as *linear search*. In this searching technique, we traverse the given array sequentially to search for the given key (say *item*). Here, we start with the first element of the array and it is compared with *item*. If both the values are not equal, then we move on to the next element in the array and it is compared with *item*. This process is repeated until we encounter a matching element in the array (a successful search) or the array is exhausted without finding a matching element (an unsuccessful search). We can use this searching technique to find an element in sorted and unsorted arrays.

3.4.1 Pseudocode

```
Procedure Linear_Search(A[1, 2, …, n], n, item)
        Input A[1, 2, …, n], n, item
        For each k from 1 to n
            If (A[k] == item)
                Print item is found at location k
                return k
            End If
        End For
        Print item is not found in the array
        return -1
End Procedure
```

3.4.2 Example

Consider the input array, A[75, 10, 7, 6, 20, 40, 50, 30, 99, 60]. Let the item to be searched is 40. Fig. 3.1 depicts the steps of linear search.

3.4.3 Complexity Analysis

The best-case scenario of linear or sequential search occurs when the item to be found is the first element of the array. Therefore, its time complexity in the best-case scenario is O(1). Its average-case complexity is O(n). The worst-case scenario happens when the item to be found is not present in the array or at the last position of the array. Since we must sequentially scan the full array, linear search's worst-case complexity is O(n).

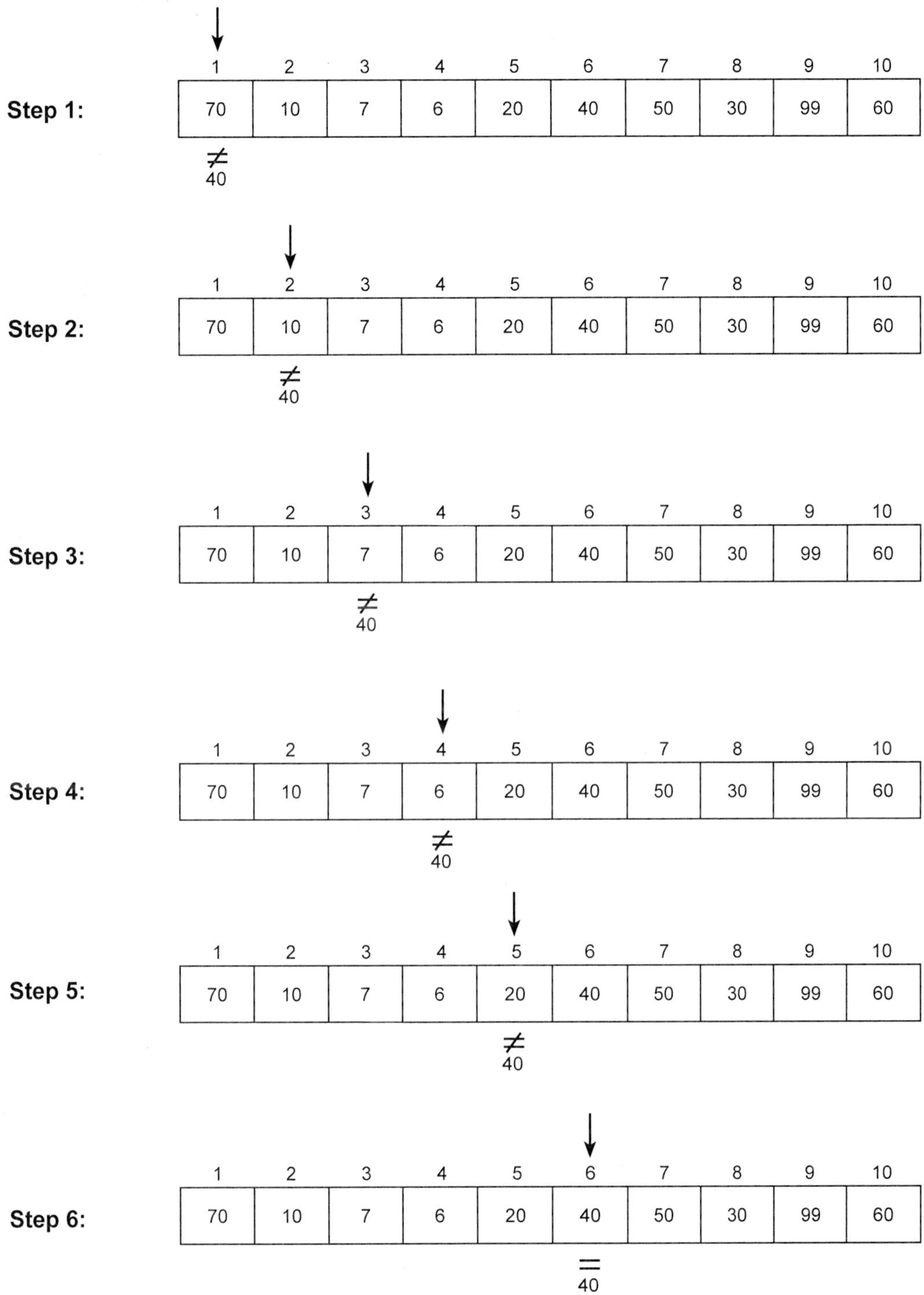

Fig. 3.1: Steps of Linear Search

3.5 BINARY SEARCH

The quickest and most effective procedure for locating a given element in a sorted array is binary search. It operates according to the divide-and-conquer strategy. Here, the algorithm first divides the given array into two halves, and then the item to be found (say, *Num_X*) is compared with the array's middle element, *A[midway]*. If both values are equal, it returns *midway*, the index of that array element. If *Num_X* is greater than *A[midway]*, *Num_X* is searched for recursively in the right sub-array of *A[midway]*. If the *Num_X* is less than *A[midway]*, the left sub-array of *A[midway]* is searched recursively for the *Num_X*. This search process is repeated until the *Num_X* is found in the array or the array size becomes one. The algorithm returns -1 if the search is unsuccessful. The input array must be sorted before using binary search, which is its main drawback.

3.5.1 Pseudocode

```
Procedure Binary_Search(A[1, 2, …, n], Num_X, first, last)
        Input A[1, 2, …, n], Num_X, first, last
        If (first > last)
                return -1
        Else
                midway = (first + last)/2
                If (Num_X == A[midway])
                        return midway
                Else If (Num_X > A[midway])
                        return Binary_Search(A, Num_X,
                                               midway+1, last)
            Else
                    return Binary_Search(A, Num_X,
                                               first, midway-1)
            End If
     End If
End Procedure
```

3.5.2 Example

Consider the input array, A[6, 7, 10, 20, 30, 40, 50, 60, 70, 99]. Let the item to be searched is 70. Fig. 3.2 depicts the steps of binary search.

3.5.3 Complexity Analysis

When the item to be located is the first middle element (in the first comparison), binary search performs best. Therefore, its time complexity in the best-case is O(1). The average-case time complexity is O(log n). The worst-case scenario happens when we have to search for the item till the array contains only one element, that leads to the complexity of O(log n).

1	2	3	4	5	6	7	8	9	10
6	7	10	20	30	40	50	60	70	99

Step 1: Midway = (first + last) / 2 = (1 + 10) / 2 = 5

				midway ↓					
1	2	3	4	5	6	7	8	9	10
6	7	10	20	30	40	50	60	70	99
↑ first									↑ last

Step 2: Compare 70 with 30 (middle element). Here 70 > 30. So discard the left sub-array and select the right sub-array.

Now first = midway + 1 = 5 + 1 = 6

midway = (6 + 10) / 2 = 8

							midway ↓		
1	2	3	4	5	6	7	8	9	10
~~6~~	~~7~~	~~10~~	~~20~~	~~30~~	40	50	60	70	99
					↑ first				↑ last

Step 3: Compare 70 with 60 (middle element). Here 70 > 60. So discard the left sub-array and select the right sub-array.

Now first = midway + 1 = 8 + 1 = 9

midway = (9 + 10) / 2 = 9

								midway ↓	
1	2	3	4	5	6	7	8	9	10
~~6~~	~~7~~	~~10~~	~~20~~	~~30~~	~~40~~	~~50~~	~~60~~	70	99
								↑ first	↑ last

Step 3: Compare 70 with 70 (middle element). Here 70 = 70. A succesful search. Return middle index (= 9) as output.

Fig. 3.2: Steps of Binary Search

Until now, we have discussed how to perform search operations on linear data structures like arrays. Now, we will discuss different specialised data structures on which we will perform operations like search, insertion, deletion, etc. The first such data structure that we will discuss is trees. Before going into its details, we will first discuss the basic characteristics of a tree data structure.

3.6 CHARACTERISTICS OF A TREE DATA STRUCTURE

A set of nodes and edges make up a *tree*, which is a type of non-linear data structure. A *node* represents a structure that contains *data* or *value* and connections to other nodes, formally called *edges* or *links*. In a tree, each node connects to zero or more nodes. A node that connects to another node through a single edge downward is known as a *parent* node, and that connected node is said to be its *child* node. The *root node* of a tree refers to a node that has no parents. The term *leaf node* refers to a node that has no offspring. Two or more nodes having the same parent are said to be *siblings*. Fig. 3.3 depicts a tree data structure.

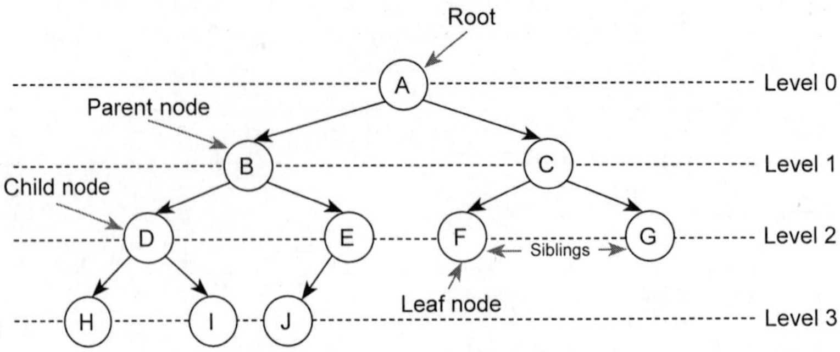

Fig. 3.3: Tree Data Structure

A sequence of connected nodes $\mathbf{N_1}$, $\mathbf{N_2}$, ..., $\mathbf{N_P}$ where $\mathbf{N_i}$ is the child of $\mathbf{N_{i-1}}$ for 1 < i <= p defines a *path* from node $\mathbf{N_1}$ to $\mathbf{N_p}$. The number of edges on this path (that is, p-1) is used to determine the *length* of the path. It may be noted that each node can be reached from the root node by exactly one path. A distinguishing characteristic of a tree is that it has no *cycle* of nodes. Node $\mathbf{N_1}$ is said to be an *ancestor* of node $\mathbf{N_2}$, and node $\mathbf{N_2}$ is said to be a *descendant* of node $\mathbf{N_1}$, if a path exists from node $\mathbf{N_1}$ to node $\mathbf{N_2}$. A node $\mathbf{N_i}$ and all its descendants constitute the *subtree* of a tree rooted at $\mathbf{N_i}$.

The path length (that is, the number of edges on the path) from the root node to a node $\mathbf{N_i}$ is the *depth* of that node $\mathbf{N_i}$. By using zero-based counting, the root node is regarded as being at zero depth. The length of the longest downward path from a node $\mathbf{N_i}$ to a leaf is referred to as the *height* of that node $\mathbf{N_i}$. Thus, all leaf nodes are considered to be at height zero. The length of the longest path from a tree's root to a leaf defines the tree's *height*. The tree's height and the root's height are identical. The depth of the deepest leaf in a tree is the *depth of the tree*, which is always equal to the height of the tree. The number of edges along the unique path from the root to a node $\mathbf{N_i}$, is referred to as the *level* of node $\mathbf{N_i}$, which is the same as the depth of $\mathbf{N_i}$. Thus, the root node is at level zero. A *node's degree* is defined as the number of offspring it has. The leaf nodes have degree zero. A *tree's degree* is equal to the highest degree attained by any of its nodes.

Consider the tree shown in Fig. 3.3. Here, nodes D, E, F, and G are at level 2; node B is at level 1, depth 1, and height 2; node G is at level 2, depth 2, and height 0; node H is at level 3, depth 3, and height 0; depth and height of the tree is 3; node E has degree 1; nodes A, B, C, and D have degree 2; all other nodes have degree zero; degree of the tree is 2.

3.6.1 Linked Representation of a Tree

As discussed above, each node in a tree connects to zero or more nodes. A node in a tree contains a *data* or *value field* as well as *reference* or *link fields* to other nodes. These link fields connect a node to its children. Fig. 3.4 shows the pictorial representation of a node. The number of link fields in a node is determined based on its degree. For example, if the degree of a node $\mathbf{N_i}$ is 3, then $\mathbf{N_i}$ has three link fields, each pointing to one of its children.

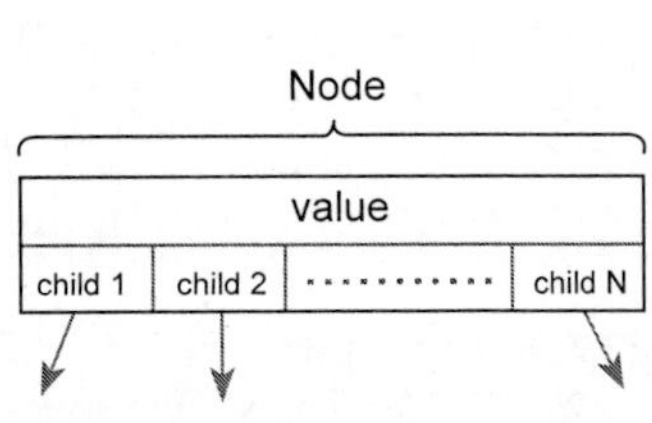

Fig. 3.4: Node of a Tree

Note: The concept of *pointers* in data structure is essential to understand the implementation structure of a node and a tree. So, we direct the reader to refer to the 'Know More' section of this unit to have a familiarity with the basic concept of *pointers* in data structure.

The following structure defines a node of a tree:

```
struct Tree_Node {
int value; // key value or data of a node
struct Tree_Node *child1; // pointer to node child1
struct Tree_Node *child2; // pointer to node child2
...
struct Tree_Node *childN; // pointer to node childN
};
```

If a tree has a degree ***K***, then each node of the tree is provided with ***K*** link fields. The unreferred link fields are filled with ***NULL***. Fig. 3.5 depicts a tree and its linked representation.

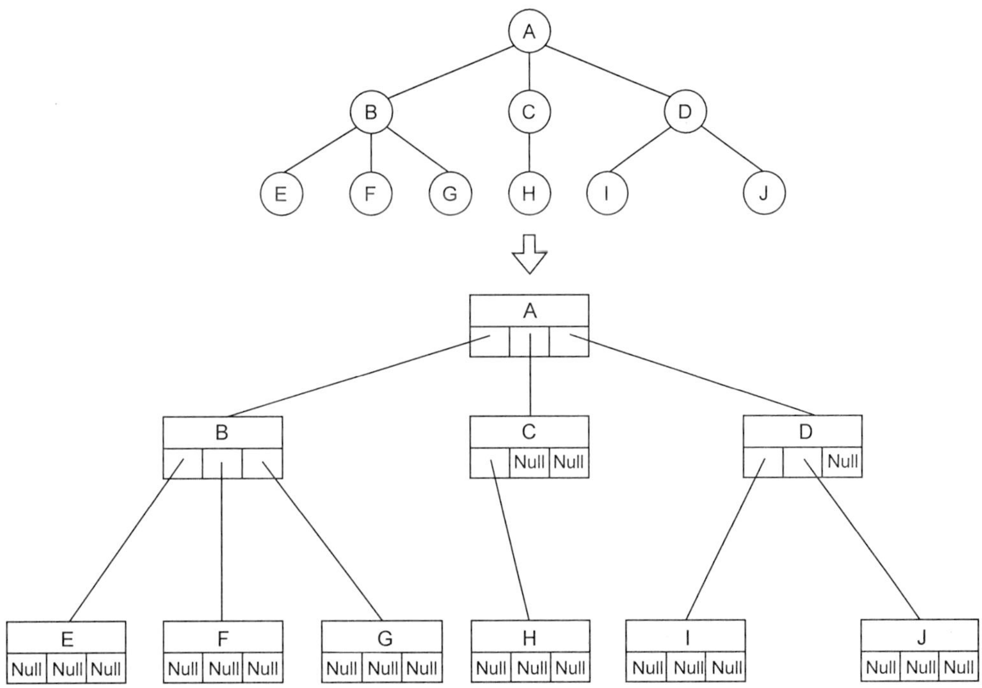

Fig. 3.5: Linked Representation of a Tree

3.6.2 Searching a Node in a Tree

To search for a given element (say '*e*') in a generic tree, *e* is first compared with the key value of the root node. If root is NULL, that is, if the tree is empty, the search returns with 'failure'. The search procedure returns with 'success' if *e* is equal to 'root.value'. However, if *e* is not matching with the current 'root.value', the search proceeds in each child node of the root node. The same sequence of operations is conducted at the child node. This procedure is repeated either until the element is found and the search is successful, or a leaf node is reached and the element is not found (when the search procedure returns with 'failure').

3.6.2.1 Pseudocode

```
Procedure Tree_Search(*root, e)
        Input struct Node *root, int e
        If (root == NULL) // for an empty tree
                return False
        Else // if tree is not empty
                If (root.value == e)
                        return True
                End If
                For each child of Node root
                  boolean b = Tree_Search(child, e)
                  If (b)
                          return True
                  End If
            End For
        End If
        return False
End Procedure
```

3.7 BINARY SEARCH TREES

After having a look at search strategy on lists arranged as a general tree, let us focus our attention on the *binary search tree* data structure which allows us to perform binary search for fast lookup, addition, and removal of data elements. Binary search trees are also referred to as *sorted* or *ordered* binary trees. In a binary tree, any tree node is restricted to have at most two children (0, 1 or 2 immediate successors) whereas in a general tree, a node of the tree may have any number of children. A list of values or keys, A[75, 10, 7, 6, 20, 40, 50, 30, 99, 30] arranged as a binary tree, can have the following look (see, Fig. 3.6):

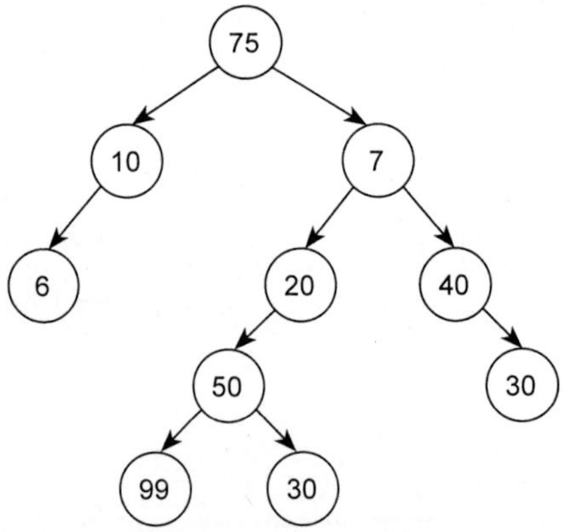

Fig. 3.6: Binary Tree

A binary tree is called a *binary search tree* (BST) or an ordered/sorted binary tree if each internal node's key is larger than or equal to every key in its left subtree and less than all of the keys in its right subtree.

This condition is called the *BST property*. There can be many BST representations for a given set of elements. For example, Fig. 3.7(a) and 3.7(b) depict two alternative BST representations for the list of values A[75, 10, 7, 6, 20, 40, 50, 30, 99, 30].

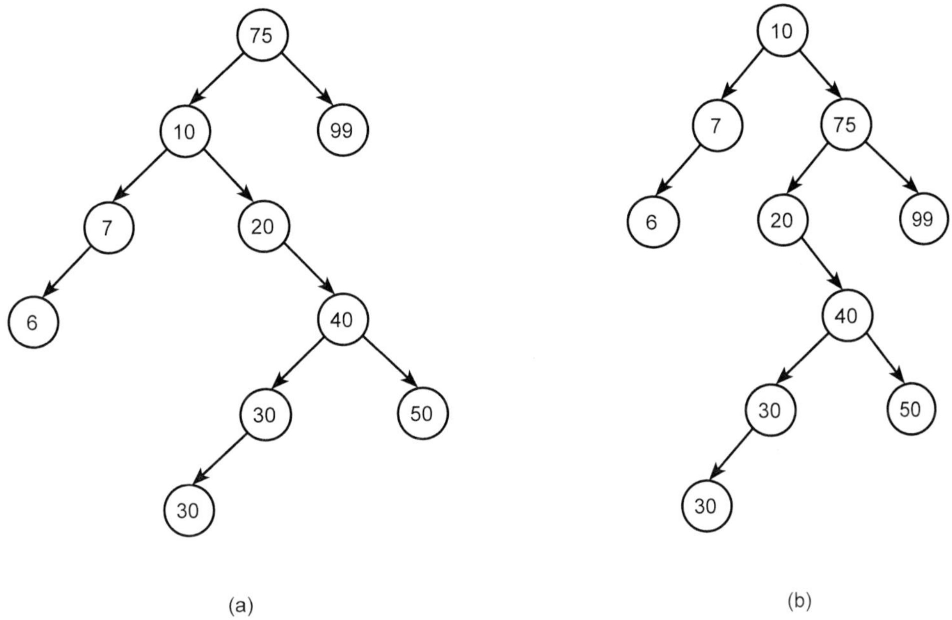

Fig. 3.7: (a) & (b) BST Representations

3.7.1 Representing BSTs in Memory

A BST node is best described as:

```
struct BST_Node {
        int value; // Key value of a node
        struct BST_Node *left; // Location of left child
        struct BST_Node *right; // Location of right child
};
```

A particular BST is identified through its root node and it is declared as:

```
struct BST_Node root;
```

3.7.2 Searching in a given BST

To search for a given element or node value (say '*e*') in a BST, *e* is first compared to the root node's key value. If this value is NULL, the search returns with 'failure'. The search procedure returns with 'success' if *e* is equal to 'root.value'. However, the search proceeds on to the root node's right subtree if e is greater than 'root.value.' If not, searching proceeds in the root's left subtree. The same sequence of operations is conducted at the root of the left or right subtree depending on where the search proceeds. This process is repeated either until the element is found and the search is successful, or a leaf node is reached and the element is not found (when the search procedure returns with 'failure').

3.7.2.1 Pseudocode

```
Procedure BST_Search(*root, e)
        Input struct BST_Node *root, int e
        If (root.value == NULL)
                return 'False'
        Else If (root.value == e)
                return 'True'
        Else If (root.value > e)
                return BST_Search(root.left, e)
        Else If (root.value < e)
                return BST_Search(root.right, e)
        End If
End Procedure
```

3.7.3 Insertion in a BST

The following procedure *BST_Insert()* may be used to insert an element having value 'e', into a BST rooted at 'root'. If the BST is empty (root = NULL), a new BST node is created with 'e' as the key value of this node and 'root' is made to point to this new node. Otherwise, we search the BST for the element 'e' in a similar fashion as 'BST_Search'. If we find 'e' in the BST, there is nothing more to do as the element that is required to be inserted already exists in the BST. During the search for 'e', if a NULL pointer is reached, we replace this pointer with a new node having 'e' as its key value.

3.7.3.1 Pseudocode

```
Procedure BST_Insert(*root, e)
        Input int e, struct BST_Node *root
        If (root == NULL)
                root = New struct BST_Node
                root.value = e
                root.left = NULL
                root.right = NULL
                return
        Else If (root.value > e)
                return BST_Insert(root.left, e)
        Else If (root.value < e)
                return BST_Insert(root.right, e)
        End If // If root.value = e, nothing to do
End Procedure
```

3.7.4 Deletion from a BST

Deletion from a BST is slightly more complicated compared to search and insertion. If the value (say 'e') to be deleted is in a leaf node, we can simply delete the leaf and there is nothing more to be done.

However, if this node is an internal node of the BST, simply deleting this node will disconnect the tree. If the internal node containing 'e' has only one child, we can just replace this node by the child node. This action deletes the node containing 'e' and appropriately readjusts the BST. If the internal node containing 'e' has two children, the following actions appropriately conduct the deletion operation: *Find the lowest-valued element (say 'g') in the right subtree of the node containing 'e', replace 'e' by 'g' (so that the node having value 'e' will now hold the key value 'g') and finally, delete the node in the right subtree containing the value 'g'.* Instead of the lowest-valued element in the right subtree, the above operation can also be performed with the highest valued element in the left sub-tree.

3.7.4.1 Pseudocode

```
Procedure BST_Delete(*root, e)
      Input struct BST_Node *root, int e
      If (root != NULL) {
            If (root.value > e)
                  return BST_Delete(root.left, e)
            End If
    Else If (root.value < e)
            return BST_Delete(root.right, e)
   // Here, the node containing 'e' has been found.
    Else If (root.right == NULL) and (root.left == NULL)
        root = NULL
    Else If (root.left == NULL)
        root = root.right
    Else If (root.right == NULL)
        root = root.left
    Else // Both children are present
        root.value = Del_Min(root.right)
    End If
End Procedure
```

```
Procedure Del_Min(*root)
      Input struct BST_Node *root
      If (root.left == NULL) {
      // root points to the lowest element
            temp = root.value
            root = root.right
            Return temp
      Else
         Return Del_Min(root.left)
    End If
End Procedure
```

3.7.4.2 Example (Deletion)

Suppose we want to delete the value '20' in the BST shown in Fig. 3.8.

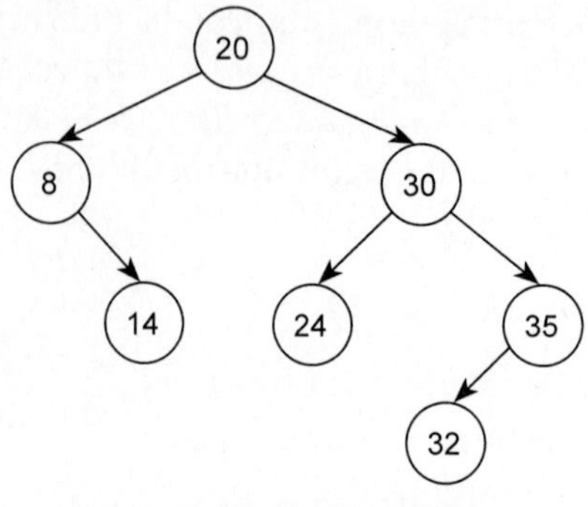

Fig. 3.8: BST before deletion

As the node containing 20 has both a left and a right child, we call Del_Min() in line no. 17 of procedure BST_Delete(). This call returns the value 24 and also deletes the node containing 24 in the right subtree of the node holding 20. The resulting BST after deletion of 20 is shown in Fig. 3.9.

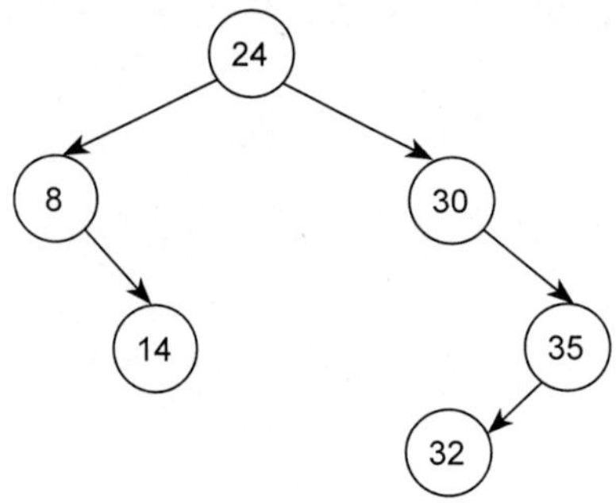

Fig. 3.9: BST after deletion

3.8 BALANCED SEARCH TREES

Operations on a BST can be accomplished in O(log n) time if any node's right and left subtree heights are equal. However, as may be inferred from the discussion on BSTs above, a series of insertions and/ or deletions on the BST can make it unbalanced. In the extreme case, the BST may become similar to a linear list in structure making the BST operations lower in their efficiency (O(n) complexity). In 1962, Adelson-Velskii and Landis introduced height-balanced BSTs, commonly called *AVL trees*, in which the height of the right and left subtree of any node never differ by more than 1.

In its simplest form, an AVL tree node has the form:

```
struct AVL_Node {
        int value; // Key value of a node
        int BF;    // Balance Factor. Can hold -1, 0, or 1
        struct AVL_Node *left; // Location of left child
        struct AVL_Node *right; // Location of right child
};
```

It may be observed that compared to BST, an AVL tree node has an additional field BF (Balance Factor) which is defined to be equal to 'h_L - h_R', where h_L and h_R denote the heights of the left and right subtrees of the node. A BST is said to be balanced, that is the BST is an AVL tree, only if the BF values of all nodes in the tree are either -1, 0 or 1. The tree must be rebalanced if the BF value of a node becomes '+2' or '-2' subsequent to insertion or deletion of a node. For example, Fig. 3.10 shows a scenario where the AVL becomes unbalanced after insertion of a node having value 26. The number above each node shows the BF value of the node. It may be observed that in this case, the BF of the node with value 12 becomes -2 after the insertion with its right child having a BF value of -1.

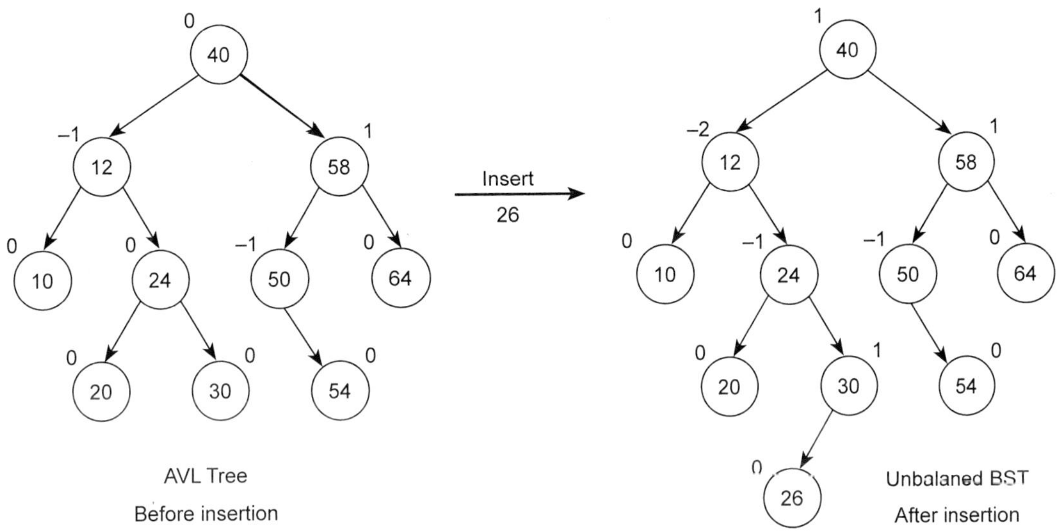

Fig. 3.10: AVL tree insertion (insert 26) operation

To rebalance this tree, a left-rotation of the node having value '12' must be performed. After the rotation, the node containing '12' becomes the left child of the node with value '24', and the node having value '20' becomes the right child of the node containing '12'. Fig. 3.11 depicts the AVL tree after this rebalancing.

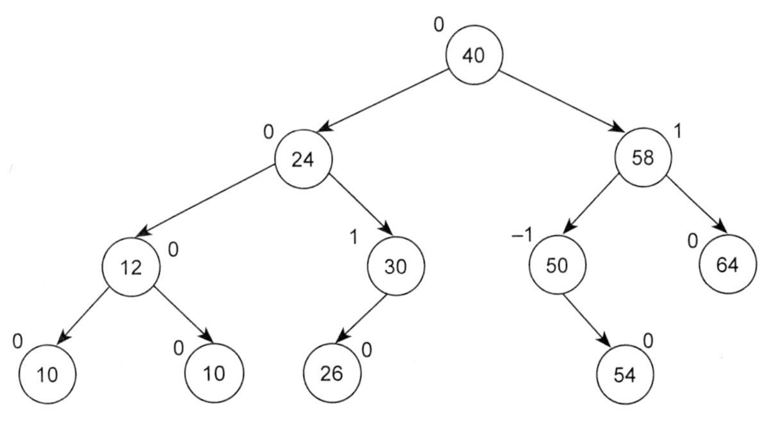

Fig. 3.11: AVL tree after rebalancing

Let us now assume that instead of '26', we insert the value '22'. Fig. 3.12 shows this scenario.

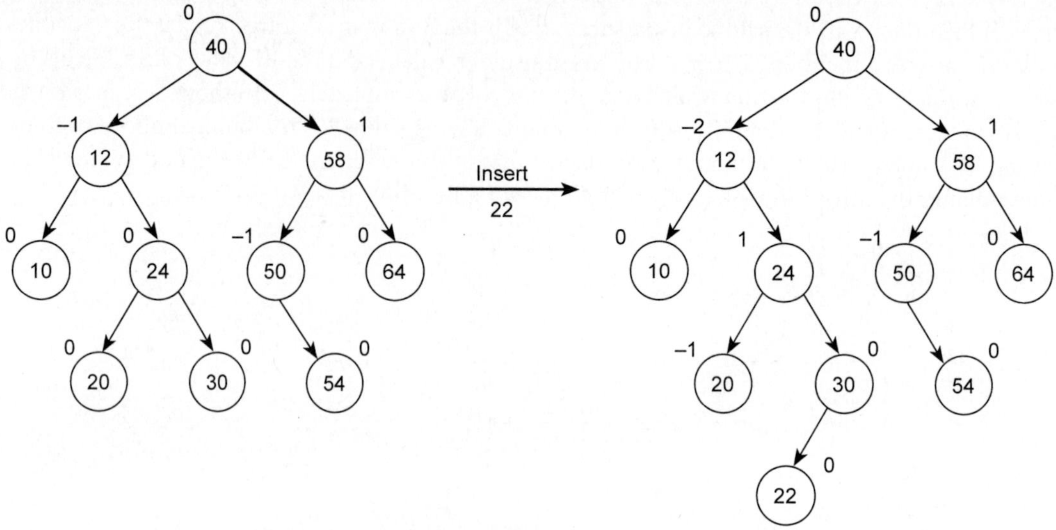

Fig. 3.12: AVL tree insertion (insert 22) operation

To rebalance this tree, first a right-rotation along the node containing '24' has to be performed. This action makes '20' the right child of '12', '24' the right child of '20' and '22' the left child of '24'. Fig. 3.13 depicts the AVL tree after this rebalancing.

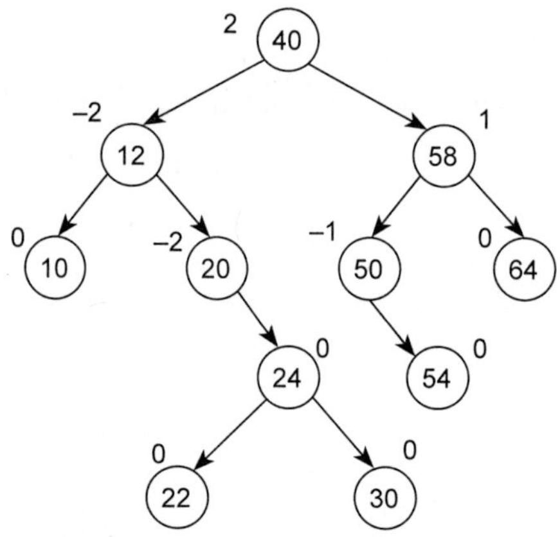

Fig. 3.13: AVL tree after right-rotation

Now, the tree must be left-rotated along the node having value '12'. As a result of this action, '20' becomes the left child of '40' and'12' becomes the left-child of '20'. The resultant tree is now balanced and is shown in Fig. 3.14. This balancing mechanism which involves first a right-rotation and then a left-rotation is called *double rotation.*

In general, there are four cases to consider:

Case 1: A subtree gets negatively unbalanced (BF = -2) with its right-child having a negative balance factor (BF = -1). Fig. 3.15 illustrates this scenario. A simple left-rotation (referred to as *LL Rotation*) rebalances the tree.

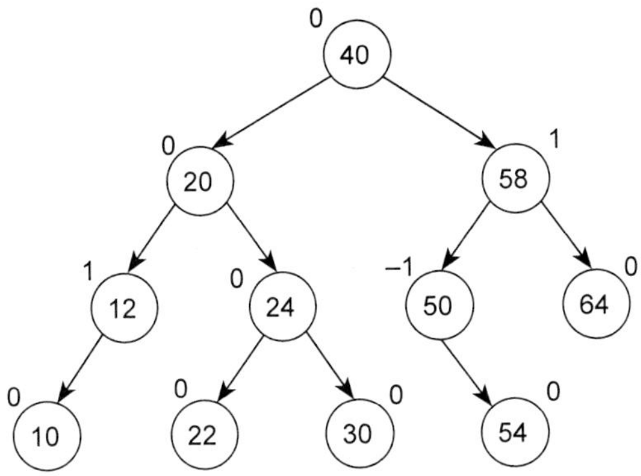

Fig. 3.14: AVL tree after left-rotation - balanced form

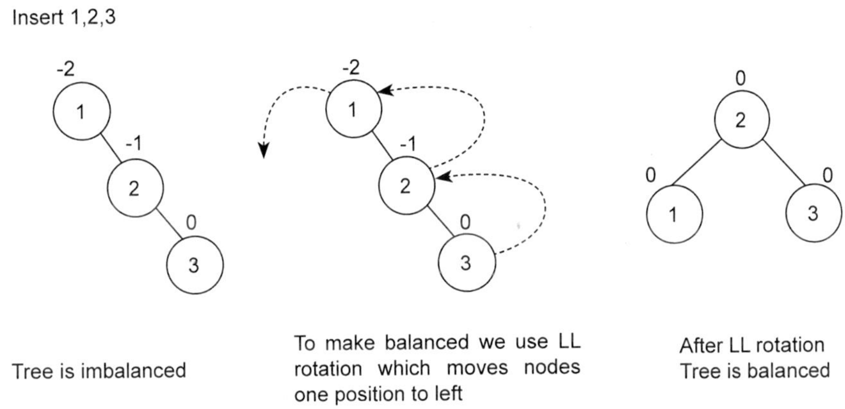

Fig. 3.15: AVL tree - LL Rotation

Case 2: This is a mirror image of case 1. A subtree gets positively unbalanced (BF = 2) with its left-child having a positive balance factor (BF = 1). A simple right-rotation (referred to as *RR Rotation*) rebalances the tree. Fig. 3.16 depicts this scenario.

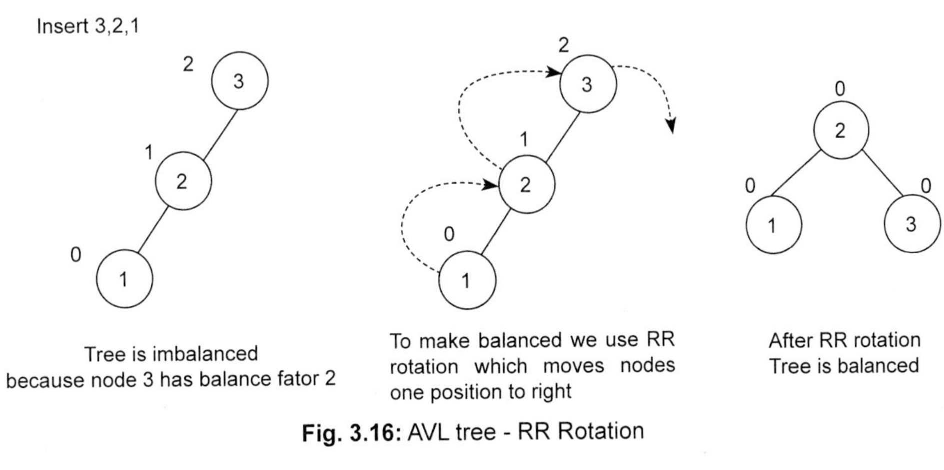

Fig. 3.16: AVL tree - RR Rotation

Case 3: A subtree gets negatively unbalanced (BF = -2) with its right-child having a positive balance factor (BF = 1). Fig. 3.17 illustrates this scenario. A double rotation which combines a right-rotation followed by a left-rotation (referred to as *RL Rotation*) rebalances the tree.

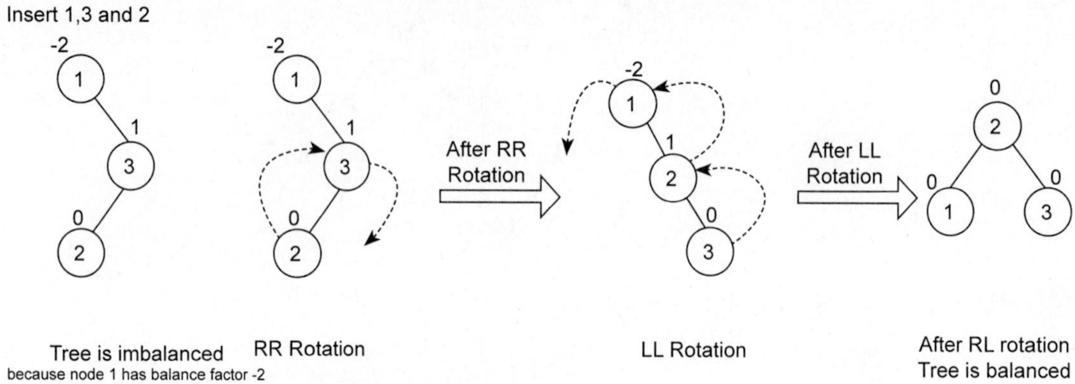

Fig. 3.17: AVL tree - RL Rotation

Case 4: This is a mirror image of case 2. A subtree gets positively unbalanced (BF = 2) with its left-child having a negative balance factor (BF = -1). A double rotation which combines a left-rotation followed by a right-rotation (referred to as *LR Rotation*) rebalances the tree. Fig. 3.18 depicts this scenario.

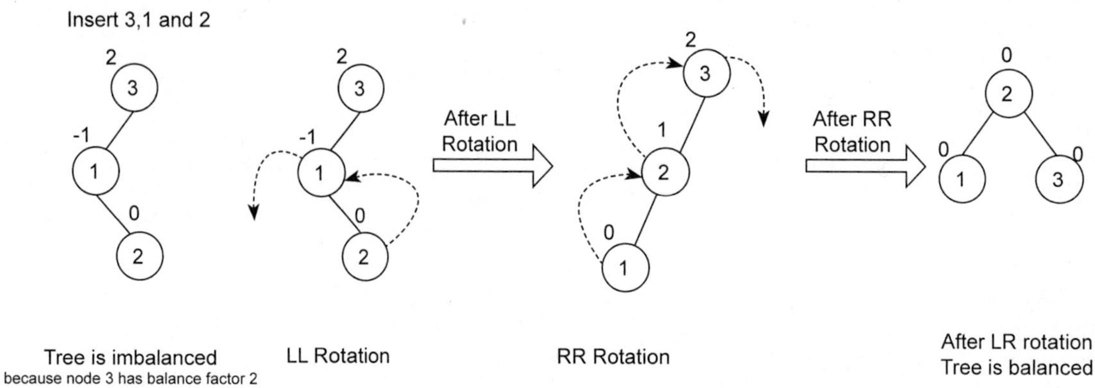

Fig. 3.18: AVL tree - LR Rotation

It may be noted that the fundamental idea behind AVL trees is to make operations such as search, insertion and deletion, more efficient. There are other variations of self-balancing trees with variations in the structure of the tree, definition of *balance* etc. but with the same fundamental idea behind them. Two examples of such self-balancing trees include *2-3 trees* and *B-trees*.

3.9 HASH TABLES

This section discusses a special data structure called *hash table* and its usage in the searching problem.

3.9.1 Direct-Address Table

As discussed earlier, the purpose of a symbol table data structure is to store a set of <key, value> pairs, so that a value associated with a given key can be searched. If the keys are small integers such that they can be accommodated within the available memory in the given system, then we can use arrays to implement symbol tables. Specifically, *key* can be used as an index to an array such that the value corresponding to *key i* can be stored in the ith position of the array. This approach is called the *direct-address table.*

To illustrate the direct-address table, let us consider the following example (as shown in Fig. 3.19) in which the number of possible keys ranges from 1 to 10. Among them, only a few values are actual key values that are being used. Suppose we have a memory to accommodate all possible keys (i.e., 1 to 10). Then, we can simply use an array to store the values. Here, key can be used to index the array.

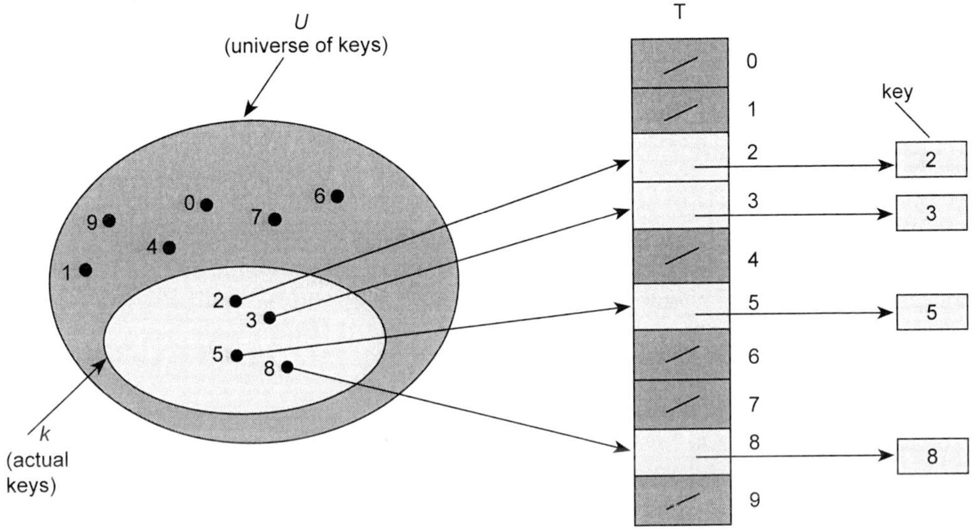

Fig. 3.19: Usage of a Direct-Address Table

In this situation, the operations such as inserting an element and searching for an element will take constant (O(1)) time. Specifically, if we want to insert the key-value pair <5, 100> into array T, then we can set T[5] = 100. Similarly, if we want to retrieve/search for the element at the key 5, we can simply use T[5] to print the value at index 5 in the array T.

However, it may be possible that the amount of memory available is limited in many real-world scenarios. In such cases, we cannot afford to allocate memory for all possible key ranges. Further, the actual keys being used may be much lower than the maximum possible key value. For example, 10000000 can be the maximum possible key value. However, the actual key value may be around 100. In this case, allocating an array to store 10000000 elements will lead to a huge amount of memory wastage. So, a **hash table** can be used when the number of actual keys that need to be stored is substantially less than the set of all possible key values.

3.9.2 Hash Table

In the direct-address table approach, we have seen that a given <key, value> pair with key k gets stored in the index/position/slot k of the input array. In case of a hashtable, this pair gets stored in position h(k). Here, h is called as a **hash function** which maps the set of all possible key values (say, U) into anyone of the m slots of a hash table T [0,1, 2, …, m-1]:

$$h: U \rightarrow \{0, 1, 2, 3, \ldots, m-1\}$$

Interpretation:

hash function: Set of all possible key values → anyone of the m slots of a hash table T

Here, m is the size of the hash table T, which is smaller than the total size of all possible key values |U|. We say that the pair <key, value> with key k **hashes** into position h(k) in the hash table T. Also, h(k) is called the **hash value** of k.

A **hash function** transforms the given key value into the index/position/slot in the hash table T and it is expected to meet the following assumption (known as *simple uniform hashing*): Each key has an equal chance of hashing to any of the m indices, regardless of where the other keys have hashed. In literature, there are different types of hashing functions. In this book, we will discuss division and multiplication based hashing functions.

3.9.2.1 Division Method

This method divides the key k by m and the remainder of this division is used to map key k into a hash table. That is, h(k) = k % m. Let us consider the following example: The key k = 100 and the size of the hash table m = 8. Then, h(k) = 100 % 8 = 4. So, the key 100 will be stored in location 4 in the hash table. An advantage of the division approach is that it only needs one division operation which is quick.

3.9.2.2 Multiplication Method

It is a two-step approach. The first step multiplies the input key k by a constant X, where 0 < X < 1, and extracts the fractional part of kX. In the next step, the value from the previous step gets multiplied by m and then takes the floor of this result. That is, h(k) = floor (m (kX % 1)). For example, let m = 10, k = 1000, X = 0.12345. Then, kX = 123.45, kX%1 = 0.45, m (kX % 1) = 4.5, floor (m (kX % 1)) = 4. The multiplication approach has the benefit that m's value is not critical.

The basic idea of a hash table is illustrated in Fig. 3.20.

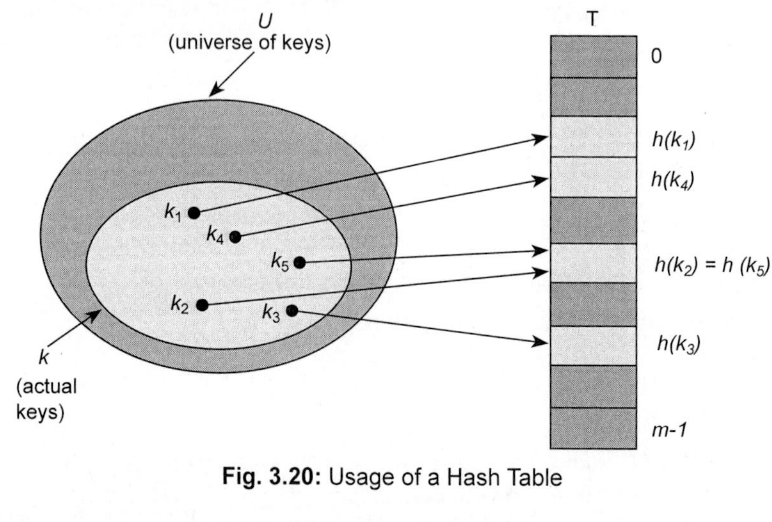

Fig. 3.20: Usage of a Hash Table

3.9.3 Collision Resolution in a Hash Table

From the above figure, we can see that the keys k1, k3, and k4 map to h(k1), h(k2), and h(k4), respectively. Further, the keys k2 and k5 map to the same position/slot in the hash table. When a slot is hashed by two keys, then it leads to the **collision**. Ideally, we expect different keys to map to distinct indices/slots/ positions in the hash table. Since the total number of possible keys (|U|) is substantially more than the size of the hash table (m), it is impossible to completely avoid collisions. Typically, ***chaining*** and ***open addressing*** techniques are used for collision resolution in a hash table.

3.9.3.1 Chaining

In this approach, the keys that collide with each other are chained together in separate linked lists. An example scenario is depicted in Fig. 3.21.

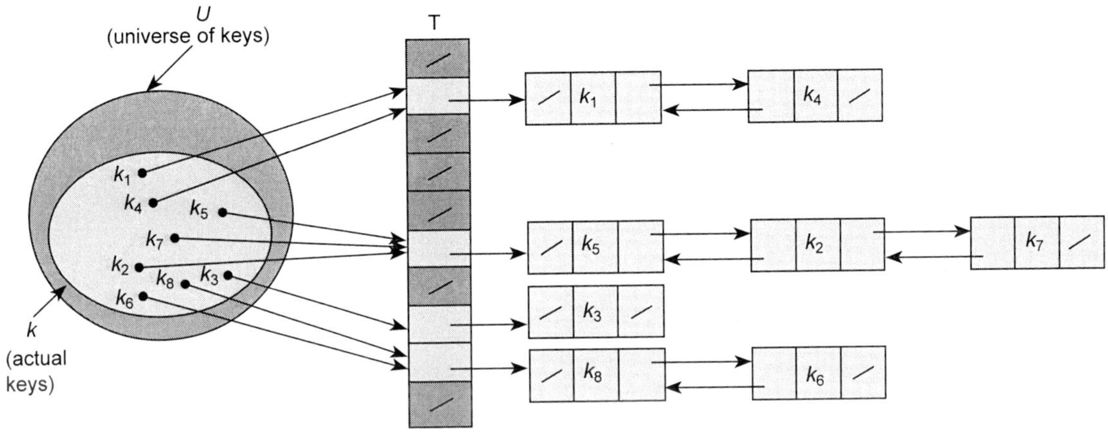

Fig. 3.21: Collision Resolution by Chaining

In the above example, h(k1) = h(k4), h(k2) = h(k5) = h(k7), h(k6) = h(k8). So, all these keys are stored in a chained fashion in the slot that they occupy in the hash table. In this approach, searching for a particular key is a two step process: First find the slot in the hash table using the hash function; Next, sequentially search through all the keys in the list of keys mapped to this slot.

3.9.3.2 Open Addressing

It is another approach for implementing hashing and this relies on empty slots in the hash table to resolve collisions. In this approach, each table entry has either a key or NIL. The easiest version of open addressing is **linear probing**. To perform insertion using linear probing, we use hashing function and compute the destination for the given key. In case of a collision, we check/probe for the next entry with NIL. This probing continues until we find an empty slot (with NIL). Unlike chaining, no key is stored outside the hash table.

3.9.4 Example

Let us consider the following set of keys {22, 28, 23, 32, 33, 43, 55, 65}. These keys are inserted into a hash table T with size 10 (index: 0, 1, 2, ..., 9; initialized with NIL) using linear probing based open addressing having hash function h(p) = p % 10. Let us sequentially insert these keys into the hash table T.

- key 22: h(22) = 22 % 10 = 2. Then, T[2] = 22.
- key 28: h(28) = 28 % 10 = 8. Then, T[8] = 28.
- key 23: h(23) = 23 % 10 = 3. Then, T[3] = 23.

- key 32: h(32) = 32 % 10 = 2. Since T[2] already contains 22, we need to find the next empty slot in the hash table. T[3] is also occupied with 23. T[4] is not yet occupied and it can be used to hold the key 32. Then, T[4] = 32.
- key 33: h(33) = 33 % 10 = 3. T[3] and T[4] are already occupied. T[5] = 33.
- key 43: h(43) = 43 % 10 = 3. T[3], T[4], and T[5] are already occupied. T[6] = 43.
- key 55: h(55) = 55 % 10 = 5. T[7] = 55.
- key 65: h(65) = 65 % 10 = 5. T[9] = 65.

The pictorial representation of the final hash table is shown in the below table.

0	NIL
1	NIL
2	22
3	23
4	32
5	33
6	43
7	55
8	28
9	65

UNIT SUMMARY

This unit first introduces the concept of symbol tables, the logical representation of structures for data storage. Symbol tables can be organized as unsorted or sorted sequential lists, trees, binary search trees, hash tables etc. on which techniques for searching, insertion and deletion are studied.

Search techniques can be categorized into linear, interval based or hash based. Linear search checks every element in a list in linear fashion. Interval based search on the other hand partitions the search area into intervals, and then explores a specific interval based on the value of the data to be searched. The unit discusses binary search or half-interval search, which are performed on sorted lists. Then it discusses search techniques on trees, binary search trees (BST) and a variant of BST called height-balanced trees. Finally, hashing mechanisms which map elements to specific symbol table entries based on a hash function, have been discussed.

EXERCISES

Multiple Choice Questions

1. How many steps will you take to search for a word linearly in a dictionary having 120,000 words, in the worst-case situation?
   (a) 19 (b) 17
   (c) 120,000 (d) 18

2. How many steps will you take to perform a binary search for a word in a dictionary with 120,000 words, in the worst-case situation?
   (a) 19 (b) 17
   (c) 120,000 (d) 18
3. Consider an all possible key set, U = {1, 2, …, 1000}, and an actual key set being used P = {1, 2, …, 100}. System memory has a capacity to hold 10000 keys. Which data structure is suitable to store these keys?
   (a) A simple array (b) A hash table
   (c) Both of them (d) None of them
4. Consider an all possible key set, U = {1, 2, …, 1000}, and an actual key set being used P = {1, 2, …, 100}. System memory has a capacity to hold 200 keys. Which data structure is suitable to store these keys?
   (a) A simple array (b) A hash table
   (c) Both of them (d) None of them
5. The complexity of search operation in the direct-address table approach in the worst-case is __.
   (a) k log k (b) k^2
   (c) k (d) 1
6. What do you mean by a hash function?
   (a) It is a map from a set of all possible key values to any of the hash table's slots.
   (b) It is a map from a set of odd natural numbers to any of the hash table's slots.
   (c) It is used to implement stacks and queues
   (d) None of the above
7. Let us consider a hash table with total number of slots as 4 and the division method based hash function. In what slot, the key 100 will be stored in this hash table?
   (a) 3 (b) 1
   (c) 2 (d) 0
8. What do you mean by simple uniform hashing?
   (a) Each key is hashed based on its priority
   (b) In a hash table, each key equally stands a chance of fitting into any of the slots.
   (c) Every key is randomly assigned into first five slots in a hash table
   (d) None of the above
9. Consider the given key set: {10, 11, 12, 13, 14, 15, 16, 17, 18}. These keys are added into a hash table T with size 10 (index: 0, 1, …, 9) using linear probing based open addressing having hash function h(p) = p % 10. Which one of the following claims regarding the final hash table is true?
   (a) Each key hashes to a different slot in the hash table
   (b) Multiple keys hashes to the same slot in the hash table
   (c) Every key is randomly assigned into any of the hash table's slots
   (d) None of the above
10. Consider the given key set: {10, 11, 12, 13, 14, 15, 16, 17, 18}. These keys are added into a hash table T with size 10 (index: 0, 1, …, 9) using linear probing based open addressing having hash function h(p) = p % 5. Which one of the following claims regarding the final hash table is true?

(a) Each key hashes to a different slot in the hash table
(b) Multiple keys hashes to the same slot in the hash table
(c) Every key is randomly assigned into any of the hash table's slots
(d) None of the above

11. Consider the given key set: {10, 82, 80, 73, 96}. These keys are added into a hash table HT with size 5 (index: 0, 1, 2, 3, 4; initialized with NIL) using linear probing based open addressing having hash function h(p) = p % 5. What is the final hash table content after inserting all these elements?
(a) HT[0] = NIL, HT[1] = NIL, HT[2] = NIL, HT[3] = NIL, HT[4] = NIL
(b) HT[0] = 10, HT[1] = 80, HT[2] = 82, HT[3] = 73, HT[4] = 96
(c) HT[0] = 10, HT[1] = 82, HT[2] = 80, HT[3] = 73, HT[4] = 96
(d) HT[0] = 10, HT[1] = 82, HT[2] = 80, HT[3] = 73, HT[4] = NIL

Answers for Multiple Choice Questions

1. (c), 2. (b), 3. (c), 4. (b), 5. (d), 6. (a), 7. (d), 8. (b), 9. (a), 10. (b), 11. (b)

Short and Long Answer Type Questions

1. Differentiate linear and binary search algorithms.
2. Write a short note on symbol tables.
3. Illustrate the steps involved in the linear search of an element 23 on a given input array [7, 12, 4, 34, 56, 23, 11].
4. Illustrate the steps involved in the binary search of an element 36 on a given input array [4, 8, 12, 16, 20, 24, 28, 32, 36, 40].
5. Write down the procedure of binary search for finding an element on a reverse sorted array.
6. Illustrate the steps involved in the binary search of an element 45 on a given input array [50, 45, 40, 35, 30, 25, 20, 15, 10, 5].
7. Define the following entities of a tree data structure.
   (a) a node's height
   (b) a tree's height
   (c) a node's depth
   (d) a tree's depth
   (e) a node's degree
   (f) a tree's degree
   (g) a tree's level
8. Explain binary search tree (BST) with an example.
9. Write down the steps involved in searching a BST.
10. Explain the procedure of insertion and deletion operations in a BST.
11. Write a short note on the balanced search tree.
12. How do a balanced search tree differ from a binary search tree.
13. What is the hash function?

14. Explain division method based hash function along with an example.
15. Explain multiplication method based hash function along with an example.
16. What is meant by collision in a hash table? Explain it with an example.
17. What are the methods to handle collisions in a hash table?
18. Explain chaining and open addressing methods in a hash table.
19. Consider the given key set: {10, 51, 62, 73, 84, 95, 85, 82, 42}. These keys are added into a hash table HT with size 10 (index: 0, 1, …, 9; initialized with NIL) using linear probing based open addressing having hash function h(p) = p % 10. What is the final hash table content after inserting all these elements?

    Hint: HT[0] = 10, HT[1] = 51, HT[2] = 62, HT[3] = 73, HT[4] = 84, HT[5] = 95, HT[6] = 85, HT[7] = 82, HT[8] = 42, HT[9] = NIL.
20. Consider the given key set: {10, 82, 80, 73, 96, 92, 98, 9, 11}. These keys are added into a hash table HT with size 10 (index: 0, 1, …, 9; initialized with NIL) using linear probing based open addressing having hash function h(p) = p % 10. What is the final hash table content after inserting all these elements?

    Hint: HT[0] = 10, HT[1] = 80, HT[2] = 82, HT[3] = 73, HT[4] = 92, HT[5] = 11, HT[6] = 96, HT[7] = NIL, HT[8] = 98, HT[9] = 9.

KNOW MORE

This section talks about a set of additional information that helps the reader to improve the knowledge on the topics discussed in Unit-3.

Basics of Pointers

As you all know, every variable declared in a program has a memory location or address where the actual value or data of that variable is stored. The memory address of these variables can be accessed using the unary operator ampersand (&). For example, consider an integer variable named '*number*' that stores a value of 30 and has a memory address say, *#2000H*. Then, the representation '*&number*' gives us *#2000H*, the memory address of the variable *number*.

In many programming languages, we use a particular kind of variable called '*pointer*' to store the address of another variable. A pointer variable is generally declared as

```
datatype *variable_name;
```

Here, *datatype* is the basic data types like int, float, char, double etc., and *variable_name* denotes the pointer variable's name. Using **variable_name*, one can access the value kept in the memory address. The following example shows the declaration of a pointer variable and its usage.

```
int number = 30; // let the value 30 be stored at a memory address #2000H
int *p_v; // pointer variable declaration
p_v = &number; // #2000H, address of number is stored into the pointer variable p_v
printf("%p", &number ); // output #2000H, the address of variable number
printf("%p", p_v); // output #2000H, the address of variable number
printf("%d", *p_v); // output 30, the value stored in the memory address
```

REFERENCES AND SUGGESTED READINGS

Syllabus Referred Textbooks:

1. Algorithms, 4th Edition. R. Sedgewick, and K. Wayne. Addison-Wesley, (2011)
2. Introduction to Algorithms, Fourth Edition, Thomas H. Cormen, Charles E. Leiserson, Ronald L. Rivest and Clifford Stein, The MIT Press, (2022)
3. Introduction to the Theory of Computation, Third Edition, M. Sipser. Course Technology, Boston, MA, (2013)
4. Design And Analysis Of Algorithms, Third Edition, Gajendra Sharma, Khanna Book Publishing Company (P) Limited, (2015)

Other Textbook References:

1. Data Structures and Algorithms Made Easy, Second Edition, Narasimha Karumanchi, CareerMonk Publications, (2011)
2. Data Structure Through C, Yashavant P. Kanetkar, BPB Publications, (2003)
3. Algorithms: Design and Analysis, Harsh Bhasin, Oxford University Press, (2015)

Dynamic QR Code for Further Reading

Scan Me

4 Graphs

UNIT SPECIFICS

Through this unit we have discussed the following aspects:

- The graph data structure along with its important types;
- Directed acyclic graphs and topological sorting on them;
- Spanning trees and techniques for determining minimum spanning trees;
- Shortest path determination using Dijkstra's algorithm;
- Flow graphs and a technique for obtaining the maximum flow;

RATIONALE

In many problems encountered in mathematics, computer science, engineering and many other disciplines, there is a need to represent relationships among data objects. In order to model relationships among data objects, we use a data structure called graph. Here, the data objects are depicted as vertices or nodes, while pairwise relationships are represented through edges between objects. Graphs can be used to simplify and quantify the representation of many systems, for example, layout of city roads where the cities could be represented as vertices and roads between cities as edges, interdependencies among different functions of a computer program, relationships among component processes in a large and complex chemical process etc.

Graphs are one of the most popular among the data structures that we have studied in this book. We start this chapter with a discussion on important terminologies related to graphs along with different types of graphs. Subsequently, we discuss various operations on graphs and algorithms for important problems involving graphs.

PRE-REQUISITES

Rudimentary knowledge of computer programming and data structure.

UNIT OUTCOMES

List of outcomes of this unit is as follows:

U4-O1: Describe various types of graphs

U4-O2: Describe spanning trees, directed acyclic graphs and flow graphs

U4-O3: Explain algorithms for finding minimum spanning trees, topological sorting and maximum network flows

U4-O4: Realize the computational complexities of different types of graph algorithms

U4-O5: Apply graphs for modelling and solving various problems in science and engineering

Unit-4 Outcome	EXPECTED MAPPING WITH COURSE OUTCOMES (1 - Weak Correlation; 2 - Medium Correlation; 3 - Strong Correlation)				
	CO-1	CO-2	CO-3	CO-4	CO-5
U4-O1	3	3	2	2	1
U4-O2	3	3	2	2	1
U4-O3	3	3	3	3	1
U4-O4	3	3	3	3	1
U4-O5	3	3	3	3	1

4.1 DEFINITIONS AND TERMINOLOGIES

This section mainly covers basic definitions and terminologies related to graphs and its associated algorithms.

4.1.1 Graph

A group of nodes (or vertices) with data and connections to other nodes (or vertices) makes up a graph data structure. In general, *graph* is a data structure denoted as a two-tuple G = (V, E) which contains

- V : collection of nodes or vertices. The terms *node* and *vertex* will be used interchangeably.
- E : collection of edges which is represented by a pair of nodes (x, y) where the nodes x, y belong to V.

Example:

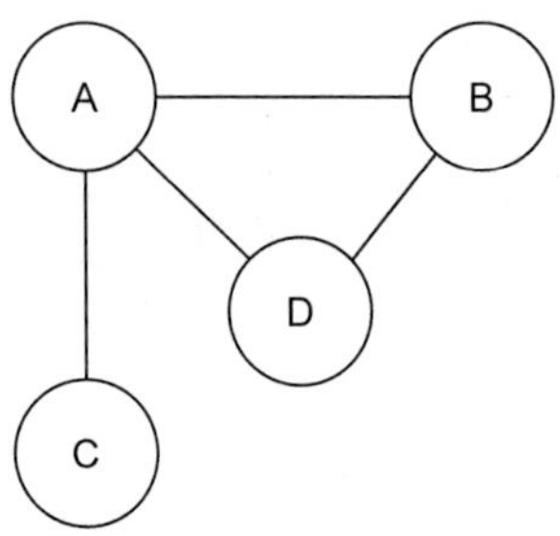

Examine G = (V, E) shown above. Here, V = {A, B, C, D} and the edge set E = {(A, C), (A, B), (A, D), (B, D)}.

4.1.2 Types of Edges

The edges are generally classified into undirected, directed and weighted. The edge between an unordered pair of nodes is usually called an undirected edge whereas a directed edge is drawn for an ordered pair of nodes/vertices. An undirected/directed edge having an integer value as a label (known as *weight*) is called weighted edge. The weight may represent distance or cost between two given vertices.

Example:

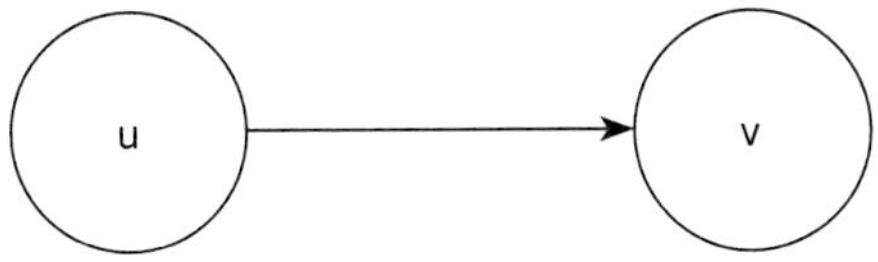

(a) Directed edge from node u to v represented as (u, v)

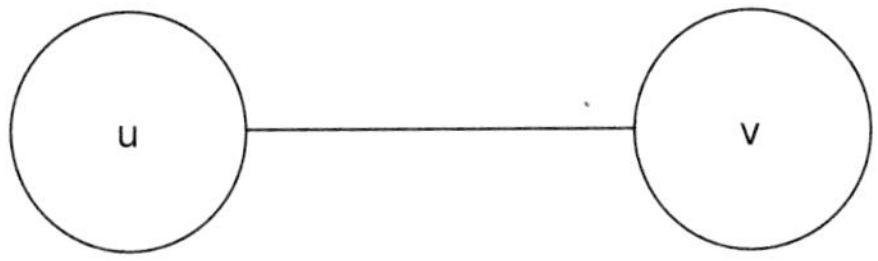

(b) Undirected edge between nodes u and v. Here, edges represented by both (u, v) as well as (v, u) are identical.

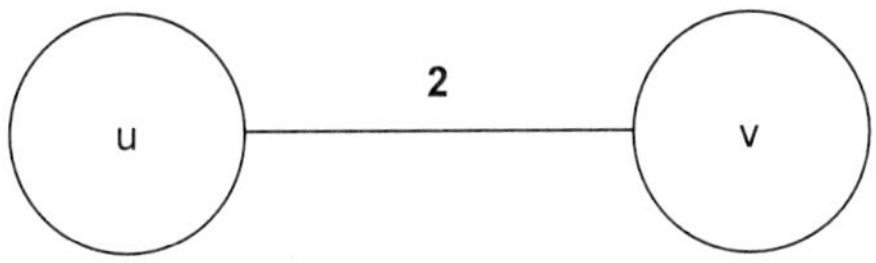

(c) Weighted undirected edge: The integer value '2' represents the weight on the edge.

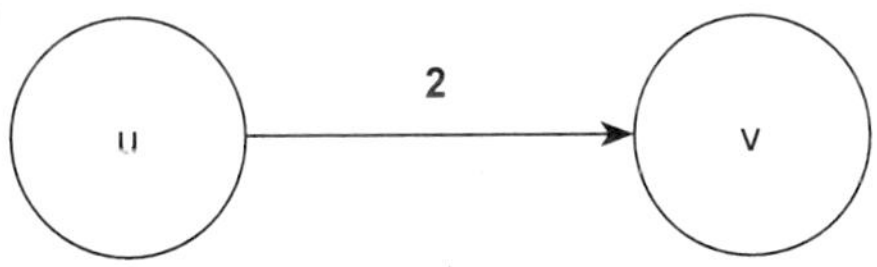

(d) A weighted directed edge (u, v). Here, the integer value '2' represents the weight on the edge.

4.1.3 Types of Graphs

Graphs are generally classified into *undirected*, *directed* and *weighted* based on the types of edges used for its creation. For a *directed* graph, all the edges are directed edges, whereas an *undirected* graph contains only edges which are undirected. An undirected/directed graph that is created using weighted edges is said to be a *weighted* graph.

Example:

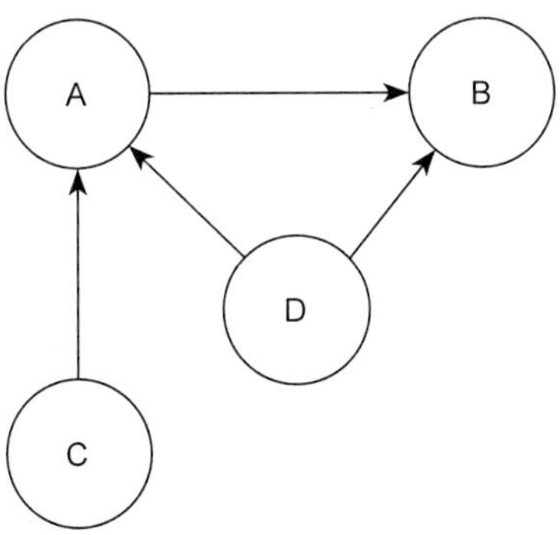

(a) Example: Directed Graph

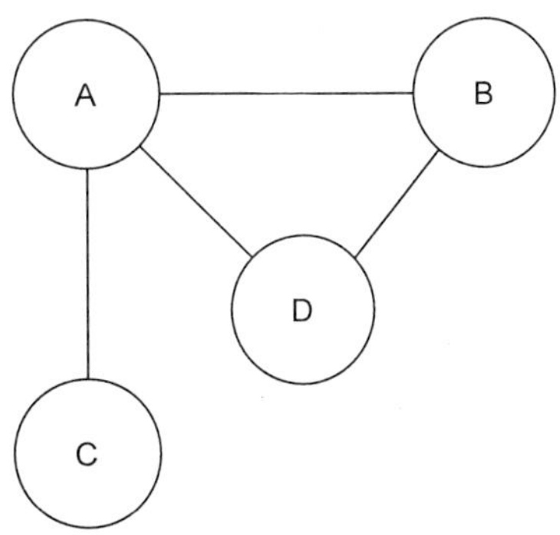

(b) Example: Undirected Graph

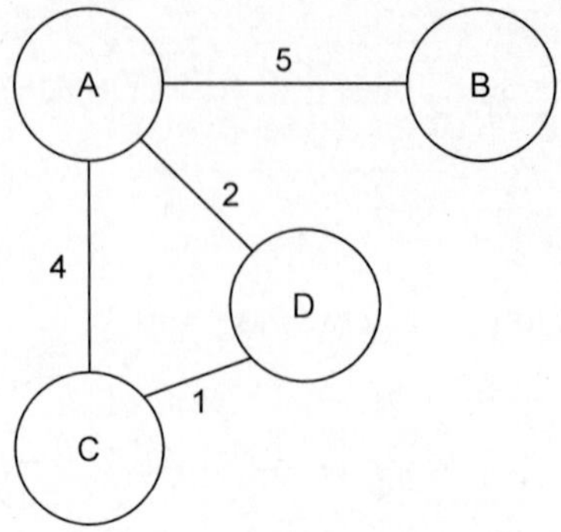

(c) Example: Weighted Undirected Graph

4.1.4 Vertex/Node Degree

In a graph, a node's degree is determined by how many edges are connected to it. The degree of node for directed and undirected graphs is determined differently. If a graph is undirected, the total count of edges incident on a node is employed to calculate a node's degree. Consider an example of an undirected graph illustrated below. Here, node A's degree is 3 as there are three edges meeting the node A. The degree of node B is 1.

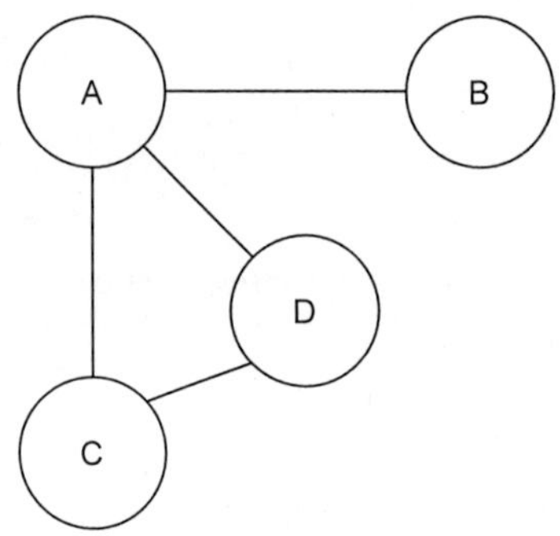

For a directed graph, each vertex has two types of degrees: an out-degree and an in-degree. The number of edges incident upon and originating from a node, respectively, is used to calculate the node's in-degree as well as out-degree of it. As an example, consider the directed graph depicted below. Here, the in-degree of A is 1 as an edge from node D is coming into node A and the out-degree of node A is 2 as two edges are going out from node A. The in-degree of vertex/node B is 2 and its out-degree is 0.

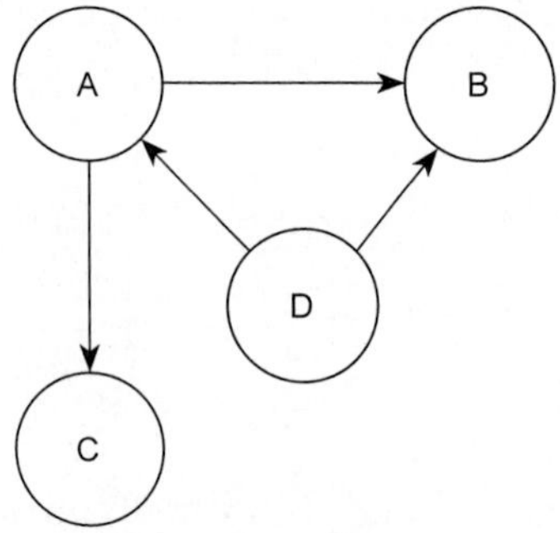

4.1.5 Path in a Graph

A sequence of non-repeated nodes (or edges) while traversing the graph is known as a *path*. A path is also referred to as dipath or directed path if the graph has directed edges. For the figure shown below, the sequence C-A-B-D and e3-e1-e4 represent the same path in terms of nodes and edges, respectively.

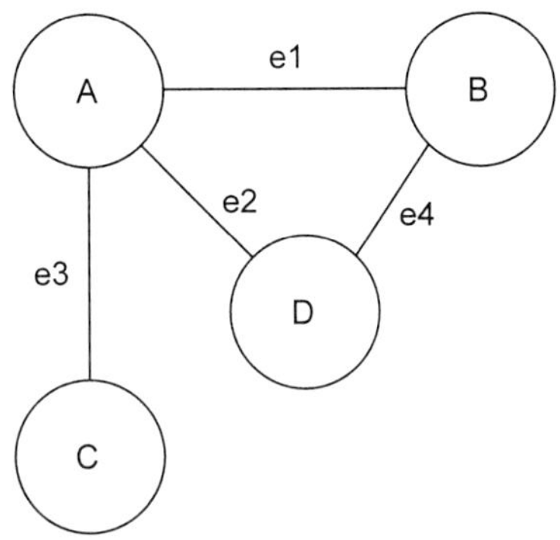

Consider the directed graph shown below. Here, A-D, A-B-D, A-C-D denote different paths in the same directed graph.

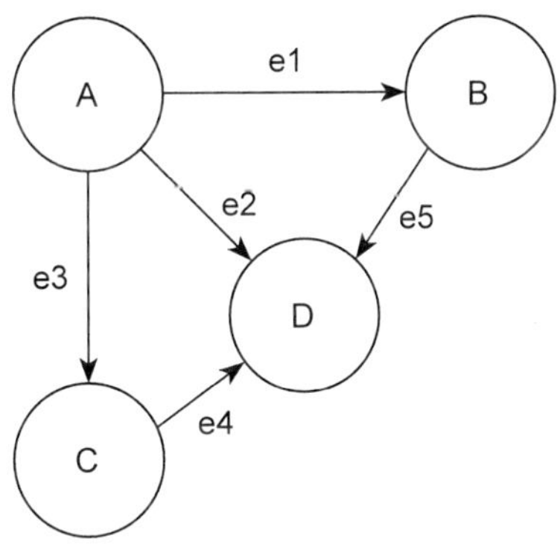

4.1.6 Cyclic Graph

A cycle is a path which originates from a given node/vertex and terminates at the same node/vertex. A cyclic graph is one that contains at least one cycle. Consider the cyclic graph shown below. Here, the series of vertices A-C-D-A result in a cycle.

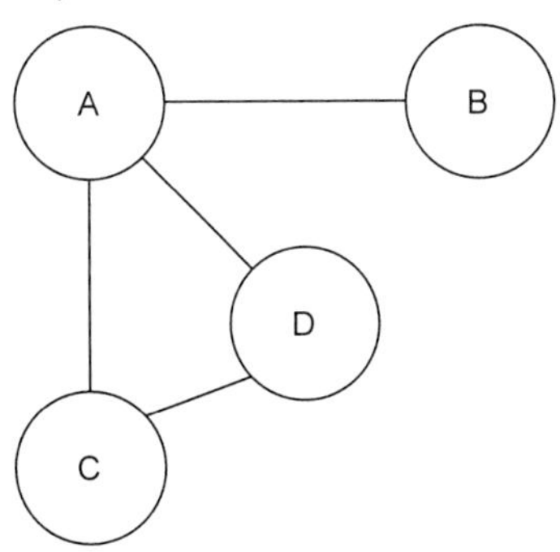

4.1.7 Acyclic Graph

A graph is said to be acyclic provided it does not include/contain any cycle. A tree is an example of an acyclic graph. For example, consider the following tree. It is an acyclic graph having no cycles.

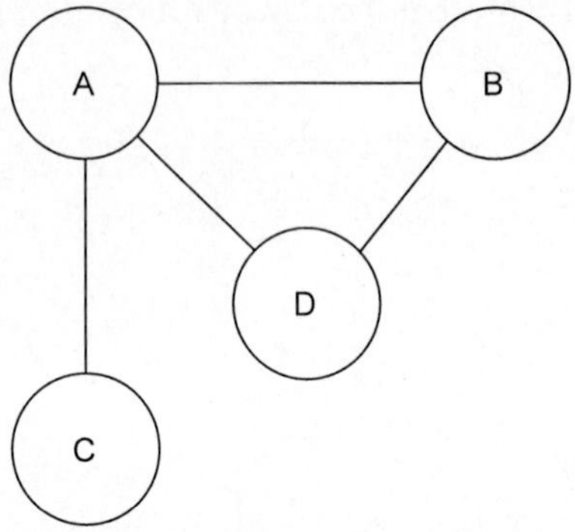

4.1.8 Directed Acyclic Graph (DAG)

From its name, we can infer that it is a directed graph without any cycles in it. For example, consider the following directed graph. Here, there exists no cycles and thus it becomes a directed acyclic graph.

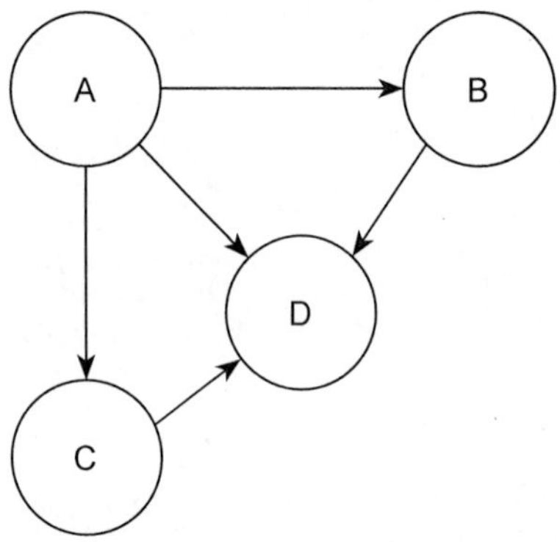

4.1.9 Connected and Disconnected Graphs

There must be at least one connecting path between each node pair in a connected graph. We can visit any one vertex from another vertex. Consider the following connected graph. Here, there exists more than one path (e.g., (A - C - B - D - F - E) or (A - C - B - D - E - F)) that connects every pair of vertices.

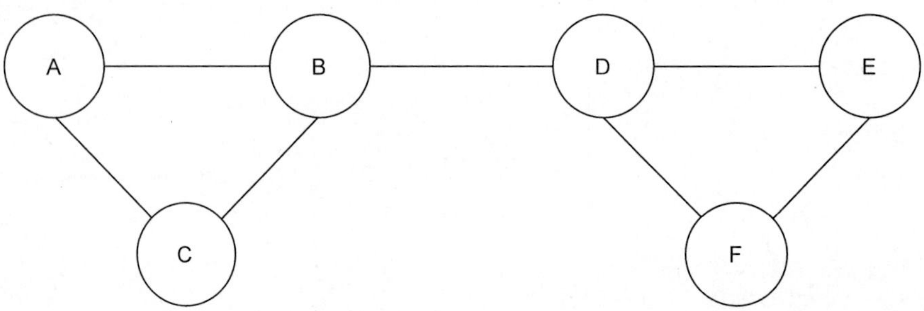

On the other hand, if there is no path connecting at least two of the graph's vertices, the graph is said to be disconnected. For example, consider the graph shown below. Here, there is no edge between the nodes B and D. This example graph has two independent components which are disconnected.

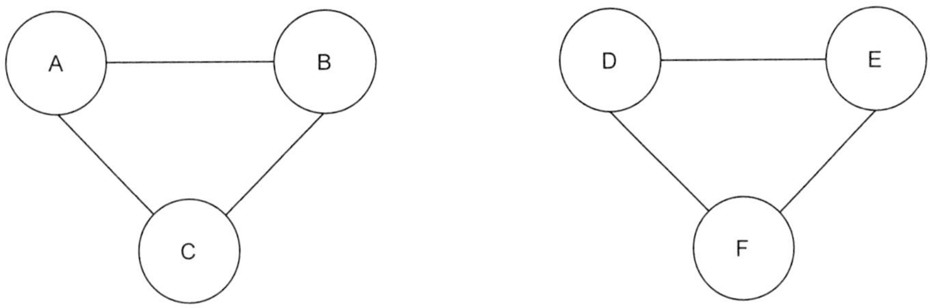

4.1.10 Forest

A forest is a graph that is disconnected, undirected, and acyclic. It is a disjoint group of trees. Although the example graph shown below appears to have two sub-graphs, it is actually one disconnected graph. Hence, we can say that it is a forest.

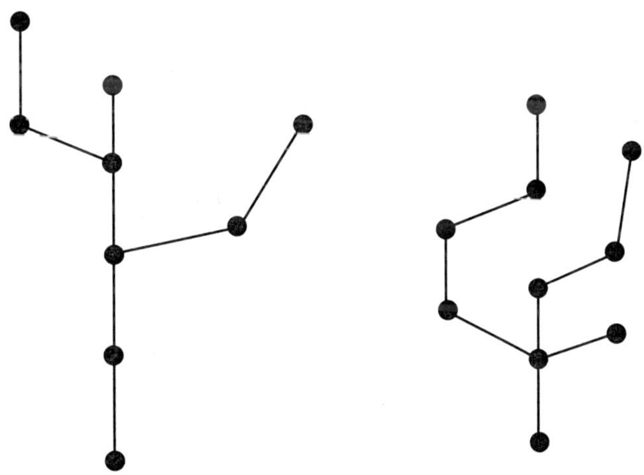

4.1.11 Spanning Trees

The subgraph of an undirected graph G that results from covering all of the vertices/nodes with the fewest number of edges is known as a *spanning tree*. Spanning trees must be connected and cycle free. In a graph which is undirected, there are at most $\mathbf{n}^{n-2}$ spanning trees, where n = |V|. For example, consider G shown below. It contains three vertices and thus a maximum of $3^{3-2} = 3$ spanning trees are possible for G. A few important properties of spanning trees are listed below.

- Multiple spanning trees may exist for a given graph G.
- For G, the same number of nodes and edges will be present in all of its possible spanning trees.
- If any one of the edges is removed from the spanning tree, then the graph becomes disconnected.
- Insertion of an extra edge into a spanning tree will introduce a loop or cycle in it.

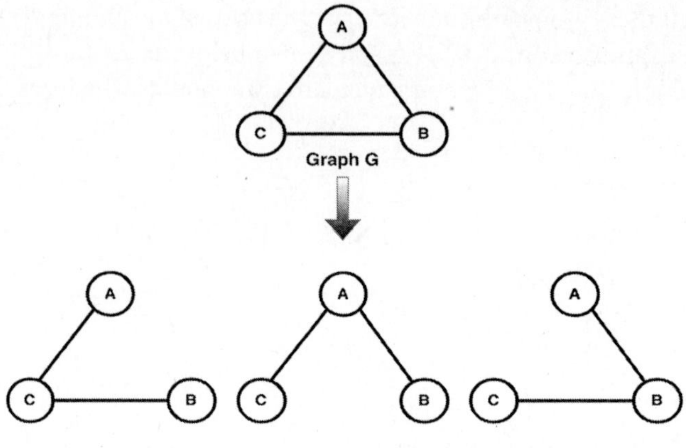

Spanning trees of G

4.2 GRAPH TRAVERSAL

To search for a vertex/node in a graph, graph traversal technique is used. There are two types of search techniques and they are: (i) Breadth-first (BFS), and (ii) Depth-first (DFS). Let us start our discussion with BFS.

4.2.1 Breadth-First Search

Consider a graph **G**. Let **u** be a node/vertex in G. BFS explores the edges of **G** in a step-by-step manner to find/discover every node/vertex that is reachable from **u**. BFS search produces a tree with the vertex **u** as a root and all the nodes that are reachable from **u**. For any node/vertex **v** that can be reached from **u**, the BFS tree contains a shortest path with the smallest number of edges. Now, let us discuss the steps to implement BFS traversal:

Input: Graph G = (V, E)

***Step 1*:** Define queue **Q**; Size of Q, $|Q| = |V|$.

***Step 2*:** Select a vertex $\mathbf{u} \in V$ as a starting point. Mark **u** as visited and add/enqueue **u** into the queue **Q**.

***Step 3*:** Find out the vertices that are adjacent to **u**, and not yet visited. Mark those vertices and add/enqueue them into the queue **Q**.

***Step 4*:** Delete/Dequeue **u** present in the front side of Q, if there are no vertices to be visited from **u**.

***Step 5*:** Repeat steps 3 and 4, until **Q** becomes empty.

4.2.1.1 Example

Consider the graph G shown below. G contains 7 nodes and 11 edges.

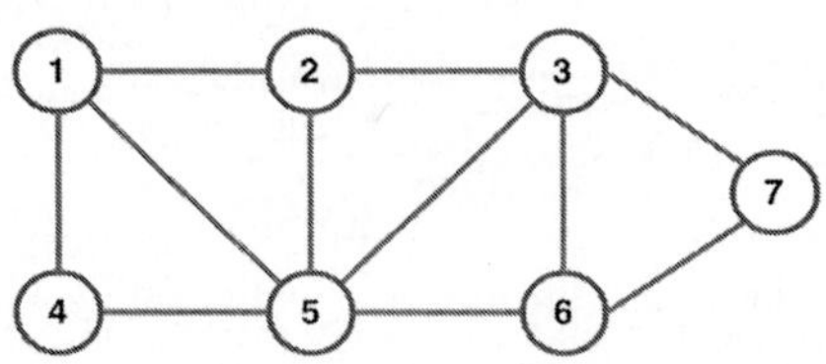

Step-1: Choose node 1 as the start node of the BFS traversal. Mark node 1 as visited and add node 1 into queue Q.

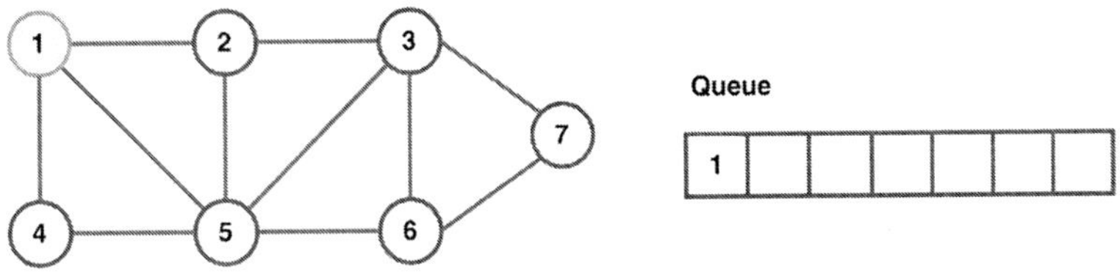

Step-2: Find out the nodes that are adjacent to node 1 and not yet visited (nodes 4, 5, 2). Mark those nodes as visited and add them to the Q. Delete node 1 from the Q.

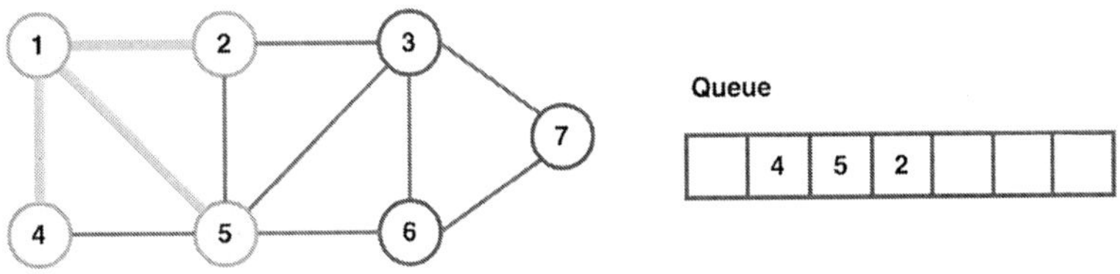

Step-3: Find out the nodes that are adjacent to node 4 and not yet visited. There is no such node. Delete node 4 from the Q.

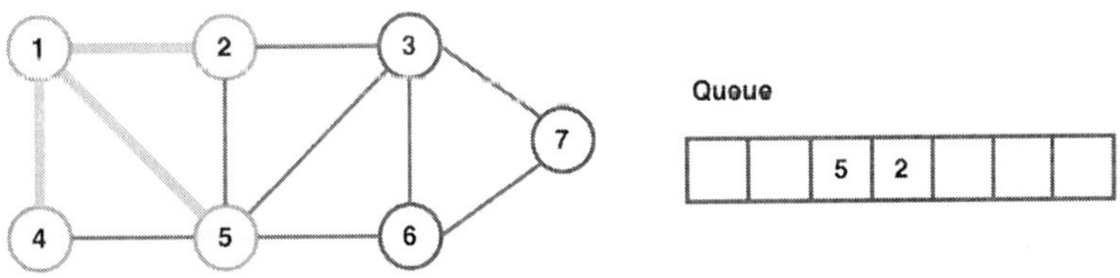

Step-4: Find out the nodes that are adjacent to node 5 and not yet visited (3, 6). Mark those nodes as visited and add them to the Q. Delete node 5 from the Q.

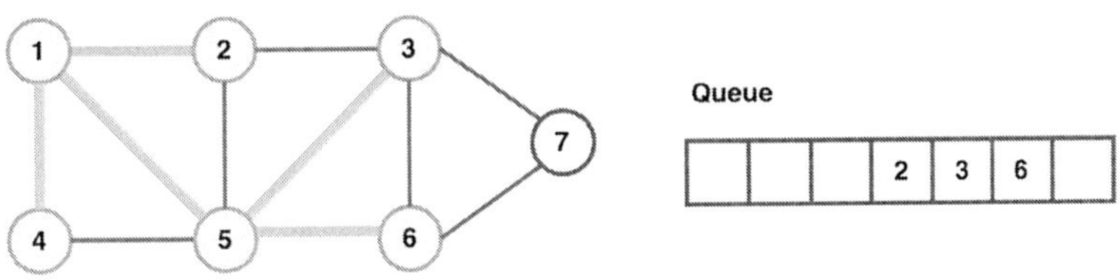

Step-5: Find out the nodes that are adjacent to node 2 and not yet visited. There is no such node. Delete node 2 from the Q.

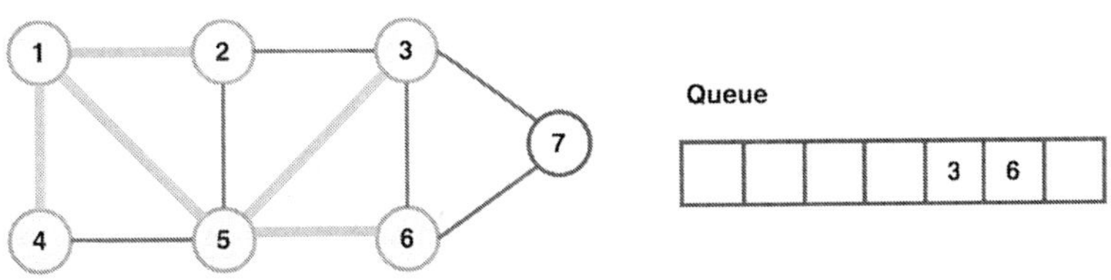

Step-6: Find out the nodes that are adjacent to node 3 and not yet visited (7). Mark node 7 as visited and add it to the Q. Delete node 3 from the Q.

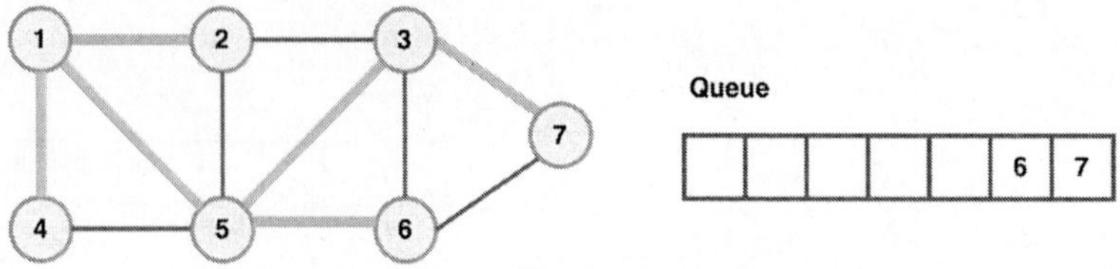

Step-7: Find out the nodes that are adjacent to node 6 and not yet visited. There is no such node. Delete node 6 from the Q.

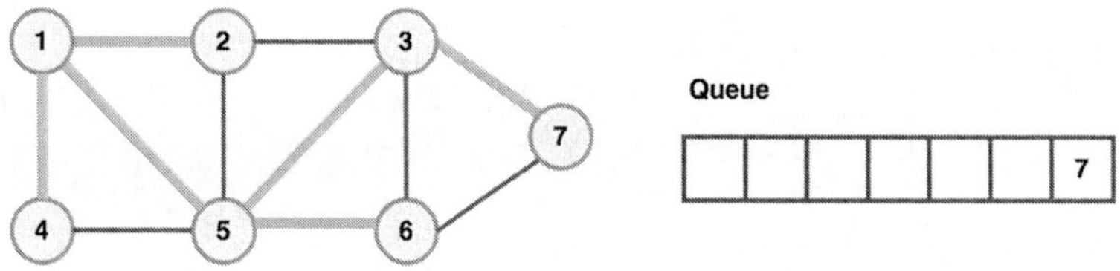

Step-8: Find out the nodes that are adjacent to node 7 and not yet visited. There is no such node. Delete node 7 from the Q.

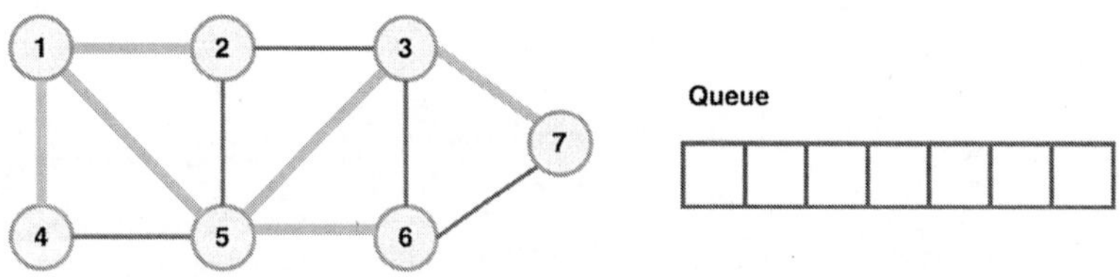

The queue Q is now empty, and the BFS traversal comes to an end. A spanning tree representing the outcome of the BFS traversal is shown below.

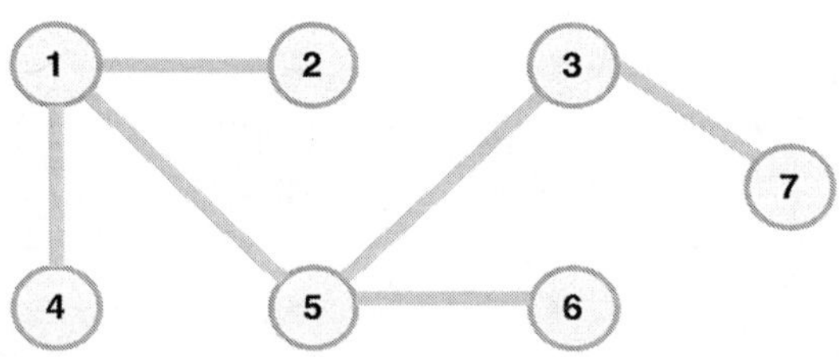

4.2.1.2 *Complexity Analysis*

The operation of adding and deleting a vertex from the queue Q consumes O(1) time. Every vertex in G is visited exactly once by BFS. Thus, BFS's complexity becomes O(V + E), when the graph is stored as an adjacency-list (refer, Know More section of the Unit).

4.2.2 Depth-First Search

Consider a graph **G**. Let **u** be a node in G. DFS explores "deeper" in the graph to find/discover every node/vertex that can be reached from **u**. Now, let us discuss the steps to implement DFS traversal:

Input: Graph G = (V, E)

***Step 1*:** Define stack **S**; Size of S, |S| = |V|.

***Step 2*:** Select a vertex **u** $\in$ V as a starting point. Mark **u** as 'visited' and add/push **u** into the stack **S**.

***Step 3*:** Find out any one of the vertices that is adjacent to **u**, and not yet visited. Mark it to be 'visited'; Push it to **S**.

***Step 4*:** Delete/Pop the vertex **u** in the top of the stack, if there are no vertices to be visited from **u**.

***Step 5*:** Repeat steps 3 and 4, until **S** becomes empty.

4.2.2.1 Example

Consider the graph G shown below. G contains 7 nodes and 11 edges.

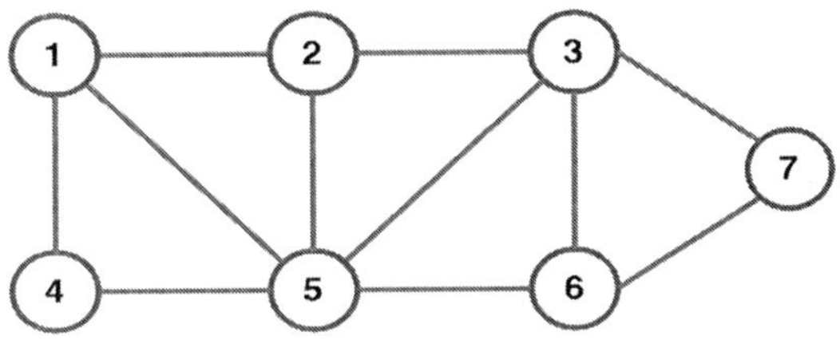

Step 1: Choose node 1 as the start node of the DFS traversal. Mark node 1 as visited and add node 1 into stack S.

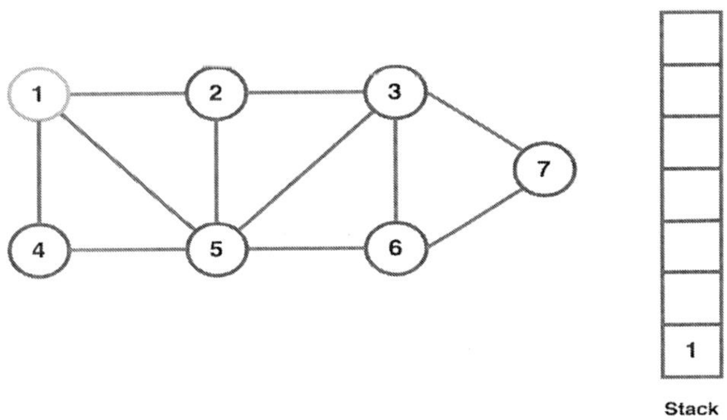

Step 2: Find out any node that is adjacent to node 1 and not yet visited (node 2). Mark node 2 as visited and add node 2 to the S.

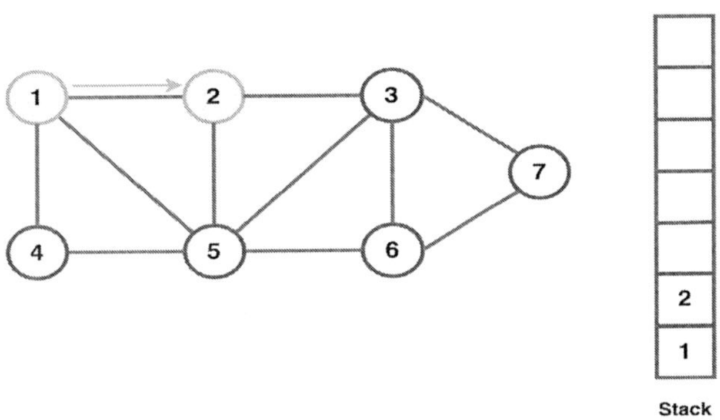

Step 3: Find out any node that is adjacent to node 2 and not yet visited (node 3). Mark node 3 as visited and add node 3 to the S.

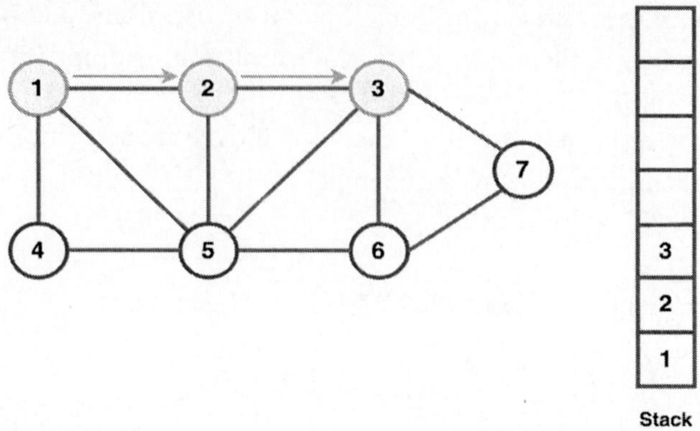

Step 4: Find out any node that is adjacent to node 3 and not yet visited (node 5). Mark node 5 as visited and add node 5 to the S.

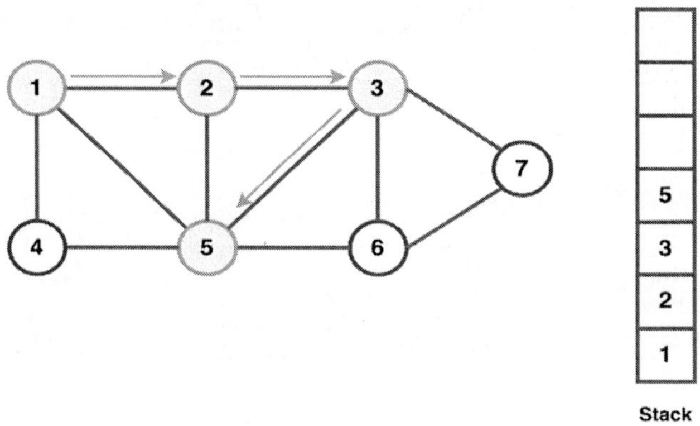

Step 5: Find out any node that is adjacent to node 5 and not yet visited (node 4). Mark node 4 as visited and add node 4 to the S.

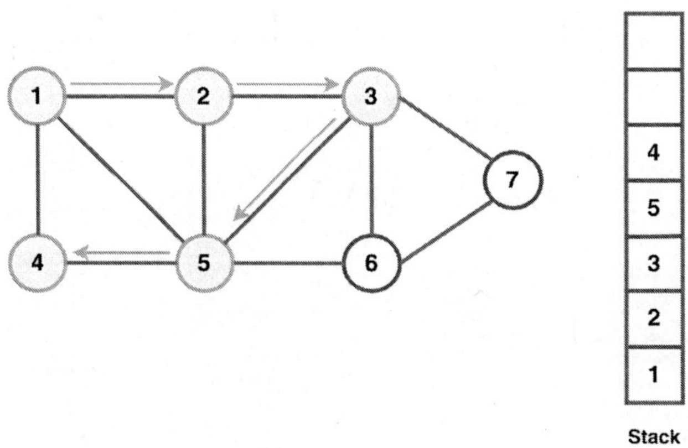

Step 6: Since node 4 does not have any adjacent node that is not yet visited, delete node 4 from the S.

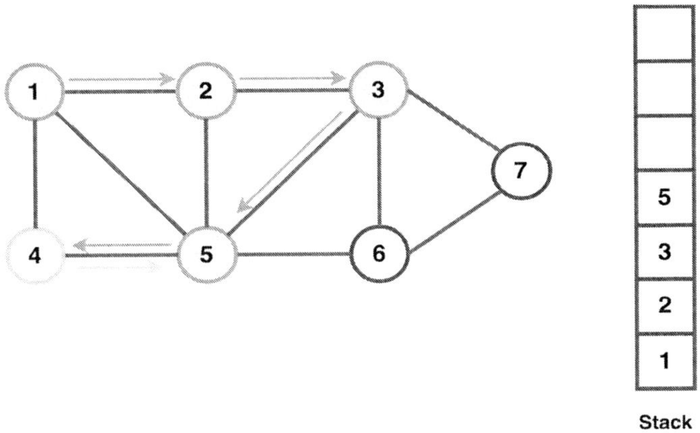

Step 7: Find out any node that is adjacent to node 5 and not yet visited (node 6). Mark node 6 as visited and add node 6 to the S.

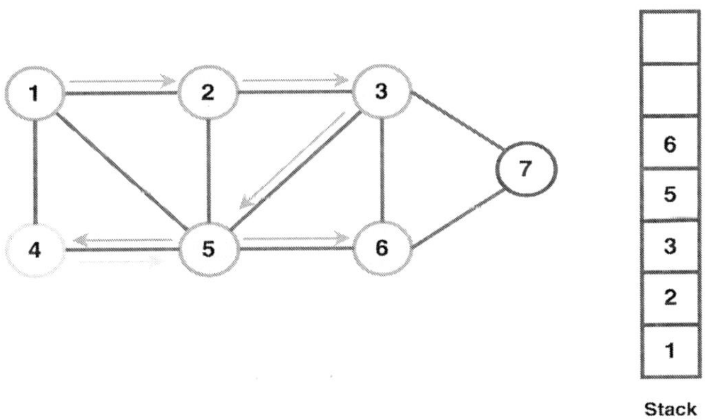

Step 8: Find out any node that is adjacent to node 6 and not yet visited (node 7). Mark node 7 as visited and add node 7 to the S.

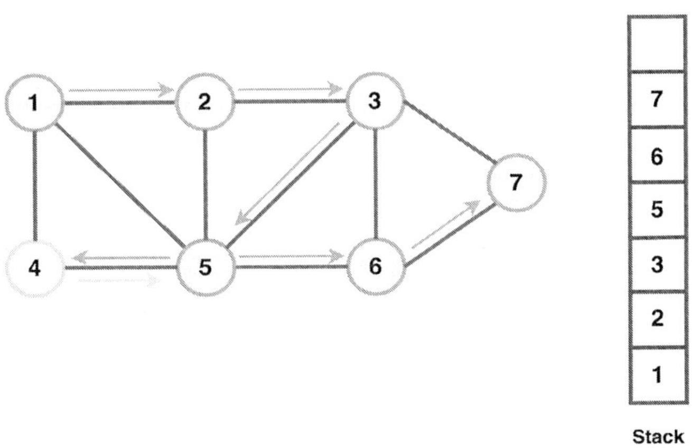

Step 9: Since node 7 does not have any adjacent node that is not yet visited, delete node 7 from the S.

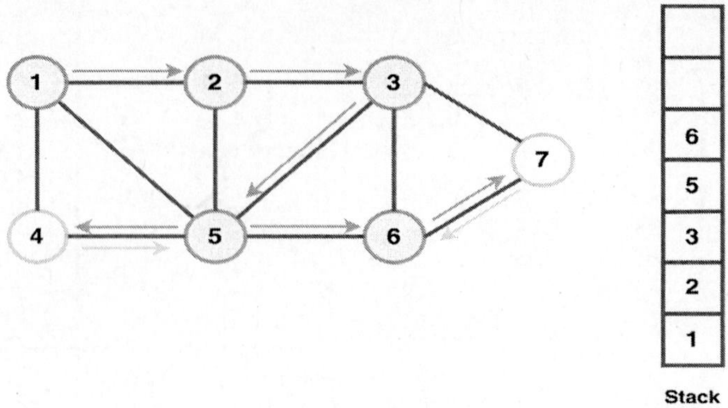

Step 10: Since node 6 does not have any adjacent node that is not yet visited, delete node 6 from the S.

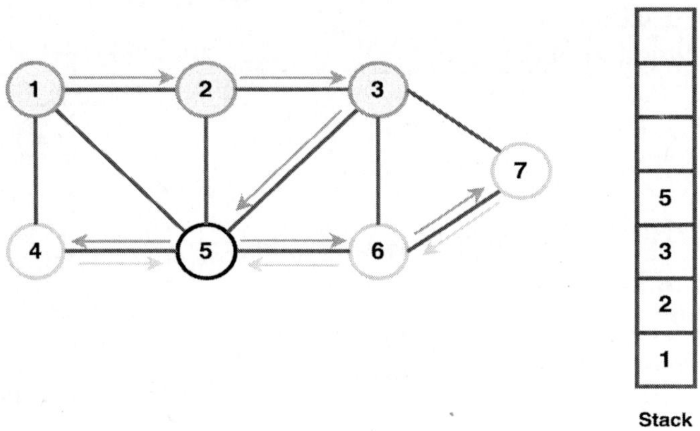

Step 11: Since node 5 does not have any adjacent node that is not yet visited, delete node 5 from the S.

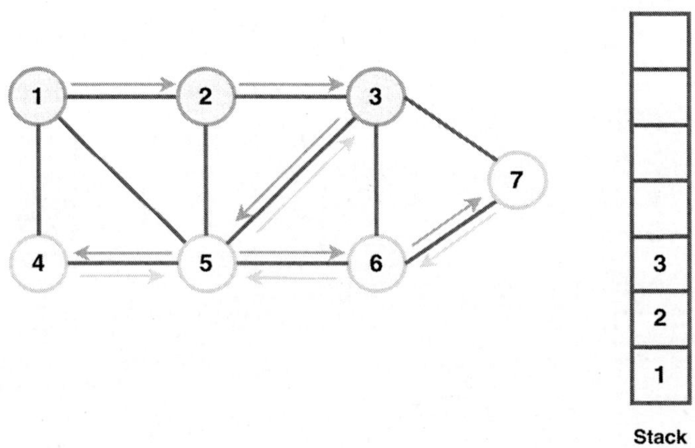

Step 12: Since node 3 does not have any adjacent node that is not yet visited, delete node 3 from the S.

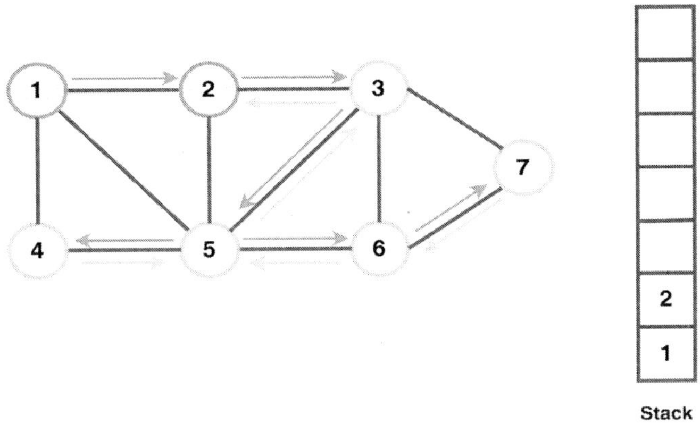

Step 13: Since node 2 does not have any adjacent node that is not yet visited, delete node 2 from the S.

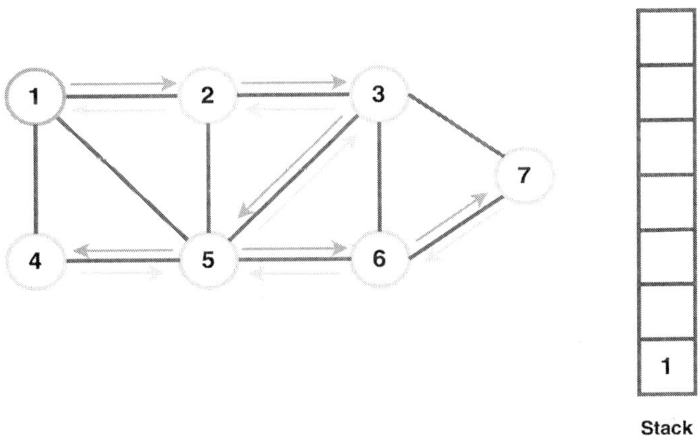

Step 14: Since node 1 does not have any adjacent node that is not yet visited, delete node 1 from the S.

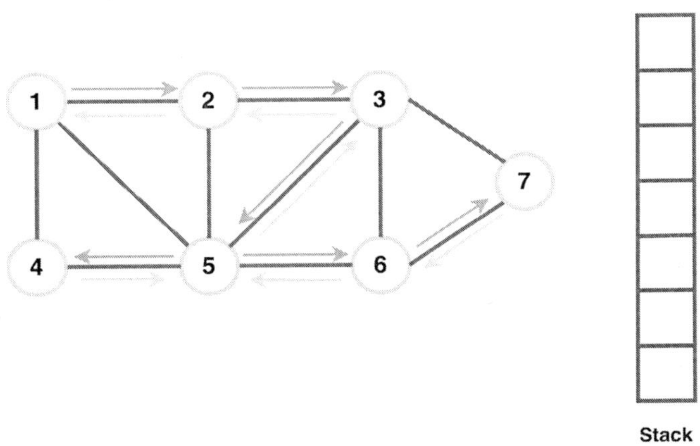

The stack S is now empty, and the DFS traversal comes to an end. A spanning tree representing the outcome of the DFS traversal is shown below.

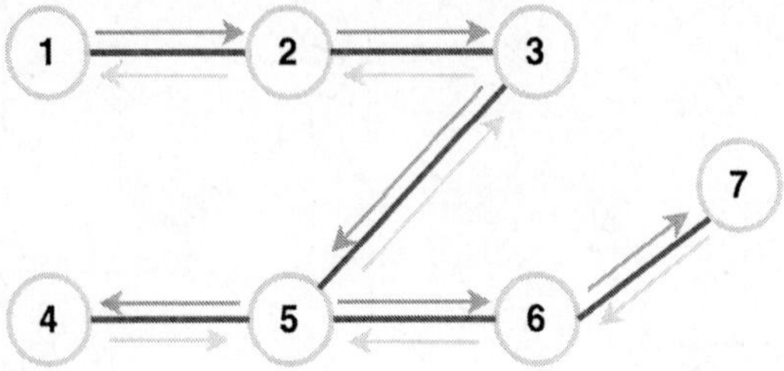

4.2.2.2 *Complexity Analysis*

The operation of adding and deleting a vertex from the stack S takes O(1) time. Every vertex in G is visited exactly once by DFS. Thus, DFS's complexity becomes O(V + E), when the graph is stored as an adjacency-list (refer, Know More section of the Unit).

4.3 TOPOLOGICAL SORTING

Topological sorting refers to the linearly ordered arrangement of nodes in a directed acyclic graph (DAG). A vertex ***u*** (source node) of a directed graph will always come before vertex ***v*** (destination node) in the ordering for every edge (***u, v***). The edges of the graph may reflect requirements that one action must be accomplished before another and the vertices may represent activities that have to be completed.

In this section, we discuss Kahn's algorithm, a simple and yet popular algorithm used to determine the topological sorting order of a graph. The algorithm first determines a node (say, X) in the graph that has no incoming edges (that is, its in-degree is zero). It then removes all the outgoing edges of X, and X is added into a sorted list (say, TOPO_L). This procedure is repeated until the graph has no more vertex. If the graph is a DAG, then the list TOPO_L gives us its topologically sorted order. This order is not always unique, that is, multiple topologically sorted order exists for a given DAG. On the other hand, if the graph contains any cycle, it is impossible to generate its topologically sorted order. Topological sorting is mainly used to a) determine cycle in a graph, and b) detect deadlock in operating systems.

4.3.1 Pseudocode

```
Procedure Topo_Sort()
        Input G, the directed graph
        Declare two lists: TOPO_L,INDE_L
        For each node X in G
               Calculate X's in-degree
               If X's in-degree is zero
                      Add X to INDE_L
               End If
        End For
        While INDE_L is not empty
               Remove a node X from INDE_L
```

```
                Add X to TOPO_L
                For each node Y having an edge E from X
                    Remove E from G
                     If Y has no other incoming edges
                          Add Y to INDE_L
                     End If
                End For
           End While
           If G has edges
                Return False //G has at least one cycle
           Else
                Return TOPO_L
           End If
      End Procedure
```

4.3.2 Example

Consider the directed graph shown in Fig. 4.1. Different topological orderings are possible for this graph. They are: ABCDEF, ABCDFE, ACBDEF, and ACBDFE.

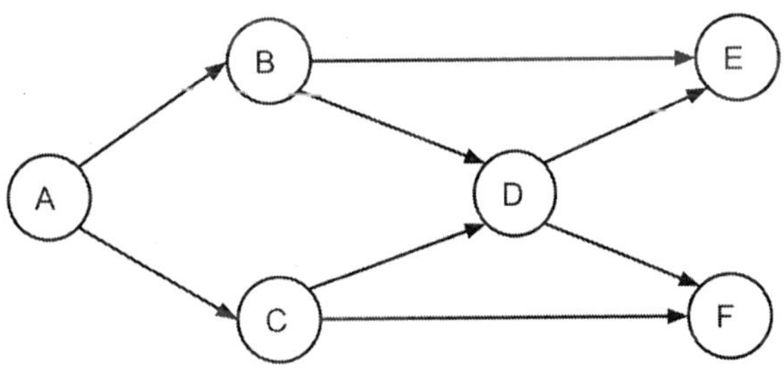

Fig. 4.1: A Directed Graph G

4.3.3 Complexity Analysis

The complexity for topological sorting is O(V + E).

4.4 MINIMUM SPANNING TREE

As discussed earlier, a spanning tree of a graph is a tree that contains no cycles and covers all nodes. In a weighted undirected graph, there exists multiple spanning trees which can be differentiated with respect to the sum of edge weights obtained by them. As the name suggests, a *minimum spanning tree* of a weighted graph is the subset of the graph's edges that avoids cycles while connecting all of the vertices with the smallest sum of edge weights. Simply, it represents a spanning tree with the smallest feasible sum of edge weights. Here, one major constraint is that the graph should be connected. It is mainly used in graph-based cluster analysis, trees for broadcasting in computer networks, image segmentation etc.

In this section, we discuss two most popular algorithms - *Prim's* and *Kruskal's algorithms*, that are used to derive a minimum spanning tree from a given weighted graph.

4.4.1 Prim's Algorithm

Prim's algorithm, a well-known greedy technique, can be used to find the minimum spanning tree for a weighted, undirected graph. This method tends to look for edges that can be used to build spanning trees and the aggregate weight of all the edges in the tree should be kept to a minimum. Beginning with one randomly selected vertex, the algorithm continues to add edges with the lowest weight until it attains its objective. The algorithm operates on two lists: the list of visited vertices, say RAND_L, and the list of unvisited vertices, say V – RAND_L. By connecting the least-weighted edge, we gradually transfer each vertex from list V – RAND_L to list RAND_L. This algorithm performs better on dense graphs.

4.4.1.1 Pseudocode

```
Procedure Prim_Algo(G)
        Input Weighted undirected graph G =(V,E)
        Declare two lists: RAND_L, TEMP_L
        Initialize RAND_L = {x1}, TEMP_L = ∅
        // x1 is the first randomly selected vertex
        While (RAND_L ≠ V)
               Find the smallest weighted edge (x,y) such
               that x ∈ RAND_L and y ∈ V - RAND_L
               TEMP_L = TEMP_L + {(x,y)}
               RAND_L = RAND_L + {y}
        End While
End Procedure
```

4.4.1.2 Example

Consider the weighted undirected graph G given below (refer, Fig. 4.2).

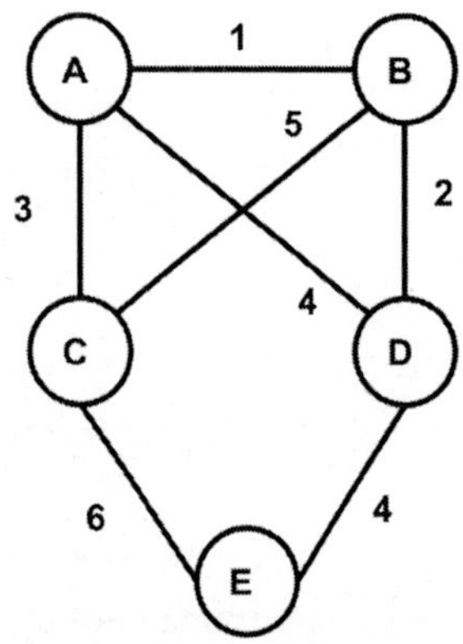

Fig. 4.2: Weighted undirected graph G

Step 1: Choose a node randomly (say, node A), and add it into the visited list, RAND_L.

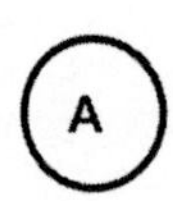

Step 2: Now, RAND_L = {A}, V – RAND_L = {B, C, D, E}. Choose vertex A's lowest weighted edge (A, B), and add node B from V – RAND_L into RAND_L.

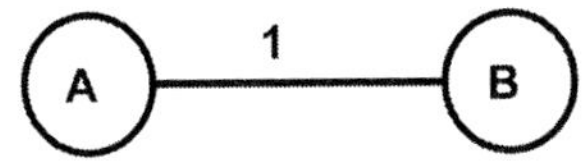

Step 3: Choose the smallest weighted edge (B, D) from a set of edges formed by the sets RAND_L and V - RAND_L. Add node D into RAND_L.

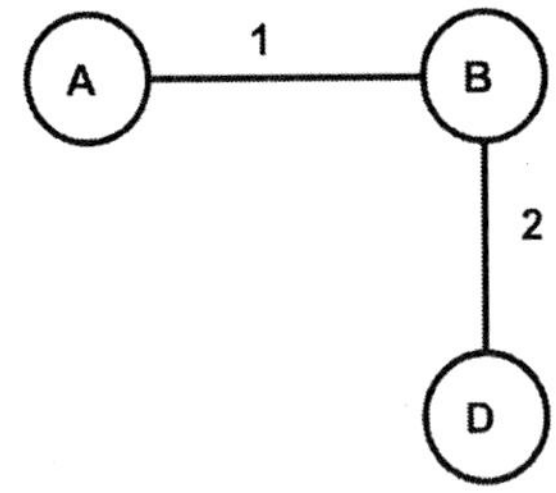

Step 4: Choose the smallest weighted edge (A, C) from a set of edges formed by the sets RAND_L and V - RAND_L. Add node C into RAND_L.

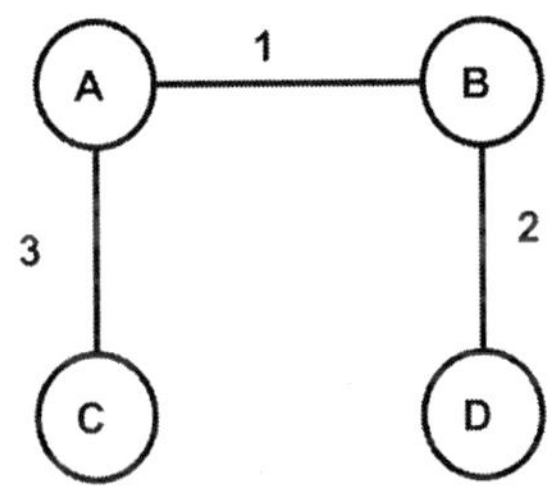

Step 5: Choose the smallest weighted edge (D, E) from a set of edges formed by the sets RAND_L and V - RAND_L. Add node E into RAND_L. Now, all the nodes are covered in the set RAND_L and the resulting tree shown below is the final minimum spanning tree.

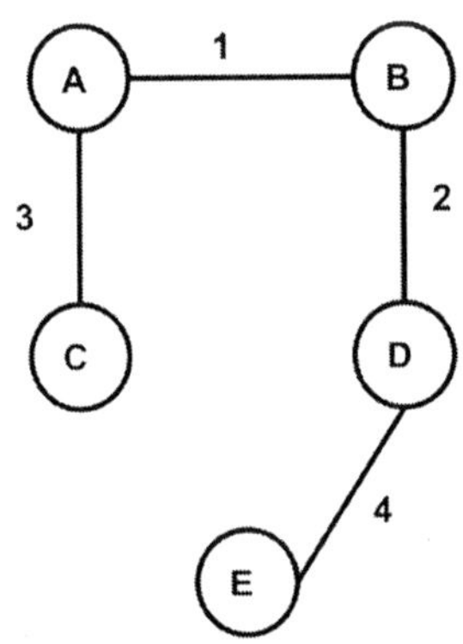

4.4.1.3 Complexity Analysis

The type of data structure that is utilized to construct Prim's algorithm will determine its running time complexity. If we use a binary heap then the time complexity is O(E log V), where V is the number of nodes and E is the number of edges in the graph.

4.4.2 Kruskal's algorithm

Kruskal's algorithm employs a greedy method, like Prim's algorithm does, to determine the undirected edge-weighted graph's minimum spanning forest. It determines the minimum spanning tree if the graph is connected. The algorithm begins with the edges that have the lowest weight and keeps adding edges until it attains the desired result. It runs faster in case of sparse graphs. The detailed steps of Kruskal's algorithm are explained below.

1. Sort the graph's edges according to their weights in a non-decreasing order.
2. Select the lowest weighted edge.
3. Verify if the chosen edge creates a cycle with the spanning tree that has been created so far.
4. If not, add this edge into the spanning tree. Otherwise, drop it.
5. Repeat from step 2 until the resulting spanning tree has (V-1) edges.

Initially, the algorithm creates $|V|$ disjoint trees, each having a node $x \in V$ using the function CREATE-GROUP() (line number 6). The algorithm then selects each edge (x, y) from the sorted list EDGE_L one by one (line number 9), and determines whether two nodes x and y of the selected edge (x, y) belong to the same tree or not. The function DETERMINE-GROUP() is used to find the inclusion of a particular node in a tree. If two nodes of an edge belong to different trees (line number 10) then the edge (x, y) is added to the final spanning tree list TEMP_L (line number 11), and the algorithm combines two corresponding trees using the COMBINE() function (line number 12).

4.4.2.1 Pseudocode

```
L1:  Procedure Kruskal_Algo()
L2:        Input Weighted undirected graph G =(V,E)
L3:        Declare two lists: EDGE_L, TEMP_L
L4:        Initialize EDGE_L = E, TEMP_L = ∅
L5:        For each node x ∈ V
L6:             CREATE-GROUP(x)
L7:        End For
L8:        Sort EDGE_L in non-decreasing order of edge weights
L9:        For each edge (x, y) ∈ sorted list EDGE_L
L10:            If DETERMINE-GROUP(x) ≠ DETERMINE-GROUP(y)
L11:                 TEMP_L = TEMP_L + {(x, y)}
L12:                 COMBINE(x, y)
L13:            End If
L14:       End For
L15:       Return TEMP_L
L16: End Procedure
```

4.4.2.2 Example

Fig. 4.3 depicts a weighted undirected graph G. There are 13 edges and 8 nodes in this graph. The minimum spanning tree that is created from G has (8 - 1) = 7 edges.

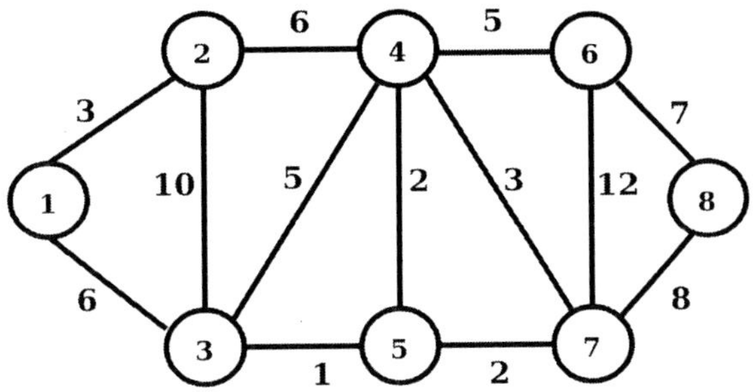

Fig. 4.3: Weighted Graph G

Now, we create a list of edges that are sorted according to increasing weights, as shown in the table below. Go through this ordered list of edges and choose each edge one by one.

Source Node	3	4	5	1	4	3	4	1	2	6	7	2	6
Destination Node	5	5	7	2	7	4	6	3	4	8	8	3	7
Weight	1	2	2	3	3	5	5	6	6	7	8	10	12

Step 1: Select the first minimum weighted edge (3,5) from the list. Edge (3,5) should be included in the output tree because it is not forming a cycle.

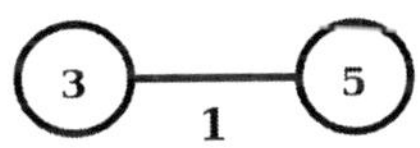

Step 2: Select the next minimum weighted edge (4,5) from the list. Edge (4,5) should be included in the output tree because it is not forming a cycle.

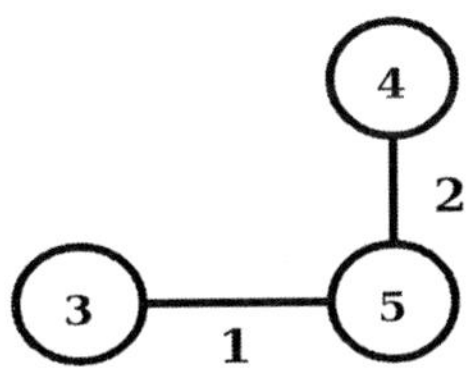

Step 3: Select the next minimum weighted edge (5,7) from the list. Edge (5,7) should be included in the output tree because it is not forming a cycle.

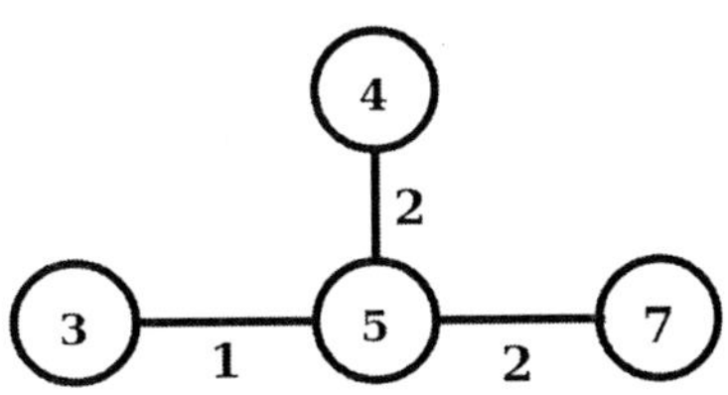

Step 4: Select the next minimum weighted edge (1,2) from the list. Edge (1,2) should be included in the output tree because it is not forming a cycle.

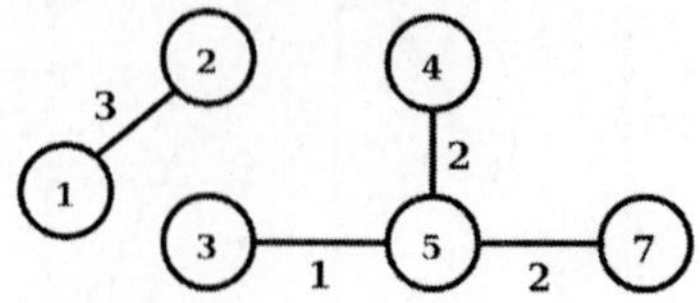

Step 5: Select the next minimum weighted edge (4,7) from the list. Edge (4,7) should be discarded because it is forming a cycle.

Step 6: Select the next minimum weighted edge (3,4) from the list. Edge (3,4) should be discarded because it is forming a cycle.

Step 7: Select the next minimum weighted edge (4,6) from the list. Edge (4,6) should be included in the output tree because it is not forming a cycle.

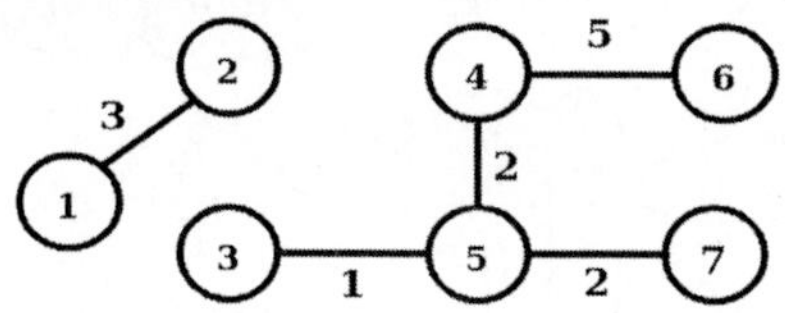

Step 8: Select the next minimum weighted edge (1,3) from the list. Edge (1,3) should be included in the output tree because it is not forming a cycle.

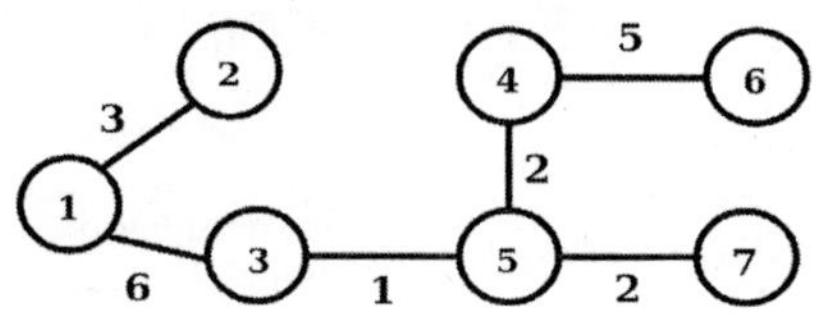

Step 9: Select the next minimum weighted edge (2,4) from the list. Edge (2,4) should be discarded because it is forming a cycle.

Step 10: Select the next minimum weighted edge (6,8) from the list. Edge (6,8) should be included in the output tree because it is not forming a cycle.

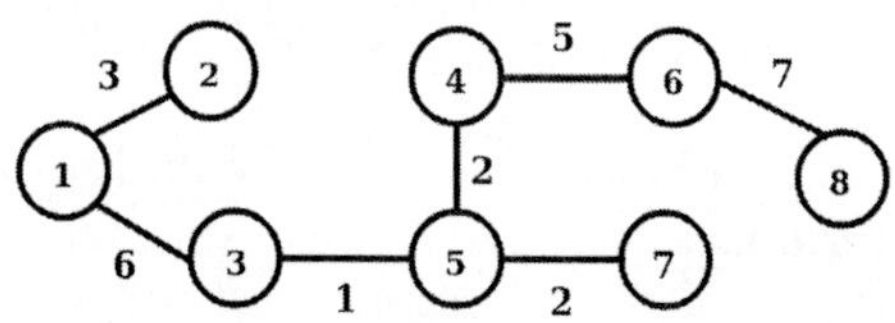

Step 11: Discard edges (7,8), (2,3) and (6,7) since the inclusion of these edges creates a cycle in the output tree. The figure below depicts the resulting minimum spanning tree.

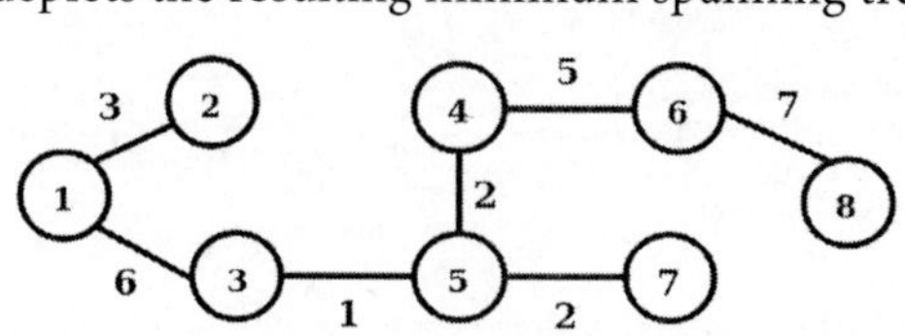

4.4.2.3 *Complexity Analysis*

Sorting of edges mentioned in line number 8 takes O(E log E) time. The disjoint set operations DETERMINE-GROUP and COMBINE also take a total of O(E log E) time. Thus, the total time complexity of Kruskal's algorithm is O(E log E). Since $|E| < |V|^2$, we have log |E| = O(log V), and thus the overall complexity associated with Kruskal's algorithm can be represented as O(E log V).

4.5 SHORTEST PATH ALGORITHMS

Consider a scenario where a graph is visualized as a real world computer network. Here, vertices of a graph represent computers, edges denote network communication links between computers, and weights on edges represent communication cost (measured in terms of geographical distance or delay time etc). There exists multiple paths (called routes in a network) that can deliver a message (say an email) from a computer (called source machine) at one end of the network to another computer (called destination machine) at the other end of the network. Algorithms that find the fastest or shortest route to send messages from a source to a destination are known as *shortest path algorithms*. Here, the shortest path is a path among a set of available paths in the network that generates a minimal communication cost. In the next two sections, we discuss two shortest path algorithms: one for unweighted graphs and another for weighted graphs.

4.6 SHORTEST PATH IN AN UNWEIGHTED GRAPH

In unweighted graphs, no weight is defined for edges. On the other hand, we can assume that all the edges are of the same weight (say, a weight of 1). If the graph is unweighted, then finding the shortest path is straightforward. We only need to count the edges in a path to measure path length. The shortest path is the one with the lowest number of edges. The strategy to determine shortest path within an unweighted graph is described in the pseudocode. This algorithm first uses a function named *determinePaths()* whose job is to traverse the given graph from a source S to a destination D and determine different paths between S and D in the graph. These paths are then compared based on their path lengths to determine the shortest one. An important point is that this algorithm is only applicable to graphs with no cycles.

4.6.1 Pseudocode

```
Procedure ShortestPathUnweighted_Algo(G, S, D)
        Input unweighted acyclic graph G, Source
                              Node S, Destination Node D
        Declare two lists: SHORTEST_L, PATHS_L
        Initialize SHORTEST_L = ∅
        Initialize PATHS_L = determinePaths(G, S, D)
        For each path in PATHS_L
                Determine pathLength, length of path
                If SHORTEST_L is empty
                        Add path to SHORTEST_L
                Else If SHORTEST_L's size > pathLength
                        Overwrite the new path onto SHORTEST_L
                End If
```

```
            End For
            Return SHORTEST_L
    End Procedure
```

4.6.2 Example

Consider the unweighted graph G shown in Fig. 4.4. Let the source and destination nodes considered for determining shortest path be 1 and 8, respectively. There exists three paths from 1 to 8, and are P1: 1-2-5-8, P2: 1-3-8, and P3: 1-4-6-7-8. The length (number of edges) of these paths P1, P2, and P3 are 3, 2, and 4, respectively. Therefore, the shortest path between 1 and 8 is P2: 1-3-8, and has a length of 2.

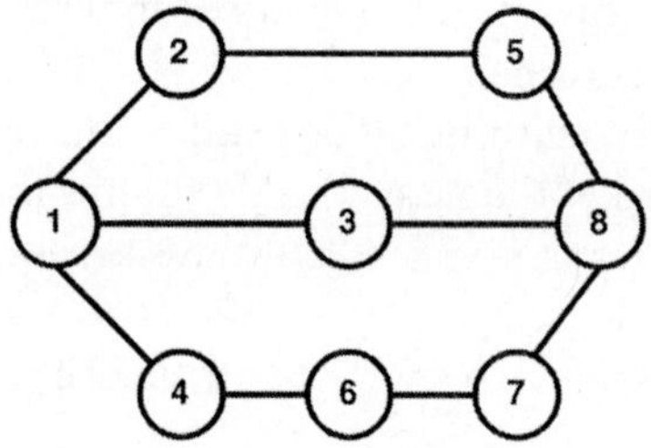

Fig. 4.4: Unweighted Graph G

4.6.3 Complexity Analysis

The time overhead associated with the above-discussed strategy depends on the generalised function *determinePaths()* that finds all the paths in the graph. There are many approaches that implement the function *determinePaths()* in different ways. Therefore, the complexity of *determinePaths()* also varies from the perspective of implementation. If one such implementation takes O(|V|!) time, then the overall time overhead associated with the algorithm also becomes O(|V|!).

4.7 SHORTEST PATH IN A WEIGHTED GRAPH

As discussed earlier, a weighted graph has weight labels on its edges that represent the communication cost between two nodes involved in the formation of the corresponding edge in the graph. Given a weighted graph, there exist many algorithms to find the shortest path. However, *Dijkstra's shortest path algorithm* is known to be a simple and efficient technique among these algorithms. It was formulated by a famous Dutch computer scientist named Dr. Edsger W. Dijkstra. In general, the objective of Dijkstra's algorithm is to calculate the shortest path between a specific source node and each of the remaining nodes in the graph. A shortcoming for this algorithm is that it works only for graphs having positive edge weights.

Dijkstra's algorithm uses two data structures: an array (say, SHORT_L) that stores the current distance from a source node to other nodes in the graph, and a queue (say, Queue) of all nodes in the graph. The algorithm first starts with a source node ***s*** and initializes the array SHORT_L as SHORT_L[s] = 0 for a source node ***s***, and SHORT_L[v] = ∞, for all other nodes **v** in G. It then adds each vertex ***v*** of the graph into Queue. Whenever Queue is not empty, the algorithm selects a vertex (say, ***u***) that has least SHORT_L[u] value and is deleted from Queue. For each neighbor ***v*** of ***u***, the algorithm determines a path from the source node to ***v*** through ***u***, and its length (say, *new_dist*) is measured as SHORT_L[u] + w(u, v), where w(u, v) is the assigned weight on the edge (u, v). If *new_dist* is smaller than the length of the present shortest path obtained for the node *v*, then the present path is substituted with the newly generated path.

4.7.1 Pseudocode

```
Procedure ShortestPathWeighted_Algo(G, S)
        Input Weighted Graph G, Source Node s
        Declare an array SHORT_L
        Initialize SHORT_L[s] = 0
               For each vertex v in G
               If v ≠ s
                      SHORT_L[v] = ∞
               End If
               Add v to Queue
        End For
        While Queue is not empty
               Find a vertex u in Queue with minimum
                                                  SHORT_L[u]
               Delete u from Queue
               For each neighbor v of u
                      new_dist = SHORT_L[u] + W(u, v)
                      If new_dist < SHORT_L[v]
                             SHORT_L[v] = new_dist
                      End If
               End For
        End While
        Return SHORT_L[]
End Procedure
```

4.7.2 Example

Consider a weighted undirected graph G shown in Fig. 4.5. Now, we determine the shortest path from the source node 1 to all other nodes in G.

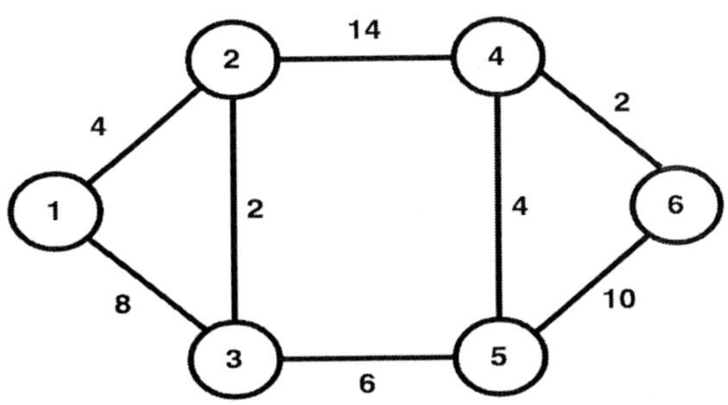

Fig. 4.5: Weighted undirected graph G

Step 1: Initialize the distance to the source vertex 1 as zero and all other vertices as infinity values. Add all the vertices of G into the queue. Select the least distance valued vertex (node 1) and delete it from the queue. The following figure depicts this scenario.

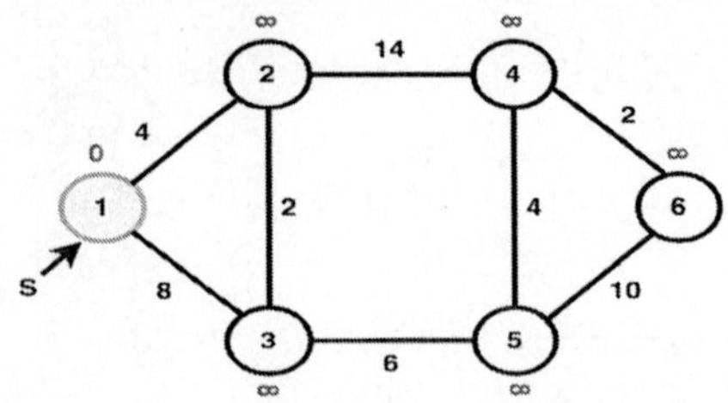

Step 2: Update the path distances from node 1 to its neighbor nodes 2 and 3. Select the next node with minimal distance (node 2) and delete it from the queue. The following figure depicts this scenario.

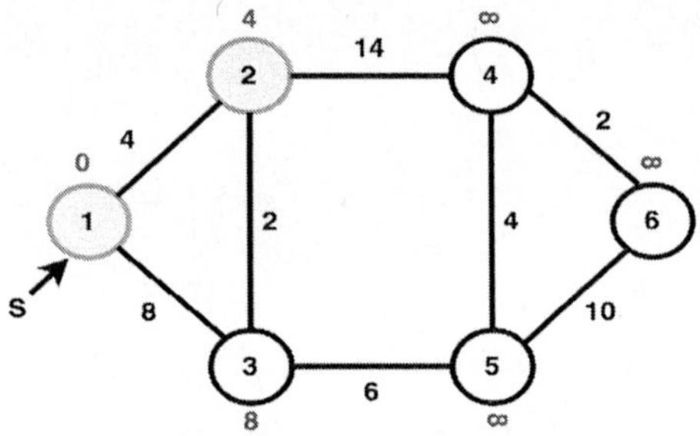

Step 3: Update the path distances of the neighbor nodes (3 and 4) of node 2. Select the next node with minimal distance (say, node 3) and delete it from the queue. The following figure depicts this scenario.

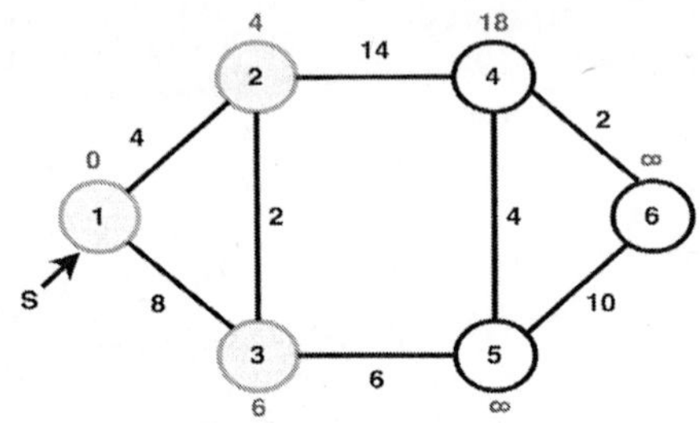

Step 4: Update the path distance of the neighbor node (5) of node 3. Select the next node with minimal distance (say, node 5) and delete it from the queue. The following figure depicts this scenario.

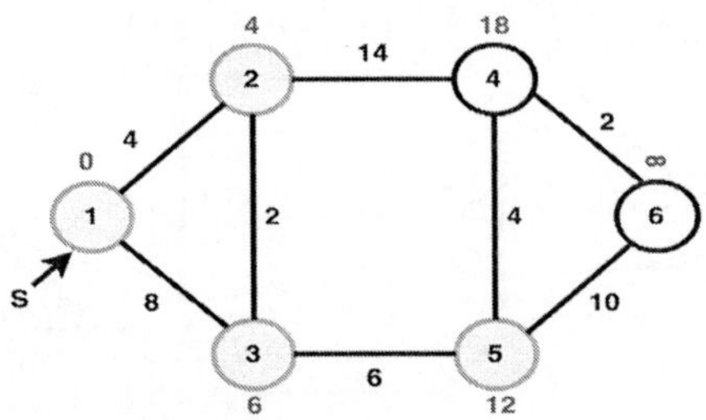

Step 5: Update the path distances of the neighbor nodes (4 and 6) of node 5. Select the next node with minimal distance (say, node 4) and delete it from the queue. The following figure depicts this scenario.

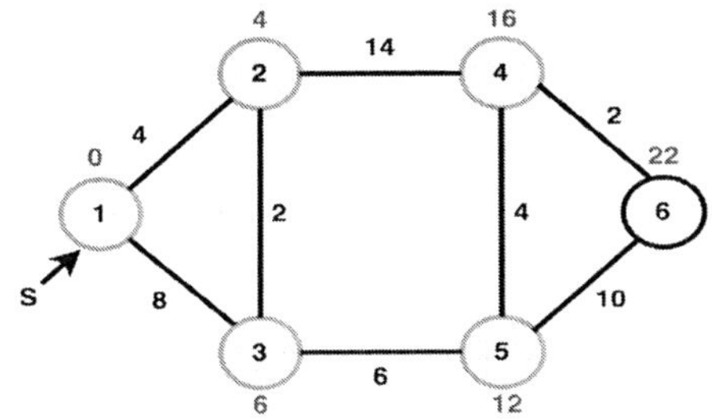

Step 6: Update the path distance of the neighbor node (6) of node 4. Select the next node with minimal distance (say, node 6) and delete it from the queue. Now, the queue becomes empty and the algorithm stops exploring further. The following figure depicts this scenario.

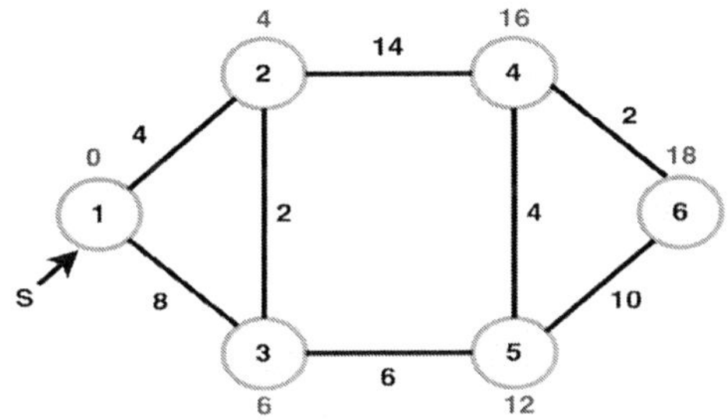

The algorithm returns the shortest path distances from source node 1 to all other nodes, as shown in the following table:

Vertex	2	3	4	5	6
Distance	4	6	16	12	18

4.7.3 Complexity Analysis

There exists two nested loops (an outer *while* loop and an inner *for* loop) in the algorithm that determine its complexity. If Queue is implemented with a normal queue data structure, the total time complexity of the strategy becomes $O(V^2)$. However, this complexity can be improved to O(E log V), if we use a binary heap to construct Queue.

4.8 NETWORK FLOW

A flow network (also referred to as transport network) is defined as a directed graph G = (V,E) with two marked nodes/vertices s (source) and t (sink) and a function c(u,v) which defines edge's capacities. The number of nodes/vertices are $n = |V|$ while the number of edges are $m = |E|$. Flow networks are often used for modeling material flow. We aim to determine a numerical flow value f(u,v) corresponding to each edge (u,v) (while not violating edge capacity, c(u,v)), such that incoming flow is equal to outgoing flow at all vertices except s and t.

Real-life scenarios concerning flow networks may include problems like modeling the maximum rate of liquid flow from s to t through a network of pipes, flow of current through wires and delivery of goods through a network of roads.

Flow networks satisfy the following properties:

Capacity constraints	$\forall(u,v) \in E: f(u,v) \leqslant c(u,v)$	The flow corresponding to any edge should not be beyond its capacity.
Skew symmetry	$\forall(u,v) \in E: f(u,v) = -f(v,u)$	The net flow f(u,v) from u to v is equal to the opposite net flow f(v,u).
Flow conservation	$\forall u \in V: u \neq s$ and $u \neq t \Rightarrow$ $\sum_{w \in V} f(u,w) = 0$	The net flow on a node is NIL, barring s, the source that initiates flow, and t, the sink that "consumes" flow.
Value of flow	$\sum_{(s,u) \in E} f(s,u) = \sum_{(v,t) \in E} f(v,t)\}$	The total flow leaving s should be the same as the total flow arriving at t.

4.8.1 Maximum Flow Problem

Here, we endeavour to maximize the flow value from s to t. The Ford–Fulkerson Algorithm (FFA) published in 1956, is a very well known greedy technique for determining the maximum flow in a flow network.

The FFA strategy is founded on the following simple idea: While there exists a path p from s to t, such that all edges in p have residual capacity, we push the maximum flow along p. Such paths *p* having available residual capacities, are referred to as *augmenting paths*. In order to easily find augmenting paths, it is helpful to define a *residual graph*. A residual graph $G_f(V, E_f)$ is one where an edge (u,v) has a capacity $c_f(u,v) = c(u,v) - f(u,v)$ (called *residual capacity*), and zero flow.

It may be noted that given a directed edge (u,v), a backward flow v→u is allowed in the residual graph (even though such a flow is not permitted in the initial network), if: $f(u,v) > 0$ and $c(v,u) = 0$. Hence in this case: $c_f(u,v) = 0 - f(v,u) = -(-f(u,v)) = f(u,v) > 0$. In other words, given a residual graph, augmenting paths can be formed through a sequence of edges where each edge (u,v) can either be a non-full forward edge, or a fully filled backward edge.

If an augmenting path from *s* to *t* can be found in the residual graph, then it is possible to add flow in the original network. The maximal flow which may be driven through an augmenting path p is determined by $c_f(p)$, its residual capacity. $c_f(p)$ is represented as: $c_f(p) = \min\{c_f(u,v) : (u,v) \in p\}$.

We now present the pseudo-code for a basic version of the Ford–Fulkerson algorithm (FFA).

4.8.2 Pseudocode

```
Procedure FFA()
    // Initialize maximum total flow in G
    max_flow = 0
    While an augmenting path p exists in G
      max_flow = max_flow + cf(p)
      Update residual graph Gf(V,Ef)
    End While
    Return max_flow
End Procedure
```

In line no. 4 of the above algorithm, an augmenting path can be obtained in many ways, for example through a BFS/DFS search in the residual graph $\mathbf{G_f(V, E_f)}$.

4.8.3 Example

Determine the maximum flow through the flow network, shown as the figure below.

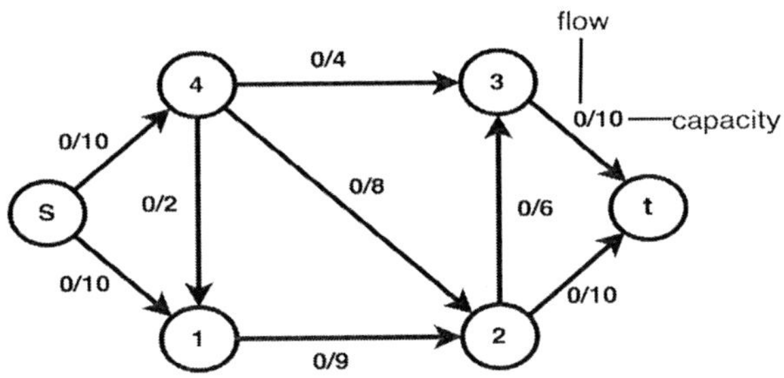

Step 1: max_flow = 0; Let us choose 'p = s -> 4->2->t' as the augmenting path.
$c_f(p)$ = min(10, 8, 10) = 8; max_flow = 0 + 8 = 8 (refer the following figure).

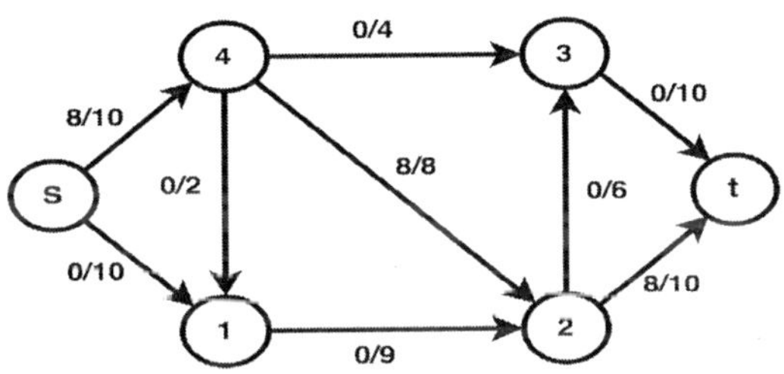

Step 2. Next residual graph: $G_f(V,E_f)$ (refer the following figure).

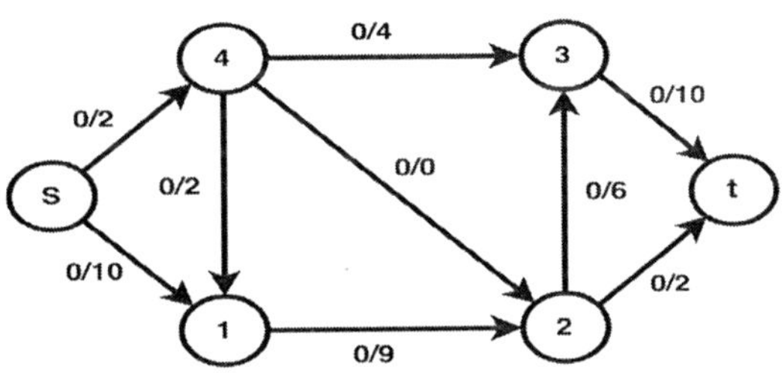

Let the next augmenting path be 'p = s->1->2->t'.
$c_f(p)$ = min(10, 9, 2) = 2; max_flow = 8 + 2 = 10 (refer the following figure).

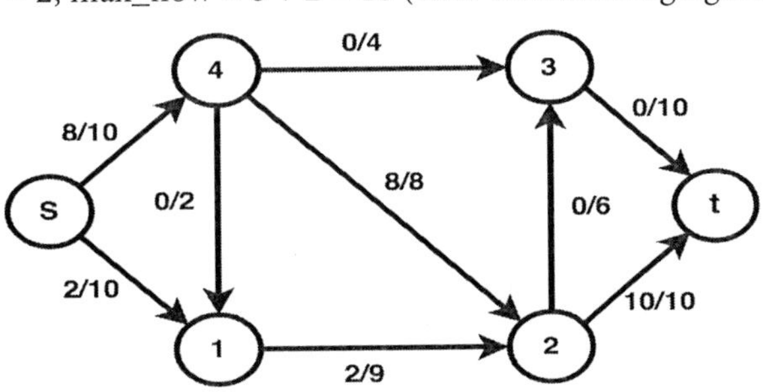

Step 3. Next residual graph (refer the following figure).

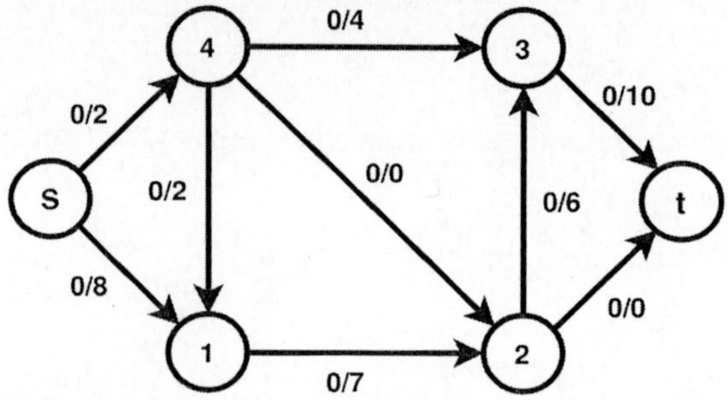

Let the next augmenting path be 'p = s->1->2->4->3->t'

This path contains a backedge from 2 to 4; f(2, 4) = –8 (refer to the figure shown in step 2); $c_f(2, 4) = 8$.

$c_f(p) = \min(8, 7, 8, 4, 10) = 4$; max_flow = 10 + 4 = 14 (refer the following figure).

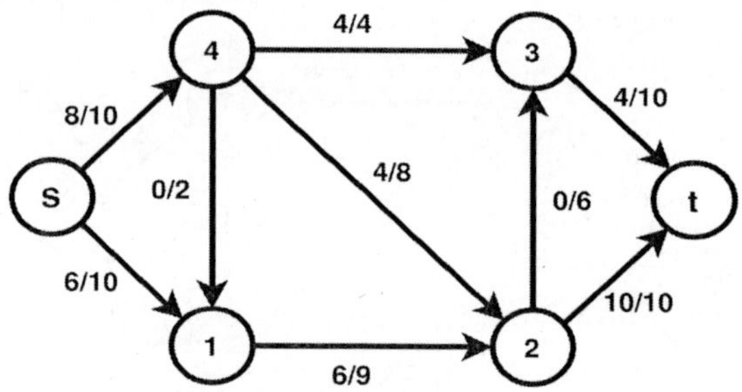

Step 4. Next residual graph (refer the following figure).

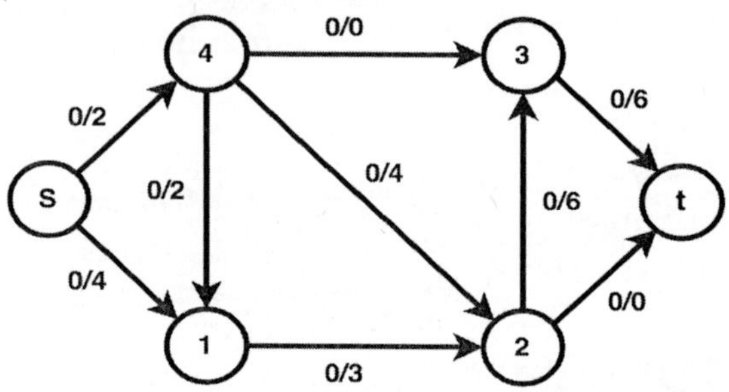

Let the next augmenting path be 'p = s->4->2->3->t'

$c_f(p) = \min(2, 4, 6, 6) = 2$; max_flow = 14 + 2 = 16 (refer the following figure).

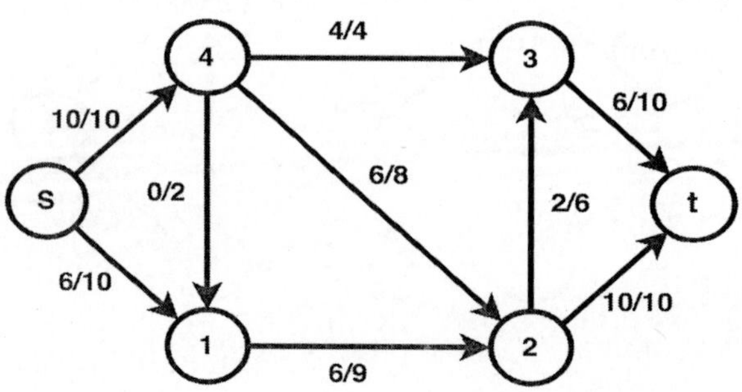

Step 5. Next residual graph (refer the following figure).

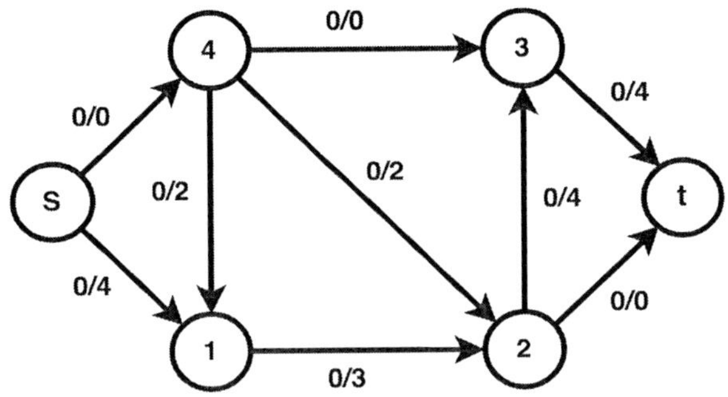

Let the next augmenting path be 'p = s->1->2->3->t'

$c_f(p) = \min(4, 3, 4, 4) = 3$; max_flow = 16 + 3 = 19 (refer the following figure).

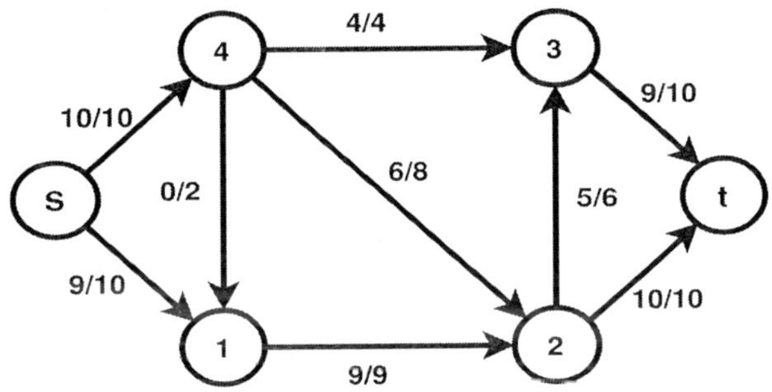

No more augmenting paths are possible. Hence, maximum flow through the given flow network is 19.

4.8.4 Complexity Analysis

The loop over lines 4 to 7 in FFA is executed till an augmenting path can be found in the residual graph. The overhead for determining an augmenting path is O(m), where *m* represents the total count of edges. In each iteration of the loop, one unit of flow can be added in the worst case. Therefore, the overall overhead of FFA becomes: O(m * max_flow).

4.8.5 Max-flow Min-cut Theorem

The maximum flow through a flow network is same as the least capacity over all s-t cuts.

Here, a *cut* refers to a set of edges removal of which disconnects the graph. An *s-t cut* is one which divides the vertex set into two partitions X and Y, in such a fashion that the source node $s \in X$ while the sink node $t \in Y$ ($V = X \cup Y$). The capacity of an s-t cut is obtained as the aggregate capacity of all edges involved in the cut.

UNIT SUMMARY

Graphs, both directed and undirected, often form a very convenient mechanism for modelling relationships among data objects. Hence, graphs have found wide usage in diverse applications including, process scheduling, path or route planning, and resource optimization, in various disciplines. This chapter starts with a discussion on important terminologies related to graphs. Then, we proceed with presentations on spanning trees, finding minimum spanning trees, directed acyclic graphs and topological sorting on them, finding shortest paths and determination of maximal flows. All the algorithms have been discussed with running illustrative examples with brief overviews on their computational complexities.

EXERCISES

Multiple Choice Questions

1. Topological sorting can be used to sort which of the following graphs?
   (a) Directed Cyclic Graphs
   (b) Undirected Cyclic Graphs
   (c) Directed Acyclic Graphs
   (d) Undirected Acyclic Graphs
2. Choose the correct topological ordering of the graph given below.

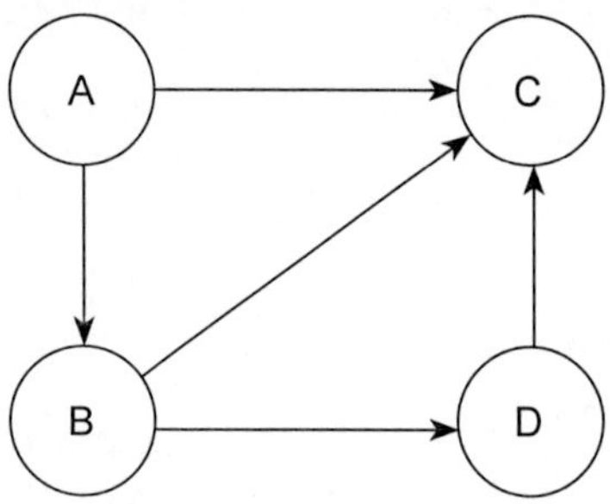

   (a) ABDC
   (b) ADCB
   (c) ABCD
   (d) DABC
3. Topological sorting has a time complexity of __.
   (a) V*E
   (b) V+E
   (c) V
   (d) E^2
4. The algorithm that is not used to find the MST of a graph is
   (a) Prim's
   (b) Kruskal's
   (c) Bellman–Ford
   (d) All of the above
5. Identify the correct statement for Prim's algorithm?
   (a) It is an approximation algorithm
   (b) It is a greedy approach
   (c) It follows dynamic programming scheme
   (d) It is based on divide and conquer approach
6. Kruskal's algorithm has a time complexity of __.
   (a) ElogV
   (b) E logE
   (c) V logV
   (d) All of the above
7. Dijkstra's algorithm has a time complexity of __.
   (a) V^3
   (b) |V|!
   (c) V*E
   (d) E logV

8. Time complexity of Ford-Fulkerson algorithm is __
   (a) E (b) E * max_flow
   (c) V*E (d) E logV

Answers for Multiple Choice Questions

1. (c), 2. (a) 3. (b), 4. (c), 5. (b), 6. (d), 7. (d), 8. (b)

Short and Long Answer Type Questions

1. Explain the terms "in-degree" and "out-degree" for a node with an example.
2. Explain the stepwise procedure of topological sorting with an example.
3. Explain the stepwise procedure of Kruskal's algorithm with an example.
4. Find the minimum spanning tree using Prim's algorithm for the graph given below. Consider node A as the starting point.

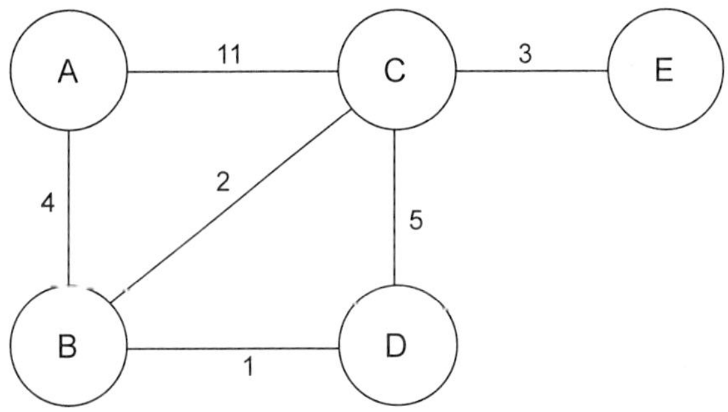

Hint:

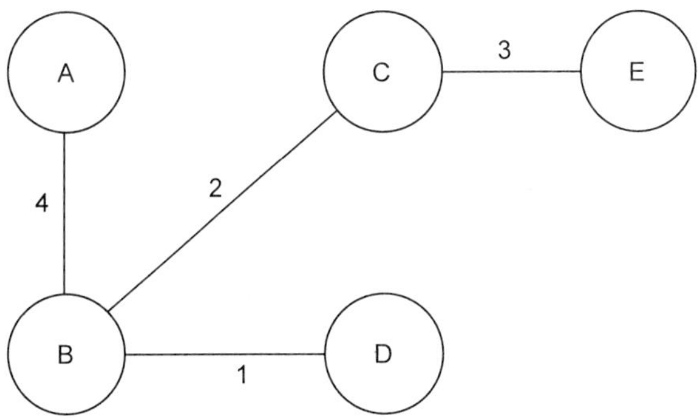

Cost of MST = 4 + 1 + 2 + 3 = 10

5. What do you mean by shortest path in an unweighted graph? Explain the concept with an example.
6. Explain the stepwise procedure of Dijkstra's algorithm with an example of your choice.
7. What is a flow network? Describe various properties of a flow network.
8. Illustrate the steps of Ford–Fulkerson algorithm with the help of an example.

KNOW MORE

This section talks about a set of additional information that helps the reader to improve the knowledge on the topics discussed in Unit-4.

Representation of Graphs in a Computer System

A method of storing a graph in a computer's memory is called a graph representation. Depending on the number of edges a graph has, the kind of operations that need to be done, and the simplicity of usage, there are various ways to optimally represent a graph.

Adjacency Matrix and Adjacency List are the two popular ways to represent graphs in computer memory.

1. **Adjacency Matrix**

   There exists adjacency matrix representations for directed, undirected, and weighted graphs. A two-dimensional array with size |V| x |V|, where |V| denotes the total number of nodes in the graph, is known as an *adjacency matrix*. Let us assume this 2D array is AM[][]. An edge joining node *a* and node *b* is indicated by a slot AM[a][b] = 1. The adjacency matrix for undirected graphs is always symmetric about the diagonal. In weighted graphs, if there is an edge with weight w from node *a* to node *b* then AM[a][b] = w. The following figure (refer Fig.4.6) depicts the adjacency matrix of an undirected graph. This representation's key benefit is that it is easy to use and implement. However, it is less efficient in terms of space and time.

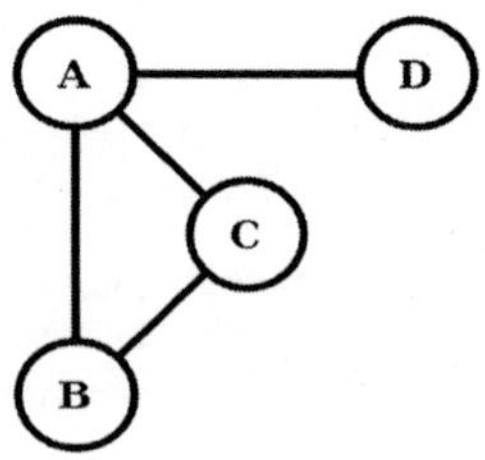

	A	B	C	D
A	0	1	1	1
B	1	0	1	0
C	1	1	0	0
D	1	0	0	0

Fig. 4.6: An undirected graph G and its corresponding adjacency matrix

2. **Adjacency List**

   In this approach, a graph is represented as an array of linked lists. The array's index indicates a node, and each item in its linked list represents the other nodes with whom it forms an edge. A weighted graph can also be represented using this method. Lists of pairs can be used to indicate the weights of edges. The following figure (refer Fig.4.7) depicts the adjacency list of an undirected graph. This method is efficient in terms of space and time.

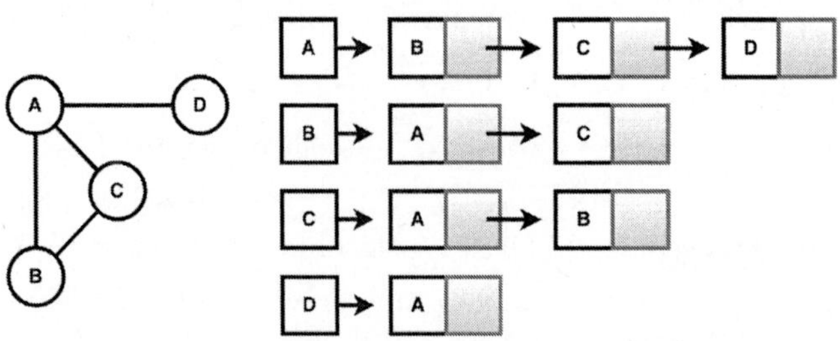

Fig. 4.7: An undirected graph G and its adjacency list

REFERENCES AND SUGGESTED READINGS

Syllabus Referred Textbooks

1. All textbooks prescribed in the syllabus.

Other Textbook References

1. Data Structures and Algorithms Made Easy, Second Edition, Narasimha Karumanchi, CareerMonk Publications, (2011)
2. Data Structure Through C, Yashavant P. Kanetkar, BPB Publications, (2003)
3. Algorithms: Design and Analysis, Harsh Bhasin, Oxford University Press, (2015)

Dynamic QR Code for Further Reading

Scan Me

5 Strings

UNIT SPECIFICS

Through this unit we have discussed the following aspects:

- Simple string sorting algorithm along with analysis on its efficiency;
- Characteristics of Trie data structure and its basic operations;
- A simple algorithm for finding substrings and an evaluation of its effectiveness;
- Concept of regular expression and its importance in string matching problems;
- Elementary data compression techniques.

RATIONALE

The most common way to describe strings is as arrays of bytes (or words) that include a series of characters. Strings are commonly considered as a data type in many programming languages. Various data structures, including ternary search trees, suffix trees, tries, suffix arrays, and many others, can be built on the foundation of a string. Strings give us immensely useful string algorithms that allow us to solve very complex problems quickly. Strings and string matching algorithms are widely used in a variety of applications such as search engines, data encoding, plagiarism checkers, DNA sequencing, spam filters, and so on.

We start this unit with a description of how to organise a string of characters in lexical or dictionary order. Subsequently, we discuss the Trie data structure, a unique tree-based data structure designed specifically for storing and searching strings. The unit also discusses the fundamentals of regular expressions, which serve as the foundation for many string matching techniques. Lastly, we talk about data compression, a crucial practical application of strings.

PRE-REQUISITES

Rudimentary knowledge of computer programming and data structure.

UNIT OUTCOMES

List of outcomes of this unit is as follows:

U5-O1: Describe the basic algorithm to sort a given string

U5-O2: Describe Trie data structure and its basic operations

U5-O3: Explain different data compression techniques through running examples

U5-O4: Realize the role of regular expressions in string matching problems.

U5-O5: Apply strings for solving various problems in science and engineering

Unit-5 Outcome	EXPECTED MAPPING WITH COURSE OUTCOMES (1 - Weak Correlation; 2 - Medium Correlation; 3 - Strong Correlation)				
	CO-1	CO-2	CO-3	CO-4	CO-5
U5-O1	3	3	2	2	1
U5-O2	3	3	2	2	1
U5-O3	3	3	3	3	1
U5-O4	3	3	3	3	1
U5-O5	3	3	3	3	1

5.1 STRING SORT

In Unit-2, we have discussed different sorting techniques. As a complementary, this section discusses how to perform sorting operations on 'string.' String sorting is the process of arranging characters in a string in ascending or descending order. For example, if the given string is 'gamer', then the resulting string after sorting in ascending order is 'aegmr.'

5.1.1 Pseudocode

```
Procedure String_Sort()
        Input gamer, the given string
        Initialize char strA[] = gamer
        Determine n, length of the given string
        For each i from 0 to n-1
                For each j from 0 to n-i-1
                        If(strA[j] > strA[j+1])
                                swap(strA[j], strA[j+1])
                        End If
                End For
        End For
End Procedure
```

Note: In the case of a string or character array, we use the index starting from 0.

5.1.2 Example

Consider an input string `gamer.' Now, we perform the string sorting operation on this input string.
Iteration 1: i = 0 and j takes values 0, 1, 2, 3

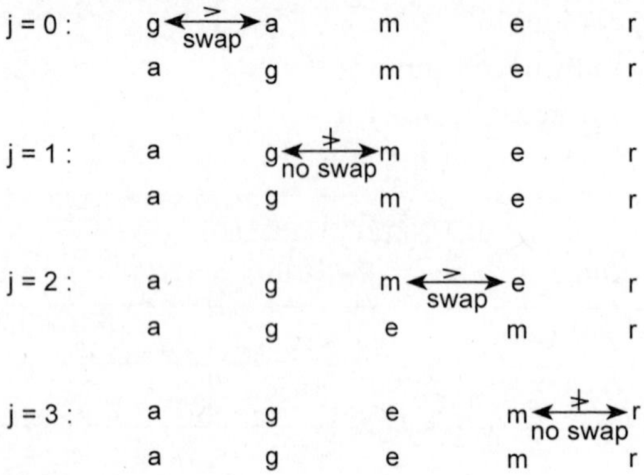

Iteration 2: i = 1 and j takes values 0, 1, 2

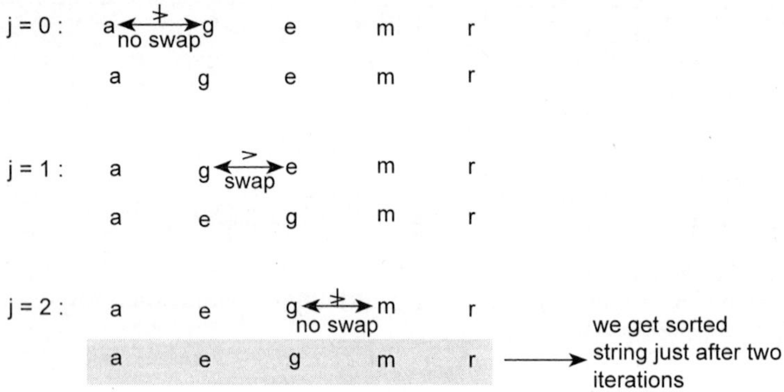

The final resulting sorted string is '*aegmr*.'

5.1.3 Complexity Analysis

The procedure String_Sort() has two *for* loops, and each loop takes at most *n* iterations. Therefore, the total time complexity of the above procedure is $O(n^2)$.

5.2 TRIES

A *Trie* is a particular kind of k-ary search tree used to store and look up a certain key from a set. It is an advanced tree-based data structure for storing and searching strings. The term "trie" is derived from the word "retrieval," that means to locate or obtain. It is also known as a *prefix tree* or *digital tree*. When it comes to storing and retrieving data, trie data structures are quicker than hash tables and binary search trees. We can efficiently perform search operations on a trie and store a huge number of strings in it. A trie can be used to determine whether a string with a specific prefix is present or not and to alphabetically sort a collection of strings. The major applications of Trie are spell checker, autocomplete features of search engines, and browser history etc. It is also useful for implementing dictionaries.

5.2.1 Properties of a Trie

As discussed above, a trie has a tree-like structure. Each Trie has a single root node that represents an empty string. A Trie's nodes denote strings and its edges represent characters. Each node is made up of an array of pointers, where each index corresponds to a character, and a flag that denotes whether any strings finish at the current node. Alphabets, integers, and special characters are all permitted in Trie data structures. However, in this unit, we will focus on strings with the English alphabet. Therefore, each node only requires 26 pointers with the 0th index representing the character "a" and the 25th index representing the character "z." Every path leading from the root to any particular node represents a string or word.

In a trie, strings are organised from top to bottom based on their prefix. The root node, which is at level 0, indicates a prefix of length 0. All prefixes with lengths of 1 are kept at level 1, those with lengths of 2 are stored at level 2, and so on.

5.2.2 Representation of a Trie Node

Each Trie node is made up of an array of character pointers (*struct Trie_Node *child[]*) where each index corresponds to a character and a flag (*bool stringEnd*) that indicates whether or not the string ends at that node. The node of a Trie is defined as follows:

```
struct Trie_Node
{
      struct Trie_Node *child[ALPHABET_SIZE];
      bool stringEnd;
};
```

Here, the boolean field *stringEnd* becomes *true* if the node represents the end of a string or a word, that is, when the node becomes a leaf node. For all intermediate nodes of a trie, the value of *stringEnd* is always *false*.

5.2.3 Example of a Trie

Consider a collection of strings {arc, art, ash, ask, mad, my}. A trie data structure used to store this set of strings is depicted in Fig. 5.1. Here, we can observe that the strings are stored lexicographically from left to right.

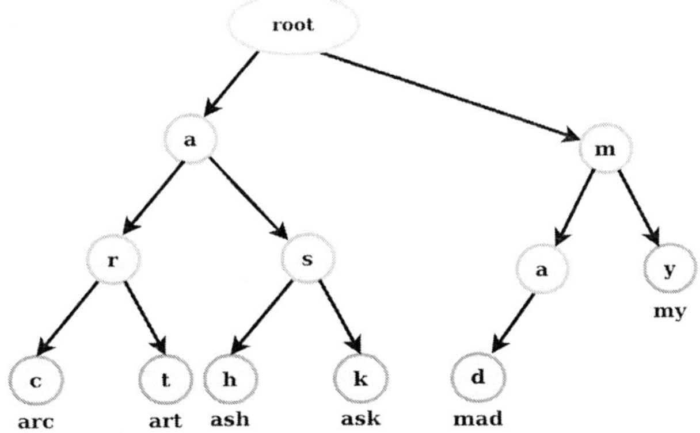

Fig. 5.1: A Trie Data Structure

5.2.4 Basic Operations in a Trie

This section discusses ideas behind the basic operations like insertion, searching and deletion of a node in a Trie.

5.2.4.1 *Insertion in a Trie*

Suppose we want to insert a string or a key into a Trie. The input string's characters are inserted as separate nodes in the Trie. If the string is new or an augmentation of an existing string, then we create new nodes for the string and mark the final (leaf) node as the end of the key. If the string is a prefix of an existing string in the Trie, then we plainly mark the final node of the string as the end of a key.

The following procedure Trie_Insert () may be used to insert a key or a string element 's', into a Trie rooted at 'root'. The algorithm first initializes the current node (cntNode) pointer with 'root' (line 3). Then it iterates over the length of the string (lines 5-12) to assign new nodes into the trie. The algorithm first checks a node in the Trie for the current character. If no such node exists, then it creates a new node and assigns the current node pointer to the newly created node. This process is repeated until all the characters of the input string are processed. After inserting the last character of the string, the algorithm assigns 'True' value to the field *stringEnd* of the last node, which indicates it as the leaf node.

5.2.4.1.1 Pseudocode

```
L1:   Procedure Trie_Insert(*root, s)
L2:         Input struct Trie_Node *root, string s
L3:         Initialize struct Trie_Node *cntNode = root
L4:         Determine n, length of the string s
L5:         For each i from 0 to n-1
L6:               int index = s[i]-'a'
L7:               If (cntNode.child[index] == NULL)
L8:                     Create a new node named newNode
L9:                     cntNode.child[index] = newNode
L10:        End If
L11:              cntNode = cntNode.child[index]
L12:     End For
L13:     cntNode.stringEnd = True
L14:  End Procedure
```

5.2.4.1.2 Example

Consider a collection of strings {arc, art}. The steps to insert the strings 'arc' and 'art' into a Trie are depicted in Fig. 5.2. Here, the strings are inserted into a Trie in lexicographical order from left to right.

5.2.4.2 *Searching in a Trie*

In a Trie, a string or key is stored by a path starting at the root node and maybe continuing all the way to the leaf node or to some other intermediate node. The following procedure *Trie_Search()* may be used to search a key or a string element 's', in a Trie rooted at 'root', and this procedure is similar to that of insertion. To search a string in a trie, we first start at the root node and move down to the next character if we find a reference match. The lack of a key in the Trie or the end of a string can cause this search to stop. If the key is missing from the Trie (line 7), the search stops without looking at all of the essential characters (line 8). The key is present in the Trie (line 12), if the value of the last node's *stringEnd* field is true.

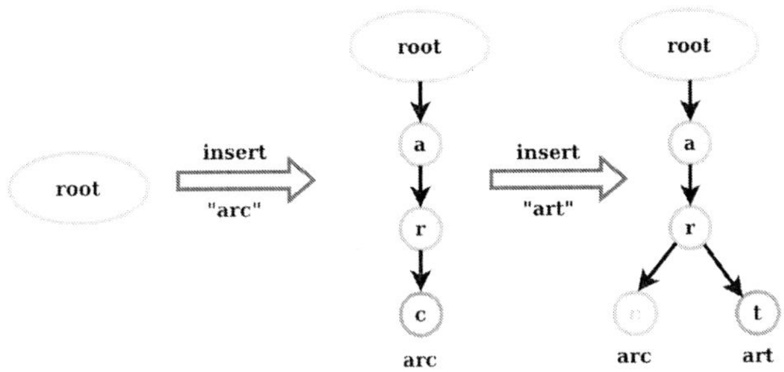

Fig. 5.2: Inserting 'arc' & 'art' into a Trie

5.2.4.2.1 Pseudocode

```
L1:  Procedure Trie_Search(*root, s)
L2:       Input struct Trie_Node *root, string s
L3:       Initialize struct Trie_Node *cntNode = root
L4:       Determine n, length of the string s
L5:       For each i from 0 to n-1
L6:            int index = s[i]-'a'
L7:            If (cntNode.child[index] == NULL)
L8:                 return false
L9:         End If
L10:        cntNode = cntNode.child[index]
L11:    End For
L12:    return (cntNode.stringEnd)
L13: End Procedure
```

5.2.4.2.2 Example

Consider the following Trie shown in Fig. 5.3. The key that needs to be searched is "mad". The steps to search the string "mad" in the given Trie are highlighted in Fig. 5.3.

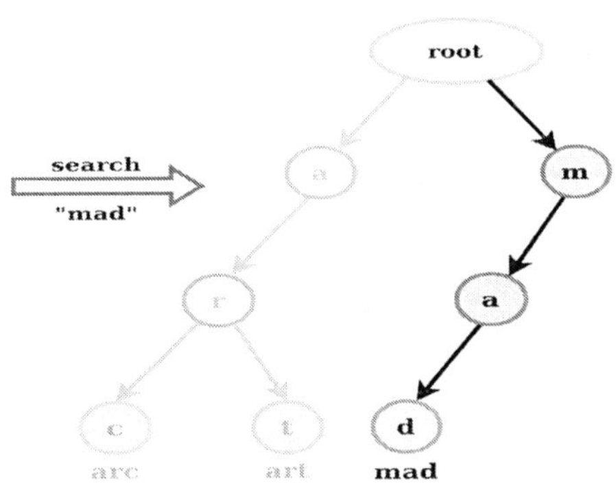

Fig. 5.3: Searching the key "mad" in a Trie

5.2.4.3 Deletion from a Trie

In the deletion operation, the given string or key is deleted from the Trie in a bottom up fashion through a recursive procedure. When we perform such deletion, the following situations may occur:

(a) The string to be removed serves as a prefix for other words.

(b) The string to be removed shares a prefix in common with any other words

(c) The string to be removed does not share a prefix in common with any other words

The following procedure Trie_Delete() may be used to delete a key or a string element 's', from a Trie. Here, the initial value of *d* is set to 0.

5.2.4.3.1 Pseudocode

```
Procedure Trie_Delete(*root, s, d)
        Input struct Trie_Node *root,string s,int d
        Determine n, length of the string s
        If (root == NULL) // if Trie is an empty tree
            return NULL
        End If
        If (d == n) // if last character is being
                                                processed
            If (root.stringEnd)
                root.stringEnd = false
          End If
          If (root is empty)
              root =  NULL
          End If
          return root
      End If
      int index = s[d]-'a'
      root.child[index]=Trie_Delete(root.child[index], s, d+1)
      If (root is empty && root.stringEnd == false)
          root =  NULL
      End If
      return root
End Procedure
```

5.2.4.3.2 Example

Consider the following Trie shown in Fig. 5.4. Assume the key to be deleted is "arc". Here, both the strings "arc" and "art" share a common prefix "ar". Therefore, we delete all the nodes starting from the end of the prefix to the last character of the given string to be deleted. Hence, we delete the node *c*. The red color highlighting in Fig. 5.4 indicates this deletion operation.

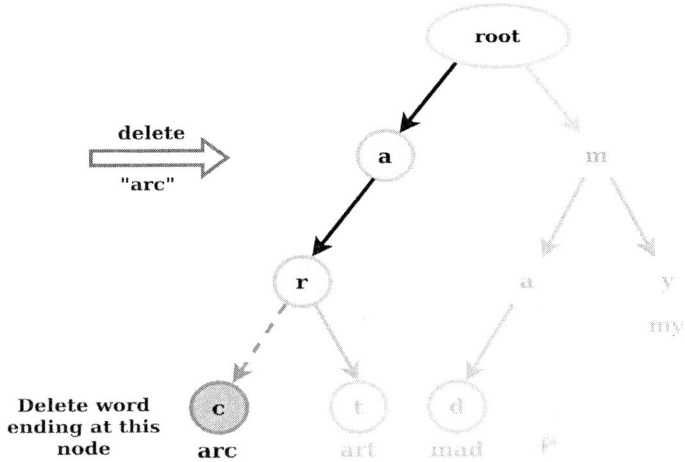

Fig. 5.4: Deleting the string "arc" from the Trie

5.2.4.4 Complexity Analysis

A string of length ***n*** can be added, deleted, and searched in the Trie data structure with a time complexity of O(n) each. If we want to create a Trie by inserting N strings into it, then the total time complexity to build a Trie is O(N * AVG_L), where N is the number of strings and AVG_L is the average length of N strings.

5.3 SUBSTRING SEARCH

A substring is a set of characters that form a continuous sequence within a string. For example, consider the string "alphabet". Some of the substrings for this given string are al, bet, hab, alpha, phabet etc. However, aph, aet, alha, albet etc., are not a substring of the given string since they do not form a continuous sequence. The following procedure *Substring_Search()* may be used to search a substring st1 within a string st2. If st1 is present within st2, then the below procedure returns the index of the first occurrence of st1. Here, we assume that the indexing of a string starts with zero.

5.3.1 Pseudocode

```
Procedure Substring_Search(st1, st2)
      Input String st1, st2
      Determine m, length of the string st1
      Determine n, length of the string st2
      For each i from 0 to n-m
            For each j from 0 to m-1
                  If (st2[i+j] != st1[j])
                        break
              End If
         End For
```

```
            If (j == m)
                return i
            End If
        End For
        return -1
    End Procedure
```

5.3.2 Example

Consider two strings: st1 = "go" and st2 = "mango." The expected output of the above procedure for these two strings is: Substring "go" is present at 3rd position of String "mango".

5.3.3 Complexity Analysis

The procedure *Substring_Search()* has two *for* loops. The outer *for* loop runs from *0* to *n – m*, and inner *for* loop runs from *0* to *m – 1*. Therefore, the total time complexity of the above procedure is O(m * n), where *m* and *n* are the lengths of strings *st1* and *st2*, respectively.

5.4 REGULAR EXPRESSIONS

In a real-world scenario, we might have created multiple files using a text editor and stored them in a computer. There may be a situation in which we may be searching for a file that contains a particular word or a sentence. So, we need a mechanism to describe the pattern to be searched. For this purpose, regular expressions are used by programmers for multiple decades.

In this section, we use the term "language" to specify a set of all possible strings. Similarly, the term "pattern" refers to a language specification. First, we discuss the basic operations associated with the regular expressions. For this purpose, let us consider three characters A, B, and C.

- **Concatenation**: The language {ABC} is obtained by concatenating A, B, and C.
- **Or**: To specify the alternative options in the pattern, Or operation is used. To denote this Or operation, we use the symbol |. For example, B | C specifies the language {B, C}. Similarly, A | B | C specifies the language {A, B, C}. Note that the concatenation operation takes precedence over Or operation. For example, AB | BC corresponds to the language {AB, BC}.
- **Closure**: To allow the arbitrary number of repetitions (including zero) of a pattern, closure operation is used. This operation is represented by the symbol *. Further, closure has a higher priority than concatenation. For example, BC* corresponds to the language consisting of strings of the form B followed by 0 or more Cs: {B, BC, BCC, BCCC, …}. Similarly, B*C corresponds to the language {C, BC, BBC, BBBC, …}.
- **Parentheses**: To override the default priority rules, parentheses can be used and it is represented by (). For example, A (BC | B) A corresponds to the language {ABCA, ABA}. Similarly, (AB)* represents {**ε**, AB, ABAB, ABABAB, …}. Here, the symbol "**ε**" represents the empty string.

Note-1: If M1 and M2 are regular expressions, then their concatenation M1M2 is also a regular expression. Similarly, M1|M2, M1*, M2* are also regular expressions.

Note-2: NULL represents an empty set ({ }). On the other hand, "**ε**" is an empty string and contains one element ({**ε**}). Therefore, "**ε**" is not NULL.

Examples of regular expression:

1. Regular expression (W | X) (Y | Z). This expression matches strings from the following language {WY, WZ, XY, XZ}. It does not match any other strings.
2. Regular expression X (Y | Z)* = {X, XY, XZ, XYYZZYZ, …}

Definition: A *regular expression* is either

- empty
- a single character
- enclosed in parentheses
- followed by the closure operator (*)
- two or more concatenated regular expressions
- two or more regular expressions separated by the **Or** operator (|)

The above definition captures the syntax of a regular expression and guidelines related to a legal regular expression.

Shortcuts: In order to form compact expressions, there are a set of shortcuts used. Now, we will discuss such shortcuts.

Name	Notation	Description	Example
wildcard	.	Any single character	X.Y (. can be replaced by any character)
specific set	enclosed in [ ]	Any character from a specific set	[WXYZ] (Any character from W X Y Z)
range	enclosed in [ ] separated by -	Any character from the specific range	[A - Z] (Any character from the range A to Z)
complement	enclosed in [ ] preceded by ^	Excluding any character from this set	[^ABCD] (Excluding A B C D)

As discussed earlier, closure operator (*) specifies any number of occurrences of operands enclosed within it. In real-world situations, we want to specify the number of occurrences of operands. Such a flexibility is provided by following symbols: the plus sign (+) represents at least one copy of the operand enclosed within *. Similarly, the question mark (?) specifies zero or one copy, and a range within braces ({}) specifies a given number of copies.

option	notation	example	shortcut for	in language	not in language
0 or one time	?	(XY)?	ε | XY	{ε, AB}	any other string
at least one time	+	(XY)+	(XY)(XY)*	{XY, XYXY, …}	ε, YYXXYX
specific count	count in {}	(XY){2}	(XY)(XY)	{XYXY}	any other string
range	range in {}	(XY){1-2}	(XY) | (XY)(XY)	{XY, XYXY}	any other string

Apart from the shortcuts discussed above, there are metacharacters (such as \, |, *, .,) that are used to form regular expressions. To separate metacharacters from the characters in the alphabet, escape sequences that begin with a backslash character \ can be used. For example, \\ represents \. Here, the first backslash denotes the escape sequence and the next backslash represents the actual character. Now, let us discuss the applications of regular expressions in terms of validity checking.

Validation of an email address: Usually, a valid email address starts with a prefix (username), followed by @ symbol and ends with a domain name (email.com). To validate such a pattern, let us formulate a regular expression. The username contains one or more characters from "a to z". This can be represented by [a-z]+. Similarly, the domain name can be represented by [a-z]+\.com. So, the final regular expression to validate an email address of the form username@email.com is as follows: [a-z]+@[a-z]+\.com. Suppose an email address contains multiple domains. That is, username@subdomain.domain.com or username@subdomain.domain.in. Then, the regular expression will be of the form: [a-z]+@([a-z]+\.)+(in|com). Further, the username may contain one or more occurrences of ".". To capture such a scenario, the regular expression can be updated as follows: ([a-z]+\.)+@([a-z]+\.)+(in|com).

Validation of a mobile number: Typically, a mobile number starts with a country code (+91 for India) followed by a whitespace and a digit number. This can be represented using the following regular expression: \+[0-9]{2}\ [0-9]{10}. Here, \+[0-9]{2} represents a country code, and [0-9]{10} represents a digit number.

context	regular expressions	matches
email address	[a-z]+@([a-z]+\.)+(in|com)	aicte@iit.ac.in
mobile number	\+[0-9]{2}\ [0-9]{10}	+91 9123456780
substring search	.*FIRST.*	THIS IS OUR FIRST MATCH

From the above examples, it can be seen that the regular expression is a powerful tool that provides concise and precise expression of the set of all valid strings.

5.5 ELEMENTARY DATA COMPRESSION

Data storage, management, and transfer are becoming increasingly important in many data-driven and data communication systems. The data must frequently be compressed, that is, shrunk down to a smaller size while maintaining all or most of the original information, in order to use the computing and storage resources like ROM, RAM, GPU etc, effectively. The data used for compression can be in the form of text, numbers, photos, audio, video, or even software and computer programmes. Redundant data, or duplication of information that is not necessary, is eliminated during a compression process. Thus, data compression can increase file transfers' speed, utilise less network bandwidth, and save up storage space.

A compression program employs an algorithm or a formula to determine how to minimize the amount of data. A formula may contain a pointer or reference to a string of 0s and 1s that the programme has already seen, or it may replace a larger string of 0s and 1s in a string of bits or 0s and 1s with a smaller string by converting between the two using a dictionary. The text can be compressed by eliminating any unnecessary characters, replacing frequently occurring bit strings with smaller ones, and inserting a single repetition character to represent a string of repeated letters.

When it comes to data transmission, compression can be applied to the entire transmission unit, including header data, or just the data content. While sending or receiving data over the internet, larger files may be conveyed in a ZIP, GZIP, or other compressed format. These formats can be used to send or receive larger files, either separately or in conjunction with other files as part of an archive file.

5.5.1 Basic Data Compression Model

The basic model for data compression comprises two primary components: a *compress* box that transforms a bitstream S into a compressed version C(S), and an *expand* box that transforms C(S) back into S. Here, the main objective is to minimize the *compression ratio*, which is given as |C(S)| / |S|, where |S| is the number of bits in a given bitstream. Fig. 5.5 depicts the basic model for data compression.

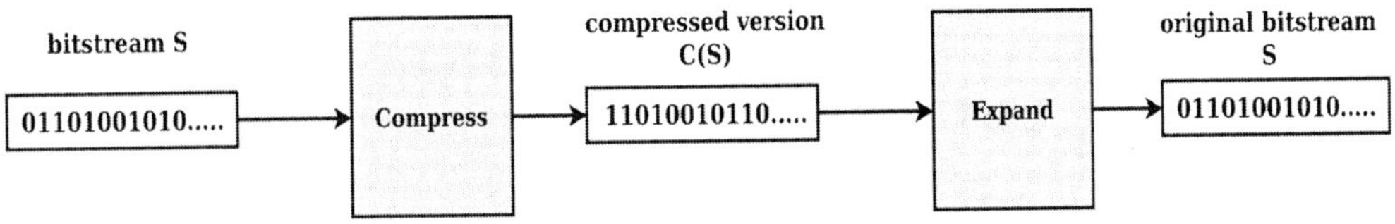

Fig. 5.5: Basic Data Compression Model

5.5.2 Data Compression Methods

Lossless and *lossy* are the two basic categories of data compression techniques. Lossy compression shrinks data by removing unnecessary parts, while lossless compression modifies data by encoding it with a formula or logic. Now, we discuss each of these techniques in detail.

5.5.2.1 Lossless Data Compression

A file can be recovered to its original form after being compressed using lossless compression since no data is lost. Lossless compression is usually used when compressing executable, text, and spreadsheet files because removing any numbers or letters would modify the data. If the data is already compressed, further compression will have little to no effect on its size. Moreover, it is less effective for larger file sizes. Portable Network Graphics (PNG), a raster-graphics file format, allows lossless image data compression. The different algorithms used for lossless data compression (refer, Fig. 5.6) include: a) Run Length Encoding, b) Huffman Encoding, and c) LZW Encoding.

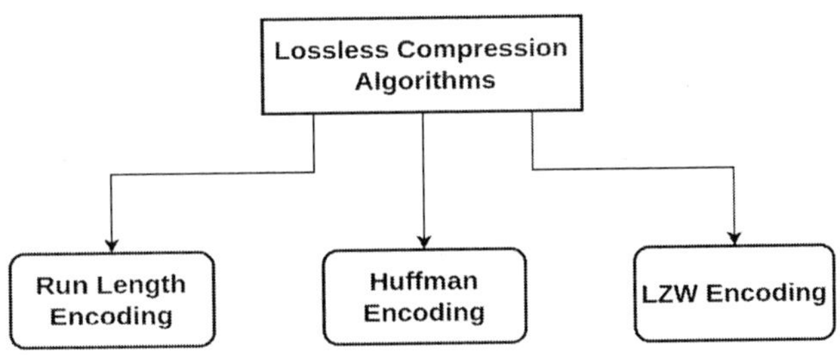

Fig. 5.6: Lossless Compression Techniques

5.5.2.1.1 Run Length Encoding

This encoding method finds recurring character sequences called "*runs*" by scanning through the contents of a file. Then the *run* is compressed into a few bytes, usually two. The first byte, also known as the "*run value*," represents the actual character in the *run*. The number of characters in the *run* is stored in the second byte, known as the "*run count*." Simple graphics and animations with lots of redundant pixels are best suited for this form of compression. This method can increase the file size rather than decrease it for complicated graphics and animations if there aren't many duplicate portions. The following are the steps to perform run length encoding.

1. Select the first character in the input (source) string.
2. Add the selected character to the output (destination) string.
3. Count the number of times the selected character appears consecutively and add its total sum to the output string.
4. Continue with steps 2, 3, and 4 until the string's final character is reached.

Example

Consider the input source string "aaabbcccc" that need to be compressed. Fig. 5.7 depicts the steps for run length encoding. Here, the source string is having "a" three times. So, we append "a" to the destination string followed by the count value "3" which is the number of occurrences of "a". Similarly, we repeat the steps for the characters "b" and "c". The final resulting destination string is a3b2c4.

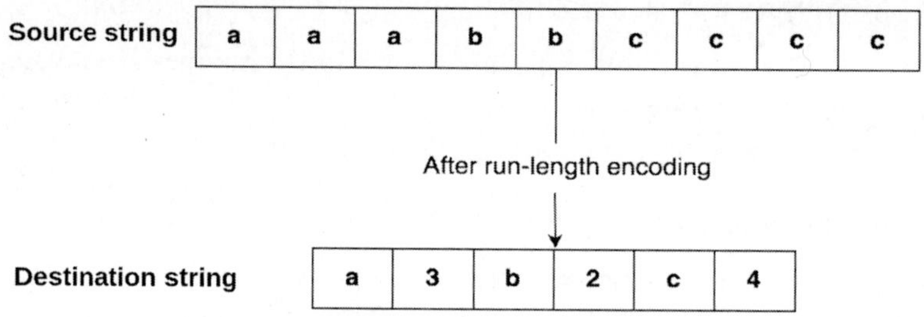

Fig. 5.7: Run Length Encoding

5.5.2.1.2 Huffman Encoding

Huffman encoding (or simply *Huffman coding*) is a lossless compression method. This encoding method assigns variable-length codes to input characters, and the lengths of such codes are decided based on the frequency of the matching characters. These variable-length codes are referred to as *prefix codes*. Here, the codes are assigned in a way that prevents the prefix of one code from becoming the code assigned to any other character. Using this strategy, Huffman coding makes sure that the produced bitstream cannot have any ambiguities in it when it is decoded. This technique is typically effective to compress data that contains frequently occurring characters.

Let us examine prefix codes using a counter example. Let A, B, C, and D be four characters, and their corresponding variable-length codes be 0, 1, 00, and 01. If we use these codes, the decompressed output for a compressed bit stream of 0001 might be "AAAB," "AAD," "ACB," or "CD," which causes ambiguity. This is because the code given to A is the prefix of the codes given to C and D.

In Huffman encoding, there are primarily two key processes to follow: a) Create a Huffman Tree using the input characters, and b) Allot codes to characters as you traverse the Huffman Tree. These two processes are described in detail through the following steps:

Step 1: Count the number of times (also called *frequency*) each character appears in the string.

Step 2: Arrange the characters in the ascending order of their frequency counts and store them in a priority queue, *Queue*.

Step 3: Create a leaf node for every distinct character.

Step 4: Construct an empty node N. The left child of N is assigned with the first minimum frequency, and the right child of N is assigned with the second minimum frequency. These two minimum frequencies should be added to determine the value of the node N.

Step 5: Add the resulting sum of these two minimum frequencies into Queue after removing them from it (the symbol + is used to represent the internal nodes in the illustrative figures).

Step 6: Now, insert node N into the Huffman tree.

Step 7: Follow steps 4 through 6 until a single tree is formed from all characters.

Step 8: Assign the left edge to 0 and the right edge to 1 in the generated Huffman tree.

Example

Let the input string that needs to be sent over the network be CBDDAAABBDBDBDB. With each character being represented by 8 bits, the total number of bits needed to transfer these 15 characters is 15 * 8 = 120 bits. Now, we apply the Huffman encoding scheme to reduce the size of the string to be transferred. The following steps are used to perform huffman encoding on the given input string:

Step 1: Arrange the characters in the ascending order of their frequency counts and store them in a priority queue, *Queue*. Create a leaf node for every distinct character, which is represented using a square.

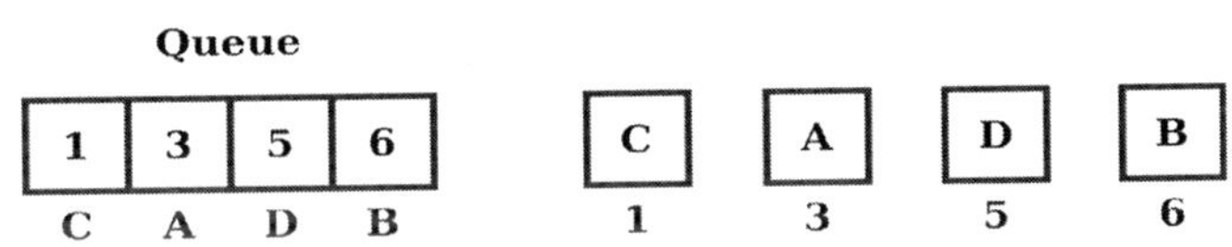

Step 2: Create an internal node (represented by a circle) with value 4 by adding the current two minimum frequencies (1 and 3) in Queue. Make leaf nodes C and A as the children of this internal node. Remove the entries 1 and 3 from Queue and insert their resulting sum 4 into Queue.

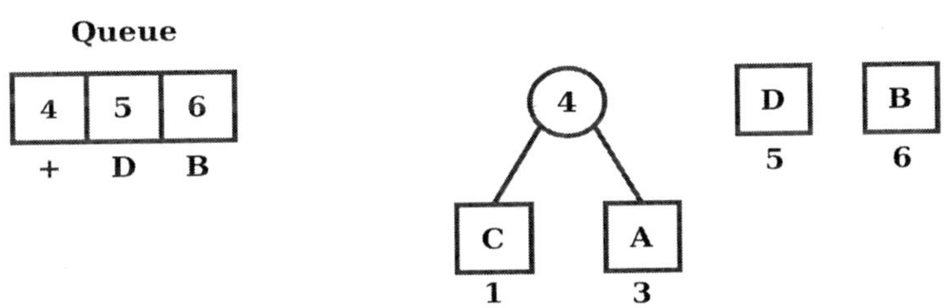

Step 3: Create a new internal node with value 9 by adding the current two minimum frequencies (4 and 5) in Queue. Make nodes 4 and D as the children of this internal node. Remove the entries 4 and 5 from Queue and insert their resulting sum 9 into Queue.

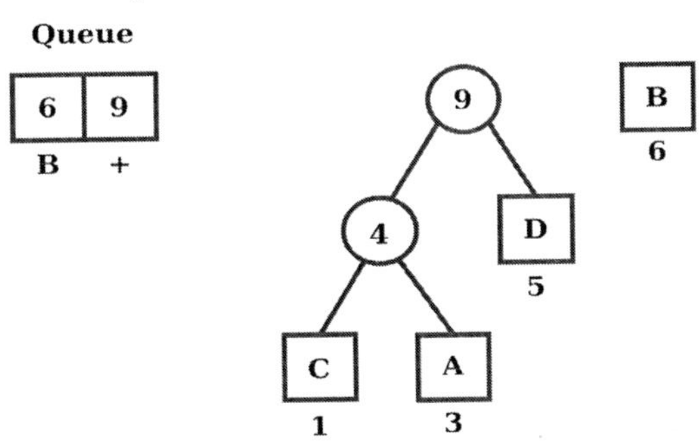

Step 4: Rearrange the nodes based on the frequency order in Queue.

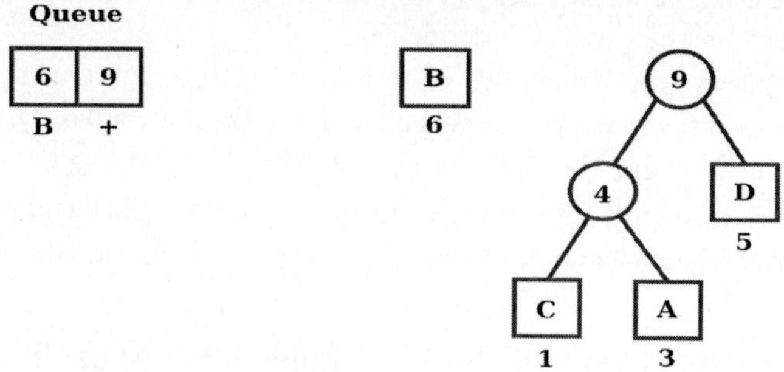

Step 5: Create a new internal node with value 15 by adding the current two minimum frequencies (6 and 9) in Queue. Make nodes B and 9 as the children of this internal node. Remove the entries 6 and 9 from Queue and insert their resulting sum 15 into Queue. Now, there are no more nodes that may be added to the tree, and the resulting tree is known as *Huffman tree.*

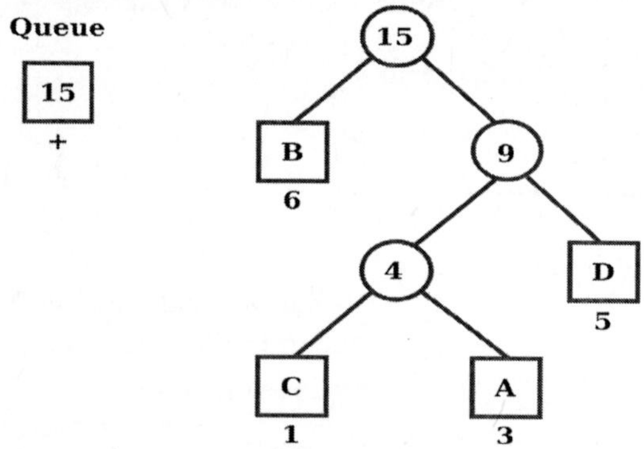

Step 6: Traverse the tree. Assign the left edge to 0 and the right edge to 1. Generate code for the characters by reading the edge label from the root to the character leaf node.

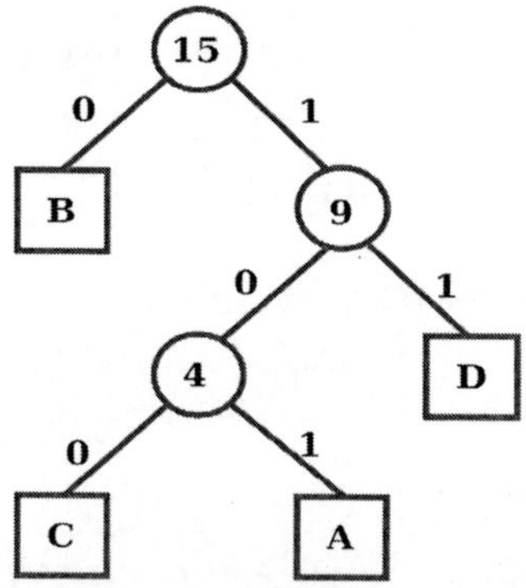

Here, the codes generated for characters A, B, C, and D in the given input string are 101, 0, 100, 11, and are represented through 3 bits, 1 bit, 3 bits, and 2 bits, respectively. Therefore, the total number of bits required to represent the given input string after the Huffman encoding is determined as: 3 * 3 + 1 * 6 + 3 * 1 + 2 * 5 = 28 bits. This reduction of the number of bits from 120 to 28 emphasises the significance of Huffman encoding in the data transmission.

5.5.2.1.3 LZW (Lempel–Ziv–Welch) Encoding

The LZW encoding is the most reliable general-purpose data compression technique due to its simplicity and adaptability. This widely used compression method can potentially achieve very high throughput while implementing in hardware and is easy to implement. LZW operates by reading a series of symbols, arranging them into strings, and then transforming the strings to codes. Here, compression is achieved because the storage requirements for the codes are lower than those for the strings. LZW compression technique works as follows: while the input data is processed, a symbol table or dictionary maintains a correlation between the longest words observed (named as *key*) and a list of *codeword* values. The input file is compressed as a result of the words being replaced by their matching codes. Thus, the algorithm becomes more effective as the amount of long, repeating words in the input increases.

Example

Consider an example where we accept a stream of 7-bit ASCII characters as input and write an 8-bit byte stream as output. Here, the 128 potential single character keys are used to initialise the symbol table, and they are linked to 8-bit codewords created by adding 0 to the 7-bit value describing each character. Hexadecimal notation is used to represent codeword values, therefore 41 stands for ASCII A, 50 for P, and so on. The codeword 80 is reserved for use as the end-of-file indicator. The remaining codeword values (81 through FF) will be assigned to different substrings of the input data that we come across, beginning with 81 and increasing the value for each additional key added. The LZW compression process for the sample input ABPAEAFABPABPABPA is described in Fig. 5.8. Since the longest prefix match for the first seven characters is only one character, we produce the codeword for that character. Two character strings are correlated to the codewords 81 through 87. Then, we identify prefix matches with AB, PA, BP, and ABP, and output the cordwords 81, 83, 82, and 88, respectively, leaving the final A whose codeword is 41. There are 119 bits overall in the input, which consists of seventeen 7 bit ASCII letters. The output is a 96-bit stream of 12 codewords with a length of 8 bits each.

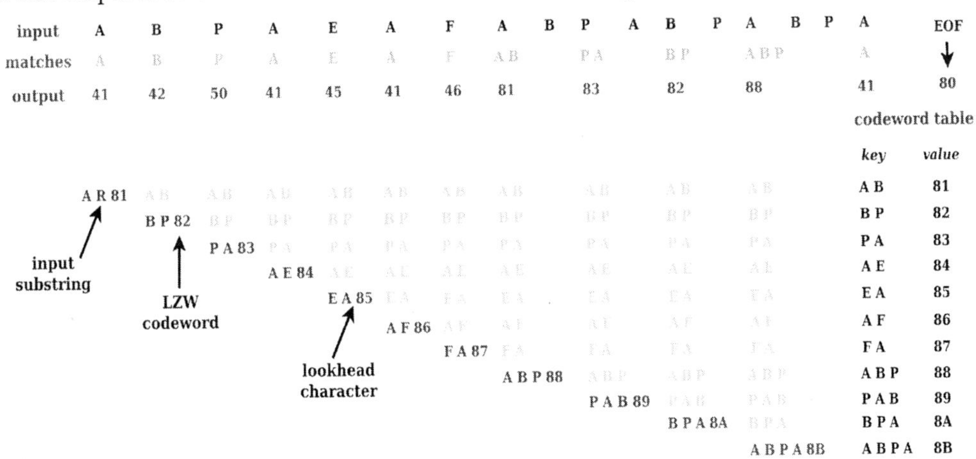

Fig. 5.8: LZW compression for ABPAEAFABPABPABPA

5.5.2.2 *Lossy Compression*

A compression technique that effectively eliminates bits of irrelevant, undetectable, or unneeded data is known as *lossy compression*. This compression method involves the loss (removal) of a certain quantity and quality of data from the original file, and hence the name *lossy* compression. When working with graphics, audio, video, and images, this strategy is beneficial since it minimizes or eliminates any visible effects on the representation of the content. Lossy compression has the advantage of being relatively quick, capable of drastically shrinking file sizes, and allowing the user to choose the compression level. The drawback is that decompressing data that has been compressed using lossy compression won't produce the exact same data (in terms of quality, size, etc.). The JPEG image, MP3 audio, and MPEG video are the most common formats that use lossy data compression (refer, Fig. 5.9).

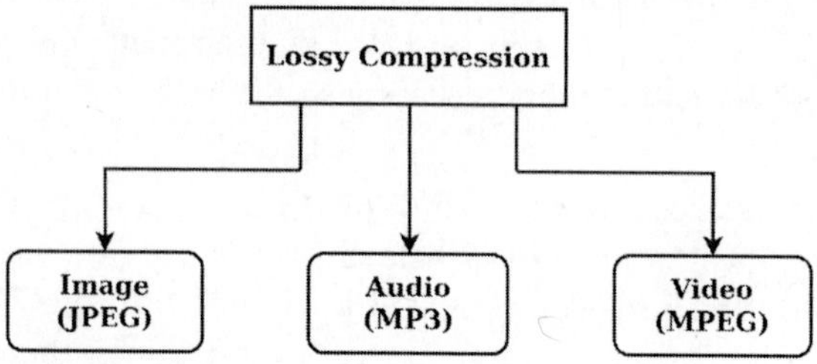

Fig. 5.9: Different Types of Lossy Compression

5.5.2.2.1 Image Compression (JPEG)

Some digital cameras reduce the image size for more efficient storage. Compression is also used to compensate for the camera speed slowdown caused by big raw images. Because of this, photos are usually saved in the jpeg format that uses a lossy data compression method, rather than the png format which uses lossless compression.

5.5.2.2.2 Video Compression (MPEG)

Digital video is compressed using a set of ISO/ITU standards known as MPEG (Moving Picture Experts Group). The MPEG system is asymmetrical. It takes longer to decompress a video in a digital TV set, computer, DVD player or set-top box than it does to compress it. Compression was therefore initially limited to the studio. Digital video recorders like Tivos can convert analogue TV to MPEG and record it to disk in real time because chips have become more inexpensive and sophisticated.

5.5.2.2.3 Audio Compression (MP3)

Lossy compression is used to compress MP3s, which are audio files. Because of lossy compression, an average MP3 file can be 90% smaller than a comparable uncompressed audio file. MP3 audio compression shrinks the size of a file by either perceptual music shaping or reducing the audio bitrate. The process of deleting undetectable noises or inaudible sounds to reduce file size is referred to as *perceptual music shaping*. The following are examples of inaudible sounds: a) quiet sounds that are obscured by louder sounds, and b) noises at frequencies that humans cannot hear. The *bitrate* in audio files refers to how many bits must be processed per second. Its unit is kilobits per second. The sampling rate, number of audio channels and bit depth are multiplied to determine the bitrate. The number of sound samples captured to represent an audio performance is known as the sample rate, and it is expressed in Hz or kHz. The bit depth measures the amount of data bits stored in each sample. The sound quality improves with increasing bitrate, but file size increases.

UNIT SUMMARY

Strings have found wide usage in diverse applications, including search engines, data encoding, plagiarism checkers, DNA sequencing, etc. This unit starts with a discussion on how to arrange a given string in lexicographical or dictionary order. Then, we proceed with presentations on Trie, a special tree-based data structure for storing and searching strings. The unit then discusses the concepts of substring search and regular expressions, which form the basis of many string matching algorithms. Finally, data compression, an important practical application of strings, has been discussed.

EXERCISES

Multiple Choice Questions

1. String sort procedure has a time complexity of
   (a) O(p) (b) $O(p^2)$
   (c) O(log p) (d) $O(p^3)$
2. Time complexity of a search operation in a Trie is
   (a) O(p) (b) $O(p^2)$
   (c) O(p log p) (d) $O(p^3)$
3. The regular expressions A|B and A|E|I|O|U represent the following languages _______ and _______, respectively.
   (a) {A, B}, {A, E, I, O, U} (b) {A, E, I, O, U}, {A, B}
   (c) {A}, {B}, {E}, {I}, {O}, {U} (d) None of the above
4. The regular expression B* matches _______
   (a) multiple occurrences of B (b) 1 or more occurrences of B
   (c) 0 occurrences of B (d) 0, 1 or more occurrences of B
5. The regular expression B+ matches _______
   (a) multiple occurrences of B (b) 1 or more occurrences of B
   (c) 0 occurrences of B (d) 0, 1 or more occurrences of B
6. The regular expression C (AC | B) E represents the following language: _______
   (a) {CACE, CBE} (b) {CE}
   (c) {CACBE} (d) {CAC, CBE}
7. The regular expression (W | Y) ((X | Y) Z) represents the following language: _______
   (a) {WXZ, WYZ, YXZ, YZZ} (b) {WXZ, WWZ, YXZ, YYZ}
   (c) {WXZ, WYZ, YXZ, YYZ} (d) {WXZ, WYZ, YYZ, YYZ}
8. Let us consider the regular expression (A+B)*B(A+B)*. Which one of the following statement is true about the language corresponding to (A+B)*B(A+B)*
   (a) The set of all substrings containing at least one (A+B)
   (b) The set of all substrings containing at most one (A+B)
   (c) The set of all substrings containing at least one B

(d) The set of all substrings containing at most one B

9. Let us consider the regular expression (A+B)*B(A+B)*B(A+B)*. Which one of the following statement is true about the language corresponding to (A+B)*B(A+B)*
   (a) The set of all substrings containing at least one (A+B)
   (b) The set of all substrings containing at most one (A+B)
   (c) The set of all substrings containing at least two B's
   (d) The set of all substrings containing at most two B's

10. Let us consider the regular expression (AB){2} | CD{1-2}. Which one of the following is equivalent to this expression:
   (a) {ABABCD, ABABCDCD} (b) {ABABCD, ABABCD}
   (c) {ABCD, ABABCDCD} (d) {AB, CDCD}

11. Let us consider the following string "HOPE IS A GOOD THING". Which one of the following regular expression can be used to search for the substring GOOD
   (a) GOD (b) .*GOOD.*
   (c) Both of them (d) None of the above

12. Let us consider the following regular expression: ([a-z]+\.)+@([a-z]+\.)+(in|com). Which one of the following patterns will be matched by the regular expression?
   (a) X.Y@A.B.COM (b) x.y@a.b.com
   (c) X@A.B.IN (d) x@a.b.in

13. Let us consider the following regular expression: a…b. Which one of the following patterns will be matched by the regular expression?
   (a) ab (b) aaabb
   (c) abbb (d) aaab

14. Let us consider the following regular expression: a[0-9][0-9]b. Which one of the following patterns will be matched by the regular expression?
   (a) a01b (b) ab
   (c) a1b (d) a0909b

15. Which one of the following statements is FALSE?
   (a) "ε" is an empty string (b) NULL is an empty set
   (c) "ε" contains one element (d) NULL contains one element

16. Typically, lossy approaches are employed to compress data that is:
   (a) Audio (b) Video
   (c) Images (d) All of the above

17. Typically, ________ compression is used by applications that cannot tolerate any change between the original and recreated data.
   (a) Lossless (b) Lossy
   (c) Both 1 and 2 (d) None of the above

18. Which of the following formats makes use of lossless compression?
   (a) JPEG (b) MP3
   (c) PNG (d) MPEG

Answers for Multiple Choice Questions

1. (b), 2. (a), 3. (a), 4. (d), 5. (b), 6. (a), 7. (c), 8. (c), 9. (c), 10. (a), 11. (b), 12. (b), 13. (b), 14. (a), 15. (d), 16. (d), 17. (a), 18. (c)

Short and Long Answer Type Questions

1. Describe the steps of sorting a given string in ascending order.
2. Explain the steps of sorting a given string in descending order.
3. Write a short note on Trie data structure with an example.
4. What are the different types of operations that can be performed on a Trie?
5. Explain the steps for the insertion of a node in a Trie with an example.
6. Describe the steps for the deletion of a node in a Trie with an example.
7. Discuss the steps for searching a node in a Trie with an example.
8. Explain the substring search operation on a given string with an example.
9. Write a regular expression to validate a mobile number of the form <country code> <10-digit number>
10. Write a regular expression to validate an email address of the form username@domain.com
11. Write a regular expression to validate an email address of the form username@subdomain.domain.com
12. Write a definition of regular expression along with an example?
13. With the help of a diagram explain the basic data compression model.
14. What is lossless data compression? Discuss its advantages and disadvantages.
15. Consider an input string AAABBCCCCDEEFFF. Generate a codeword for this string using the run length encoding scheme.
16. Explain Huffman encoding with a suitable example.
17. Write a short note on LZW encoding.
18. What is lossy data compression? Discuss its advantages and disadvantages.
19. Differentiate between lossless and lossy compression methods.
20. Explain lossy compression techniques for video, audio and image compression.

KNOW MORE

This section talks about a set of additional information that helps the reader to improve the knowledge on the topics discussed in Unit-5.

String Handling Functions

In the C programming language, there are different library functions that provide flexibility to handle strings in programs. These functions are mainly defined in two header files named "stdio.h" and "string.h". The "stdio.h" header file contains gets() and puts() library functions for reading and displaying strings, respectively. The "string.h" header file defines the following few string handling functions:

Function	Description
strlen()	It outputs the length of string
strcpy()	It copies the contents of one string into another.
strcat()	It concatenates one string (say S1) to another string (say S2) and stores the resulting string in string S1.
strrev()	It outputs the reverse of a string.
strcmp()	It compares one string with another and returns 0 if both strings are matching.
strlwr()	It outputs all the characters of a string in lowercase.
strupr()	It outputs all the characters of a string in uppercase.

REFERENCES AND SUGGESTED READINGS

Syllabus Referred Textbooks:

1. Algorithms, 4th Edition. R. Sedgewick, and K. Wayne. Addison-Wesley, (2011)
2. Introduction to Algorithms, Fourth Edition, Thomas H. Cormen, Charles E. Leiserson, Ronald L. Rivest and Clifford Stein, The MIT Press, (2022)
3. Introduction to the Theory of Computation, Third Edition, M. Sipser. Course Technology, Boston, MA, (2013)
4. Design And Analysis Of Algorithms, Third Edition, Gajendra Sharma, Khanna Book Publishing Company (P) Limited, (2015)

Other Textbook References:

1. Introduction to data compression, Khalid Sayood, Morgan Kaufmann, (2017)
2. Data Structures and Algorithms Made Easy, Second Edition, Narasimha Karumanchi, CareerMonk Publications, (2011)
3. Data Structure Through C, Yashavant P. Kanetkar, BPB Publications, (2003)
4. Algorithms: Design and Analysis, Harsh Bhasin, Oxford University Press, (2015)

Dynamic QR Code for Further Reading

Scan Me

REFERENCES FOR FURTHER LEARNING

List of some of the books / nptel course links is given below which may be used for further learning of the subject:

1. Algorithms, 4th Edition. R. Sedgewick, and K. Wayne. Addison-Wesley, (2011)
2. Introduction to Algorithms, Fourth Edition, Thomas H. Cormen, Charles E. Leiserson, Ronald L. Rivest and Clifford Stein, The MIT Press, (2022)
3. Introduction to the Theory of Computation, Third Edition, M. Sipser. Course Technology, Boston, MA, (2013)
4. Design And Analysis Of Algorithms, Third Edition, Gajendra Sharma, Khanna Book Publishing Company (P) Limited, (2015)
5. Data Structures and Algorithms Made Easy, Second Edition, Narasimha Karumanchi, CareerMonk Publications, (2011)
6. Data Structure Through C, Yashavant P. Kanetkar, BPB Publications, (2003)
7. Algorithms: Design and Analysis, Harsh Bhasin, Oxford University Press, (2015)
8. Introduction to data compression, Khalid Sayood, Morgan Kaufmann, (2017)
9. https://nptel.ac.in/courses/106106131
10. https://nptel.ac.in/courses/106102064
11. https://nptel.ac.in/courses/106104019
12. https://nptel.ac.in/courses/106106127
13. https://onlinecourses.nptel.ac.in/noc23_cs16/preview
14. https://onlinecourses.nptel.ac.in/noc23_cs39/preview

CO AND PO ATTAINMENT TABLE

Course outcomes (COs) for this course can be mapped with the programme outcomes (POs) after the completion of the course and a correlation can be made for the attainment of POs to analyze the gap. After proper analysis of the gap in the attainment of POs necessary measures can be taken to overcome the gaps.

Table for CO and PO attainment

Course Outcomes	ATTAINMENT OF PROGRAMME OUTCOMES (1- Weak Correlation; 2- Medium correlation; 3- Strong Correlation)						
	PO-1	PO-2	PO-3	PO-4	PO-5	PO-6	PO-7
CO-1							
CO-2							
CO-3							
CO-4							
CO-5							

The data filled in the above table can be used for gap analysis.

INDEX